KARMASUTRA
THE KARMA OF SEX

Karmasutra

The Karma of Sex

A non-moralizing look at the karmic laws and rules
governing consensual sexual conduct, freeing us from
years of rigid religious or dogmatic sexual conditioning

STAJU JACOB

Matador
9 Priory Business Park,
Wistow Road, Kibworth Beauchamp,
Leicestershire. LE8 0RX
Tel: (+44) 116 279 2299
Fax: (+44) 116 279 2277
Email: books@troubador.co.uk
Web: www.troubador.co.uk/matador

ISBN 978 1785890 017

Cover page design and revision of illustrations by Studio366.xx
and George Gkrekas. glenglenn33.14xp@gmail.com

British Library Cataloguing in Publication Data.
A catalogue record for this book is available from the British Library.

Printed and bound in the UK by TJ International, Padstow, Cornwall
Typeset in 11pt Aldine by Troubador Publishing Ltd, Leicester, UK

Matador is an imprint of Troubador Publishing Ltd

To the fondest memories of Rejeline Jacob and Guruji Krishnananda

and

To Kamadeva, the god of love

Namo'stu puṣpabāṇāya jagadānandakāriṇe
manmathāya jagannetraratiprītipradāyine

Homage to the carrier of flower arrows, the creator of world's joy
The stirrer of heart and the bestower of pleasure and love –
the eye of the world

CONTENTS

PART I

INTRODUCTION

1

Introduction to Karma

What is This Book All About?

Some people might question the relevance of this book. After all, sex is freely available in most Western, liberal, developed societies. In these societies, men and women are free to choose their sexual partners. However, large parts of the world are still mired in an outdated religiously-driven framework of sexual behaviour. This book advocates a paradigm of sexuality which goes beyond mere availability. It aims to remove the stigma of sex from the society. The human race, tired of its various environmentally disastrous forays into 'development' is seeking to reconcile with nature. The sexual paradigm however, continues to be driven by religious discourse. If eating and sleeping are natural activities deserving no publicity, one wonders why sex still makes news. If the President of the United States eats food from a street restaurant, no one would bother, but if he decides to have sexual pleasure with a person other than his 'legal' partner, it makes for front page news.

This book is about freeing the sexual energy within marriage. Most democratic countries have eight to ten fundamental rights, which usually include the right to free speech, freedom of religion, freedom of thought, etc. But unless there is another fundamental freedom of sexual expression, no society can be truly free and in harmony with the cosmos. This freedom, like the freedom of free speech and thought, cannot be shackled by other contracts and agreements like marriage.

The Issues Under Discussion in This Book

Is it possible to reconcile this idea to the existing paradigm of sexual exclusivity which is the bedrock of marriage, partnerships and committed relationships? If yes, as happens in couples practising 'open marriages', can it be ingrained within a socially acceptable and robust model of family? Can there be an ethical paradigm for sexual behaviour free from the influence of religious texts? After all, many of our sexual mores and ethics come from contextual writings in these texts.

Such an approach will easily integrate karmic well-being while making sex guilt-free. Can a person enjoying sexual variety aspire to spiritual upliftment and indeed experience spiritual dimensions? Can he meditate and experience the fruits of meditation? Does a high degree of sexuality bring down human capability for spiritual pursuits? Is it possible for us to imagine a world where a man (or woman) can search for sexual fulfilment as easily as he (or she) searches for a good restaurant? These and other ethical dilemmas of consensual sexual behaviour are the various questions that this book tries to address. This book has not explored the issues of coercive sexual activities such as rape or paedophilia, which are illegal in most countries of the world anyway. The immorality of these actions is well-established and there is little dissonance between the laws of countries and what is taught by most religious books when it comes to these violent one-sided sexual activities.

This book is also a book of digressions. Rooted in perspectives of cosmic harmony in sensual activities, it digresses gently into areas of spirituality, psychology and sociology. The limitation of this approach is to be a jack-of-many-peripheral-issues without being the master of any. Despite this drawback, if it adds to the perspective of people seeking fresh insights into cosmic rules, it is hoped that sociologists, psychologists and technique-oriented occultists will forgive the author for straying into their domains without earning professional spurs. If this work can be said to have any authority in any area besides sexual ethics, let it be known as a work throwing fresh light on some poorly lit areas of cosmic mysteries.

Family: a Unit of Love, Empathy and Contentment

Since most of the world still thinks of 'marriage' as the bedrock of family, we will refer to 'marriage' frequently. (In this book, a long-term partnership is also considered the equivalent of marriage in terms of expectations from both partners. Hence the same principles which govern marriage would apply. The word 'marriage' is only used frequently for readers from non-Western cultures where non-marital sensual relationships are often considered illegal, uncouth or both.)

Family, most people agree, is the constitutional unit of society. We agree that violence used against children even within the confines of the family is not morally tenable. We also understand that an environment of love and empathy within the family leads to well-being and development of individuals. Can we not, then, extend this principle of love and jealousy-free well-being to so-called 'committed' sensual relationships? Within a loving marriage or partnership, the partner is not hauled over hot coals for eating from a public restaurant instead of a home kitchen. Similarly, can we one day hope for the dawn of a liberal society where a man (or woman) can occasionally have his (or her) sexual needs satisfied from the 'market place' without having the foundations of an existing marriage or relationship shaken to its very core?

The Workplace and its Temptations

In the past centuries, men have been breadwinners while women remained confined to their homes as dutiful housewives. They often had children to tend to. The opportunities for physical intimacy with others were limited. The availability of leisure time was another constraint. Household chores often left the housewife too tired for sexual experiments. Today, the scenario is different. To create their own identity and for financial well-being, women have moved into the heart of the industrial society as workers, managers and owners. Careers have become an important consideration for women too. Even in societies like India, tied to ancient customs, women in the cities have moved out of their homes to make their mark in the productive, increasing Gross Domestic Product (GDP) economy. However, the advent of automated machines in most spheres also means that there is reduced physical activity and increasing amount of desk-based work.

It is logical that if both husband and wife work long hours in offices, in the close proximity of their office colleagues and co-workers, they are likely to develop some bonds with these co-workers. Is it not realistic for some of these colleagues to develop a bond beyond a purely platonic one? Can two such bonded people not venture into a celebration of their physical senses through a physically enjoyable relationship? Must such a relationship be wrapped in the guilt and the religious-ethical chant of 'terrible sin'? Must the spouse or partner of this 'unfaithful' one be pushed to feel the 'morally righteous' anger borne out of years of social and cultural conditioning?

The Rise of Imagination

At many levels, men and women of some creativity and imagination in so-called 'committed' relationships already fantasize sexually about different people of the opposite (*or same*) gender. Whether they reveal this to each other depends on the level of openness in their relationship. For example, does the man watching a movie and seeing Sandra Bullock making love with her on-screen hero not fantasise about Sandra Bullock doing the same with him? Even if such a fantasy is purely momentary, does it not happen? Similarly, does the young lady watching Tom Cruise kiss the heroine, not fantasize about the same happening to her? Frequently this thought may not be held long enough or explored further to create sexual arousal. At other times a prolonged on-screen love-making session would surely make the viewer want to be a part of the action. What, other than tricking the body into believing it is part of the action, is the purpose of pornography? Hence, if a person does not mind the spouse looking at pornographic images, does it really matter whether the picture in the pornographic images comes out of the 2-D screen or whether it is a multi-dimensional full-blooded person who services either one of the partners?

The Taboo of Love-Making

Can we imagine a society where a man or woman can say from the rooftops that they enjoy making love? Leave alone traditional, orthodox societies like Islamic countries or South Asia, can we expect this in the so-called 'liberal' societies of Europe, Australia or America? Can a lady, except perhaps in an anonymous internet chat room or in a drunken state, proclaim that she enjoys making love with different men, without inviting disapproval? Perhaps this declaration can also be made in jest in the presence of her equally fun-loving friends. (This is not to say that all women necessarily want to say this. Just like everyone is not a food lover to the same degree, appetite for sexual pleasure or variety might not be the same). Even in 'developed' societies, sexuality has not yet evolved to the point of it being a meaningless topic. It is so simple to tell our middle-aged friends that we had a wonderfully-done lobster for lunch. However, to say that, "A lovely escort gave me a wonderful afternoon session," becomes embarrassing in a social setting. A typical American, white, Anglo-Saxon protestant couple would still feel uncomfortable if their French or Spanish couple friends were to disrobe completely on an isolated beach and expect them to do the same. It is sad that despite the so-called 'sexual liberalization' in the West, the fact that a celebrity wants to make love with someone whom he has no intention of marrying (with the partner in question being fully aware of this) still makes the news. This freedom from sexual guilt is the paradigm that this book tries to advocate. Genuine and abiding freedom from sexual guilt can only happen when one is transparent about the karmic implications of sexual actions.

Even in the land of origin of Kamasutra, sex continues to be a big taboo. This is despite India having some of the highest numbers of HIV-positive patients in the world. Most sober Hindus today ignore the erotic and sexually liberated moorings of ancient India. The Hindu nationalist and right-wing political parties which presently govern India often highlight the spiritual and scientific achievements of ancient India while carefully avoiding any mention of their ethos of sexual liberty. In many parts of India today, police routinely intervene to prevent couples from kissing in parks or holding hands, terming it 'Western Evils'. In smaller cities, police often raid hotels to book consenting adults on the charge of adultery or prostitution. Needless to say, prostitution is illegal in India, except in designated red-light areas. Of course, with the relatively high levels of corruption in the Indian police force, implementation is often whimsical[1].

The film certification body in India does not restrict itself to certifying movies. They censor movies and delete 'objectionable' scenes from movies. Films depicting love between same sex couples are usually banned. Till the late 1990s, no Bollywood movie would dare show any sexual love scenes. The most that a curious movie-goer could expect to see would be the sight of the shirtless hero switching off the lights in a bedroom. The heroine would be shown admiring the hero with the right mix of shyness and pleasurable guilt. In stark contrast, in much of South Asia, urinating in public by men is considered acceptable behaviour, even on crowded street corners. As some journalists have noted, "Pissing is okay, but kissing is not."

Dilemmas of the Sociologist

Some 'ethico-social' thinkers might balk at the stance of these arguments. They might argue that while a mother or father is a biological relationship, marriages are merely created artificially by society and hence, for something so feeble to last, the strong foundation of fidelity is a must. The two partners must have a 'sacred' bond in their physical relationships. Despite his occasional tendencies to wander, owing probably to his evolutionary genes which keep prompting *him* to look for innumerable potential mates, the man must by and large, stick to his wife. Since there is no irrevocable biological connection, these thinkers argue, how can the man feel anchored to the family if he has too many sexual connections? Isn't it necessary that for a family to exist, the two partners must have that special sexual connection born out of strict sexual loyalty?

These are profound questions for the sociologist. Will the institution of marriage in its present form, drawing its strength mainly from the battered concept of sexual fidelity and 'special' love survive in the coming decades? Besides workplaces where men and women are often dressed attractively, people also have more time for social activities which bring them in to proximity with other attractive companions in social settings. Will the present style of marriage withstand these pressures? Or, will people who want to enjoy guilt-free sexual diversity prefer to keep opting out of one marriage or relationship to walk into another, thus enjoying the fruits of both social respectability and sexual diversity simultaneously? Even with the ease of amicable divorces, how many times can a person divorce his partner, without losing a little of his/her social respectability? Does a marriage or committed partnership have to be the death knell of sexual experimentation?

Repeated divorces also bring up other questions related to the upbringing of any children. Will children feel secure in a family of rotating stepfather or stepmother through a series of marriages? Will the more revolutionary amongst us, see the futility and hypocrisy of this situation? Will they finally pull the plugs on this institution of marriage as the only socially acceptable means of seeking sexual diversity? If this institution weakens away, are there other relationship models or forms of living together which could robustly replace marriage?

Or is the prognosis not practical enough? Maybe the theory that increasing contacts leads to greater sexual availability is not that true after all. Maybe, as Alvin Toffler and others predict, improvements in technology may create flexible work environments. Instead of more women going into the heart of corporate empires, the workplaces may start coming home. Perhaps more people staying at home to manage their work with the help of technology will make marriage stronger than ever. Increased time spent with each other, even while working from home, could easily increase the intimacy between married couples.

These are the questions for the sociologist. But this book has a different purpose and direction. This will not be an intellectual debate on the institution of marriage. This book will take the less trodden path of karmic repercussions of various sexual activities and merely as an aside (or to present the picture more holistically), foray into the sociological angles and fleetingly touch some of the thought-worthy arguments.

The Contours of Sexual Jealousy

Is our jealousy natural? Does this jealousy come out of a sense of insecurity that our 'unfaithful' partner may be on the verge of deserting us? Or is this jealousy or 'righteous anger' a result of the sociological drama of faithfulness, a drama in which the victim of unfaithfulness only acts out this role of 'righteous anger/outrage' for the benefit of society? Is it acted out from our sub-conscious sense of deep-seated 'wrong' which was created not as an instinct but merely by years of social conditioning that emphasises the concept of 'sexual partner monopoly' in marriage?

If a man says to another older woman, "I consider you as a mother," his real mother never feels outraged. Neither does this man have to say these words covertly for fear that others will hear him. He can say these words openly in most parts of the world. Similarly he can address a woman as his sister, even in the strictest Islamic countries. He might even be considered noble for saying this, especially if the woman in question is beautiful and poor. Will this man's real biological sister call him 'unfaithful' and threaten to cut off all ties? Will his real sister take him to court on the grounds that he was 'unfaithful'? The answer is *no*. A man can call any number of women his mother or sister, without really creating much of a fuss. On the other hand, can a man say openly to an unknown lovely woman, "I would like to consider you my wife," without people thinking of him as a sex-maniac and lecher? In many parts of the world, he would be beaten up ruthlessly, arrested or even end up dead.

Let us explore jealousy in a bit more detail. When the wife comes home joyously after meeting her sister or mother, the husband is usually unaffected or very happy for her. Then, why should he be jealous if she comes home after enjoying a nice sexual experience? What is it about sexuality that creates such explosive insecurity among partners? Is it, like the sociologists might say, the awareness that since such relationships are born out of sexual needs, unlike blood ties of birth, there is more likelihood of them coming to an end? Is it merely the fear that the person with whom we have developed a strong bondage, emotional relationship and comfort can leave us lonely and insecure? To add to this, of course, is the possibility of financial penury.

A similar kind of fear and insecurity may be perhaps experienced by parents who have had their children stay with them for a long time. An elderly parent who had his son or daughter staying with him or her might be worried that the son or daughter might want to move out; especially in Eastern cultures which have often traditionally encouraged joint families with young people staying together with elderly members. However, this insecurity is still much less sharp than the jealousy and insecurity experienced by a partner worried about his/her spouse's infidelity. We could easily think of three main reasons for this heightened sense of insecurity among sexual partners.

(i) In the case of parents they can always rely on the fact that no matter how wayward and rebellious their offspring might be, there can be no other physical and genetic parent. On the other hand, partners in a sensual relationship worry that a partner who goes out from their life, often goes away permanently. Needless to say, the politically correct post-divorce or post-break-up statement continues to be: 'we will remain friends'. These nice things are often said more for the sake of form and rarely meant. There are situations where old lovers do come back together, but that is more to do with fortuitous situations that might have rekindled or renewed the relationship. These reunions are rarely the result of any obligation on the part of either partner to keep the relationship alive.

(ii) As mentioned earlier, probably our entire cultural, social and religious paradigm makes it obligatory for each partner who has 'cheated' on the other to feel guilty, ashamed and defensive. The same ground rules expect the other partner to feel superior, outraged and betrayed. Clearly this feeling of 'being cheated' and 'outraged' is merely a result of our programming. After all, in some Muslim societies, where the husband has more than one wife, many of these wives often stay together harmoniously

under one roof. Similarly, let us consider the ancient
Hindu epic of *Mahabharata*. The importance of this
epic can be judged from the fact that arguably the most
significant piece of Hindu scripture, the Bhagavad Gita, is
a part of this epic. This ancient Hindu epic of *Mahabharata*
depicts five highly respected Pandava brothers (referred
commonly to as Pandavas) sharing their wife Draupadi
while maintaining the strongest fraternal love for each
other. In fact they are said to have evolved a system of
etiquette and convenience where they could share
Draupadi without any logistical difficulties. They did so
by keeping their uniquely identifiable slippers outside the
bedroom while one brother was cavorting with Draupadi.
This was a system similar to a red bulb lighting up above
the conference room door to show that it is occupied.
Despite this wife-sharing arrangement, the Hindus
regard the Pandavas and the god Krishna, their friend,
as spiritually exalted beings (in fact, the god Krishna,
the incarnation of Vishnu, is considered one of the most
popular and powerful gods in the Hindu pantheon).

(iii) Is jealousy instinctual? Is it similar to fear, greed and the
instinct for survival? Or is it a hybrid instinct born out of a
mixture of all three? If so, can we train ourselves as human
beings to be free of this somewhat primeval instinct? If
human beings can be trained to wait politely for their
turn for food and be polite in social intercourse, can they
be trained to rise above this aggressive sexual jealousy?
Till now society has only stoked the fires of jealousy by
encouraging partners to feel that jealousy is a legitimate
tool/behaviour to remind their partners/spouses of sexual
exclusivity. Can this social habit be finally buried along
with our other primitive instincts?

Possibilities of Alternative Models of 'Marriage'

Can our legal system do something to take the jealousy, insecurity and possessiveness out of relationships? Is it possible to have a better, more robust system in which the strengths of the institution of marriage are incorporated into a *sexually free* co-habitation model, without the ankle chains of sexual exclusivity? The contours of such a proposed system have been discussed in some detail in the concluding chapter of this book.

Is this Book a Green Signal for 'Sex Addiction'?

Is this book a sinful discourse encouraging promiscuity? Is this an attempt to bring the practices of fringe groups and 'weirdos' to the centre stage of our civilization? Certainly that is not the aim of this book. After all, someone suggesting that people should have the freedom to eat anywhere is not condemning the society to die of gluttony and obesity. This book merely tries to remove the stigma of sexuality from sober, freedom-loving societies forever. It also throws light on the karmic and spiritual pitfalls of sex-related actions in the spiritual plane. Thus it is an attempt to free ourselves from the perennial concept of sin based on Abrahamic faiths (Christianity, Judaism and Islam). Perhaps the injunctions on sexuality have been relevant due to practical, hygienic or social necessities during those centuries. It is high time now that the civilized world cuts this umbilical cord of sexual behaviour and spirituality.

Once this is done, it will be possible to accept that spiritually exalted human beings can have legitimate sexual needs. It would be easier even for spiritually minded Hindus to accept that Krishna, one of the celebrated Hindu gods, was both spiritually accomplished and sexually liberated. A spiritual seeker can enjoy sexuality as much as good food or a good drink, as long as this is not based on unethical practices or excesses. It must be remembered that anything in excess can become an addiction. People can possibly get into a pattern of overuse of TV, radio, internet, books, cigarettes, food or even exercise. Does the possibility of overuse make all these things evil, to be shunned by spiritually exalted human beings? Who knows, in the future, the Pope or a Dalai Lama could participate in a group sex-party without creating a tsunami in the spiritual world!

Basics of Karma: the Essentials for Understanding This Book

For a layperson trying to understand the cosmic laws governing sensuality, it is important to start with the understanding of what is karma. Followers of many Eastern religions understand this as the universal unwritten law that holds a person responsible for his actions, thoughts and words. The difference between the karmic system and the legal system is the fact that the legal system only covers the duration of our existing physical lifetime. Undoubtedly, in terms of fixing responsibilities and proportionate punishments, the judiciaries of many developed nations do a reasonably good, if not perfect, job. However, our legal system can mete out little punishment to the suicide bomber himself who kills a hundred innocent people in support of some violent ideology of hate.

So is such a suicide bomber never going to get any punishment for his crime? It is here that the laws of karma have the answer. People with a strong religion-driven sense of ethics might say that God or Allah will punish this wrong-doer by sending him/

her to hell. But in order to understand the laws of karma one does not need the crutches of any organised religion. Even an atheist can understand and appreciate these laws. If we look at life as a continuous cycle of births and deaths, then we appreciate that no one in this cosmic system can escape the responsibility and punishment for his or her deeds. We can view karma or the karmic system as the automatic cosmic judiciary. It could also be viewed as the perfect cosmic accounting system that pays a person back in his lifetime or in one of his future lives. It is not difficult to understand why many people in India and other parts of the world understand 'karma' as nothing but another word for 'fate' or 'destiny'. If we understand the laws of karma, it also becomes easy to understand why some people are born poor or disadvantaged, while others are born into great wealth, glory or endowed with extraordinary beauty.

Does karmic theory simply mean a person is born again and again on this earth? When one remembers that our Milky Way galaxy is merely a miniscule dot in the big room of the universe, we might know better than giving too much importance to this Earth. There are millions of stars like our sun and millions of solar systems in our universe. It must be remembered that being born on a planet higher or lower in advancement is like merely stepping on a higher or lower rung of a ladder. It does not mean permanent relief from the cycle of births and deaths. The complete freedom from the cycle of births and deaths only comes from absolute clearing of all karma accounts.

Some people use karma as a clothes hanger, on which they hang all their troubles. They look upon it as an excuse to avoid work. Needless to say, this comes from a poor knowledge of karma. If everything is predestined, of what use is the human initiative, goes the argument. Karma itself becomes another name for laziness and fatalism. This fallacy is put to rest in our section on 'hard' and 'soft' karma in the next chapter. Simply put, many people forget that karma is like being at a crossroad. Using our brains, we do not get to choose after our birth which particular crossroad we will be dropped at during this lifetime. However, once we are placed at a particular crossroad (our birth family and circumstances), we have to decide which further road to take. So there are definitely some parts of our present life that are strictly under our control and one should never underestimate that.

Another unintended consequence of the knowledge of karma is the way many people in the East treat their servants. The infamous ill-treatment of the lower castes in India often comes from this belief and understanding of karma. The thinking goes that since these people are merely doing these menial jobs and holding low social positions due to their previous bad karma, they truly deserve their plight and need no mercy, help or empathy. Those who have visited countries like India are often appalled by the horrific levels of poverty coexisting with amazing wealth. The feeling of karma makes the poor menial worker content with his fate, whereas the millionaire does not feel the need for any charity. It is sometimes forgotten that those who harbour such pride or negative thoughts that result in harsh actions towards fellow humans accumulate bad karma themselves.

Did Christ and the Prophet Muhammad Accept the Laws of Karma?

There is one question that troubles Christians and Muslims. If karma is such an inevitable reality, why would the Prophet

Muhammad and Jesus Christ not talk about it strongly in their teachings? We can only surmise the reasons. One reason could be that Christ's teaching of love and forgiveness ('turning the other cheek') was already quite a radical and new teaching as compared to the old law of 'an eye for an eye'. Hence he might not have wanted to overshadow this new paradigm with more complicated concepts like karma. In any case, Christ probably thought that if people even half-followed his teachings, then a lot of bad karma would automatically stop. There is also the likelihood that if Christ had mentioned karma and the cycle of births, some of his followers might have thought of the next life as a back-up option. For instance, they would say, "Even if I have killed so many in this lifetime, I will do amends in my next life.'. It might have all ended up as a second-chance approach to salvation.

These reasons notwithstanding, a careful reading of the Bible brings forth instances where Christ has implicitly admitted the impact of earlier deeds upon the present life. For instance, he heals a sick man saying that his sins have been forgiven.[2] Implicitly Christ is admitting that the man's past sins (whether from this life or from one of his previous lives is not clear) were responsible for his illness. Understandably, when the scribes of the time think of this as blasphemy, Christ promptly issues a perfunctory clarification about his choice of words and how he has the power to forgive past sins.

Another instance of this implicit admission of karma is when his disciples, seeing a congenitally blind person, want to know the cause. They pointedly ask Christ whether the cause of this defect was due to the man's 'own' sins or the 'sins of his parents'.[3] It could be safely assumed that since this person is already born blind, the disciples are referring to the sins in previous lives.

Similarly the part about parents' sins seems to acknowledge the possibilities of transfer of negative karma from parents. Christ replies to his disciples and cites other reasons for the man's illness. What is important to note here is that Christ doesn't rebuke or dismiss conclusively the possible karma speculations of his disciples, namely, the beliefs in previous lives, or the parent's karmic load passing on to the offspring.

A similar instance of biblical admission of the concept of karmic load transfer can be found at the time of Christ's crucifixion. When the gathered hostile crowd is told by Pontius Pilate clearly that he disowns any responsibility for the execution of the innocent Jesus Christ, they immediately reply in loud chorus, "His blood be on us and on our children."[4] This is a clear pointer towards the karmic load transfer agreement executed in the presence of a divine witness (in this case, Christ himself). There are some who believe that at least some of the constant tribulations faced by the Jews were the result of this karmic load transfer agreed to by their ancestors. Further, we find Christ himself probably alluding to this karmic transfer, when he tells the crowd who are wailing and crying for him on his last route to Calvary, "Weep not for me, but weep for yourselves and for your children."[5] Obviously Christ is not warning the Jews about their own safety or security in their present lives. After all, in any case, the existing law in that country would not have held them responsible for Christ's death. So is Christ not warning them about the future karmic repayment for their complicity in his death?

The reasons for the lack of karmic theory in the Quran and in Islam could be similar. In war-prone, hot Arabia, a relaxing afternoon in the shade of trees would be everyone's dream. The last thing that Muhammad must have wanted would be a surge in laziness on account of a mistaken understanding of karma. For a simple yet hard-hearted unruly group of Bedouins and other tribes in Arabia at that time, an uncomplicated message was needed. It would have to be a message simple enough to understand and execute, with clearly defined rules for most foreseeable situations of the time. Like Christ, Prophet Muhammad, during a war-torn era, wanted to emphasise the here-and-now aspect of life. In fact, this is borne out even today by the judicial system of the strictest Islamic nations. If you steal, you lose your hand: a straightforward, highly deterring punishment without unnecessary complications of deeper analysis. A non-Muslim who reads the Quran might find some of the injunctions of the Sharia Islamic law harsh, inhumane and inflexible. Many of Prophet Muhammad's seemingly harsh words can only be seen in context and discounted by all but the most fanatical followers of Islam. The tragedy is that many of the so-called hard-core Islamic nations, Saudi Arabia, Iran etc. continue to insist on following these injunctions fanatically. In order to understand Islam and the Quran better, one has to understand the social environment of Prophet Muhammad's time. With internecine wars going on in much of the region in Arabia, there is little wonder that parts of the Quran read like a war manual. Unsurprisingly, some chapters of the Quran have even detailed operational instructions for different aspects of life. Harsh punishments are prescribed for breaking the law, stealing and other misdemeanours. It is easy to understand why in such a context, introducing the subtle karmic philosophy would not have been such a great idea.

Having said this, there is a well-known passage in the Quran which also points to karmic philosophy and implies the recognition of the existence of a cycle of births and deaths:

'How can you reject faith in God? Seeing that ye were without life, he gave you life; then will He cause you to die, and will bring you again to life; and again to him will ye return'[6], seems to affirm this belief in karmic cycles.

The Concept of 'Overself' in This Book

The karma theory is often scoffed at because little of its subtlety is understood. To begin with, we have to understand that 'we' keep appearing in different worlds in different times in a cycle of births and deaths. Naturally in this process, there must be some component within 'us' that is constant. That constant component cannot be our body. Neither is it our knowledge, acquired during our time on earth. Of course some component of it does permeate the death barrier, but more of that later. Neither do our petty emotions and minor likes and dislikes cross the death barrier. (Having said this, there are some deeply abiding emotions that do cross the death barrier, but again, more about them later.) Our material possessions, titles or grandeur do not cross the death barrier either. To the disappointment of young lovers who commit suicide together, our relationships and the intensity in the same form often do not cross the death barrier.

However, there is one strong aspect of our individuality, our **unique identity** or **stamp**, which goes from birth to birth to birth. This happens till there is final relief from karmic cycles. Some spiritually enlightened people believe a union with a very advanced spiritual entity is the final stage. This super advanced 'spiritual entity' can be called God or Brahma or Allah or whatever else depending on our language or religion. It makes little difference because that is way beyond the scope of this book. In this book, we will refer to this all-powerful entity as **'cosmic intelligence'** to keep the discourse free from religious leanings.

Coming back to 'us', many religions use the word 'soul' or 'atman' for this permanent unique individuality stamp. For the sake of convenience, in this book, the word **'overself'** will be used. This will preserve the non-religious outlook of the whole work. Another problem with the word 'soul' is that the contours of its definition are slightly different in the Judeo-Christian tradition and in the Eastern Hindu- Buddhist traditions.

Having mentioned 'overself' let us have some more clarity about what we are referring to. Imagine a person born without eyes, ears, nose, tongue or the sense of touch. How does this person connect to the world? This human would have a mind but cannot hear, touch, taste or see. Despite the absence of these organs there is a throbbing life, an individual being in all its purity. To the technologically inclined, this could be likened to a brand new computer with the memory but with no software loaded into it. In other words, there is a being, well and alive, but unable to connect to the world. Now imagine that this blank entity is given the full record book of its previous births, deaths and all its karmic loads. This happens through a full transfer of cumulative memories from all births. So now we have a wise, highly knowledgeable entity with thousands of years of knowledge, wisdom and experience. For the purpose of this book, let us call this entity the 'overself'. Blank individual + loaded cumulative memory = **'overself'**.

In reality, everyone is born with overself. However, normal babies also have fully functional senses. Hence they also keep loading their own experiences of the present life. Our mind has a conscious, cognitive segment and an unconscious segment. In fact some books also mention the subconscious and the semi-conscious mind. This loaded cumulative memory, which is a part of the overself, is preserved in the deepest recesses of our unconscious mind. It is well known that a million-page document can be preserved on a small chip. Similarly, this entire file of our cumulative experiences across all births is preserved in a highly compressed form in our unconscious mind. Through our cognitive, conscious minds and sense organs, we also keep adding the load of information about our current lives. This load of information about our present existing lifetime is what can be simply called our 'ego'. This 'ego' is often bolstered by our 'achievements' and 'successes'. As the baby grows older and with the influx of information about current life, the compressed cumulative memory box is locked and pushed deep into the recesses of the unconscious mind, so that there is no easy access or intermingling of present life memories and past life cumulative memory. Although used in Freudian psychoanalytical theory, the word 'ego' or *Ahamkara* is also relevant to Karmic theory.

In time, through trained meditation and mental fine-tuning, part or full conscious connection with our overself can be made. The overself also tries to assert itself whenever we are faced with a tense decision by looking at all our previous records of eons. In fact, a strong intuition is nothing but our overself quietly checking and retrieving previous data from its ancient records and suggesting options to us. The solutions that are not available at a cognitive level are often available to the unconscious mind. The normal individual is said to be merely the sum of his experiences in the present birth. On the contrary, the overself is the normal individual, plus the cumulative memory of all births. Just like how our grandfather, if alive, will always be older than us – no matter how old we get – a person's overself too, will always be wiser and much more insightful.

Decisions that 'We' Take

Our overself takes us in an upward path through several births and eons. This karmic destiny is an arrangement to settle our accounts of previous karma. When we are born we are dealt some cards. However, we also have a willpower that can be exercised during each moment of our existence. The results of our conscious actions can be positive, negative or neutral (detached action). Is it always nice to do positive karma so that by the law of karma good things may happen to us? If we keep on doing good things, we have to keep on coming back into one or the other forms of human or higher existence to enjoy the fruits of good karma. Likewise, in the case of deeds generating a lot of negativity, we have to keep coming back to suffer and clear our account. So the best option is, as the Buddhists would say and the Bhagavad Gita will exhort us, 'to do things with detachment'. Doing things with a complete sense of detachment and out of a sense of duty, doesn't lead to a heavy accumulation of karma. Hence it spares us the trouble of having to be born again due to an un-cleared karmic balance.

Understanding the Mechanism of 'Yearning' and 'Avoidance'

Some readers might ask what is wrong in being ecstatic in pleasant situations, while they might agree that being depressed in an unfortunate situation is not a good option. The simple answer is this. When we are in a situation that is pleasant, does it not mean that this situation is much better than our daily humdrum lives? Only when there is a difference in our experience from normal experiences, we remember it. When we are sad about a situation, it means that the situation is something that doesn't occur every day and is more unpleasant than our average day.

If we look at our life as an even graph, any upward or downward swings would be remembered by us. We remember incidents that are a break from the normal routine. Some downward swings (as in unfortunate moments) or upward swings (as in joyful occasions) are remembered. When we have a joyful situation, we are thrilled and keep remembering that situation long after it is over. We keep mentally chewing the old, pleasing situation like gum. An older man might remember his younger days with a lovely lady, sometimes remembering even the love-making in great detail.

Generally most of us have the tendency to mentally recycle happy situations again. This in turn creates a **yearning**. It is not without reason that Buddha talks of how desire is the root cause of all suffering. Simply put, each desire that seeps into the subconscious starts having a life of its own. (It is important to note here that constant repetition at conscious level can cause it to seep into the subconscious level.) This acts like a virus programme in computer software that will not be destroyed until it implements itself. In other words a strong desire for a situation (created **yearning**) will die only when that situation happens as desired. Simply put, if one desires for anything long enough, one gets it, in this lifetime or the next.

Yearning: the Ancient Story of Amba – the Sheer Force of Desire

At this juncture, it is worth relating the story of Amba and Bhishma, from the *Mahabharata*, the grand Hindu epic. This story is a good example of a desire having a life of its own. King Shantanu, the widower king of Hastinapur kingdom, fell in love with an exceedingly beautiful fisherwoman on one of his hunting trips. When the King requests the hand of this lady in marriage, the arrogant fisherman father rejects the alliance citing the reason that since the king already has a son, prince Devavrata, his own daughter's son will never be first in line for the throne. Needless to say, Shantanu was a righteous king. In ancient India, most righteous and just rulers would never resort to force for their personal needs. The fact that a fisherman could audaciously put forth these conditions to a monarch without fear speaks a lot about the tolerant and benevolent form of monarchical autocracy that was in practice in ancient India.

Hearing this condition, King Shantanu became sad. Certainly, to satisfy his personal desire he could not deprive his beloved and valiant son, Devavrata, of the right to the throne. Soon enough, the prince came to know of his father's despondency. Prince Devavrata immediately went to the fisherwoman's father and made a solemn promise never to seek the throne. The shrewd fisherman was not satisfied. He retorted that it was still possible that Prince Devavrata's children could reclaim the throne. Faced with this, the young prince angrily took the additional vow to remain a *brahmachari* (completely celibate) till his death.

It is said that even the gods were touched with his sacrifice. The pleased King Shantanu married the fisherman's daughter.

He granted his beloved son Prince Devavrata the boon of 'being able to choose the time of his death'. (In those days, a boon or a curse usually always bore fruits, especially when it came from a righteous person or a god. The whole cosmic philosophy behind curses has been elaborated in Chapter 3.) Prince Devavrata was referred to as 'Bhishma' (for his 'terrible' vows) hereafter. Part of Bhishma's vow was also that he would protect the throne of the kingdom of Hastinapur. In other words, no matter who the king of Hastinapur would be, Bhishma would always protect the king.

Years pass by. The King Shantanu and fisherwoman-queen Satyavati soon have a son, Vichitravirya. In the course of time, this son grows up and occupies the throne. When he needs a bride the valiant, celibate Bhishma decides to go bride-hunting for his step-brother. There is a *swayamvara* being held in another kingdom. *Swayamvara* (meaning 'choosing your own groom') in ancient India, was a process where a beautiful princess chose her own groom. The king would send out invitations to all eligible bachelors, usually from among the royalty of neighbouring kingdoms, to attend the ceremony. Then the princess would garland the person of her choice in the assembly, held in a big hall. Often, there would be some test of strength, skill or intelligence which the aspiring groom would have to pass. Sometimes when the princess was more interested in looks or personality or had someone special in mind, she would simply go past each of the assembled men and put the *varmala* (a special floral garland) around the neck of the groom of her choice.

Bhishma attends this *swayamvara* on behalf of the king of Hastinapur. He comes to this *swayamvara* and challenges the other princes to a battle and defeats them all. Interestingly, this *swayamvara* was held for the marriage of three princesses namely, Amba, Ambika and Ambalika. After defeating all the assembled suitors, he rightfully claims the hand of the three princesses and proceeds to Hastinapur in his chariot. However, unknown to Bhishma, the eldest princess, Amba, was in love with another King Salva, from a neighbouring kingdom. Before long the chariot of Bhishma was stopped by King Salva who challenges Bhishma to a battle to decide who wins the hand of Princess Amba. However, Salva is completely defeated by the great Bhishma and retreats in shame.

The happy Bhishma finally lands in Hastinapur with the three princesses for his young king. Only at this point does Amba tell Bhishma that she is madly in love with Salva and cannot accept another husband. The other two princesses are happy to be married to Vichitravirya. Being a gentleman, Bhishma immediately sends Amba to King Salva with his compliments. Salva, already in shame, refuses to accept a gift from a person who has defeated him. Despite his love for Amba, Salva returns her to Bhishma.

By this time, Amba's love story is well known and King Vichitravirya also refuses to marry her saying that she mentally belongs to another man. Princess Amba is utterly frustrated by this turn of events and this whole situation of limbo. She blames Bhishma for the whole fiasco and asks him to marry her. Bhishma cites his irrevocable oath of celibacy and pleads helplessness. Princess Amba is incensed at Bhishma. She approaches many warriors asking them to help her kill Bhishma. Some of them do challenge Bhishma to battles, but find themselves defeated.

Having exhausted her friends and weapons, she turns to hard penance to please the gods. When the gods appear before her,

she asks for boons to kill Bhishma. The Hindu god Shiva
(the lord of destruction) grants her the boon that she will
be instrumental in Bhishma's death in her next birth. In her
impatience for revenge, Amba immediately jumps into a fire
and kills herself, to enter her next birth. In that birth, in the
great Mahabharata war she finally achieves her desire of being
instrumental in Bhishma's eventual death.

This whole story illustrates the point of desire leading to
fruition. Desires – good or bad, have a life of their own. Like
a created entity, they will end only when that desire has been
achieved. This is the power of yearning.

Manifestations of 'Avoidance' and 'Yearning'

Similar to yearning is **avoidance**. In Hindu philosophy
yearning is referred to as *raga*, while avoidance is called *dwesha*.
Guilt, depression, anger and fear are often nothing but various
manifestations of avoidance. Let us look at each of these a little
more deeply. What is guilt? Simply put, guilt is nothing but
the feeling of 'wish I had done/not done this' or 'wish this had
not happened'. This is nothing but one form of avoidance of
an unpleasant situation. We find ourselves responsible for it in
the past, partly or fully. Variations of this guilt-based avoidance
include an inferiority complex ('wish I was not like this' or
'wish I was not born here' or 'wish I was like this' etc.). The
difference is that guilt is often based on what one has been
responsible for in a direct way, whereas an inferiority complex
is related to one's existing state, which would generally not
have been caused in the present life through deliberate actions.
For instance, a person who has a heated argument in abusive
language with his girlfriend, may lose her and regret it later. He
may feel guilty about this for a long time.

Inferiority complex is different. A person may have an inferiority complex because he/she is short or bald, or has some socially less-desirable personality trait. This would be despite the awareness that physical traits are often not a result of one's own actions in the present life.

Another manifestation of this avoidance is shame. Shame is nothing but a regret of what is happening now or has happened in the past that caused acute embarrassment, and could have been best avoided. Interestingly, a somewhat mirror expression of guilt and shame can be a result of a pleasant experience too. For instance in certain cultures, a girl who has never known a boy might feel both a pleasurable sense of guilt and shame after her first kiss from a handsome boy in a dark corner. It is a guilt and shame mixed with anticipation. Yet another variation of this avoidance is a mild depression or sadness (not referring to clinical cases of depression here). This depression is often in the form of questions such as 'why did this happen to me?' or 'why did God do this to me?'.

The various manifestations of avoidance and yearning can be depicted in the figure on the following page. Excessive yearning for power could lead to arrogance or a superiority complex. Excessive yearning for sex could lead to constant lust. Excessive yearning for material possessions could lead to greed.

Differentiation of Avoidance and Yearning-based Guilt

It is important to differentiate between guilt in a pleasurable way and guilt in a depressing way. After all, their effects are different in the physical realm and the karmic realm. For instance when

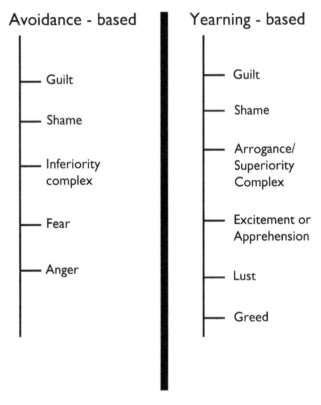

Avoidance - based	Yearning - based
Guilt	Guilt
Shame	Shame
Inferiority complex	Arrogance/ Superiority Complex
Fear	Excitement or Apprehension
Anger	Lust
	Greed

one is happy eating a generous helping of chocolate it produces a *yearning-based guilt* at having done something delightful. On the other hand, a child who had been abused sexually could harbour, besides shame or inferiority complex, an *avoidance-based* negative guilt, despite the fact that he/she is a mere victim. Like the victim of a rape who experiences an orgasm at the hands of the rapist, this person could also feel a mixture of shame, embarrassment and guilt that perhaps, he/she too somehow participated in this hateful act of shame and filth. Similarly, a reckless car driver who has hurt a person severely cannot escape his avoidance-based negative guilt. This guilt would bring him sadness. Hence avoidance-based guilt creates sadness. If severe, this often plays like a mournful dirge in the background of the life of that person. As mentioned later, this differentiation of guilt, fear etc. into avoidance-based and yearning-based also has implications for health.

One might ask, "What about spontaneous laughter?" That kind of spontaneous happiness is not a result of either avoidance or yearning. However, these kinds of amusing situations could often lead to a yearning. A woman/man who enjoys the company of the other might fall in love. Falling in love is the result of yearning at a subconscious level. The same is the case with lust.

Other manifestations of yearning include greed. When there is a strong greed for money or something material, we tend to create a strong pull for that object. The universe creates situations to fulfil that desire or yearning. This is the foundation of many recent books on the secrets of success, which emphasise the importance of **dreaming** and **visualising**. Lust for a woman or craving for food are similar to greed for money or possessions, because the pull created is the same. Till the fulfilment of the *yearned* things happen, there is no further release from the cosmic cycle. This is why the Buddha talks about containing desire. At all times as seen in the story of Amba, desires held close to the heart and caressed constantly, ultimately bear fruit.

Coming back to love, many Eastern cultures and romantics loathe to club so-called 'pure love' with 'lust'. They contend that pure love is laced with feelings of sacrifice and non-sexual joy of togetherness. On the other hand, lust is pure sexual chemistry. In fact popular romantic movies and literature in India distinguish it as '*pyaar*' (love) and '*vaasna*' (sexual desire). The same was the case with many romantic novelists. In

India, this has more to do with highly romanticized attitudes of sexual puritanism, rather than karma. This build-up of emotion while controlling the sexual urges create a strong, almost obsessive 'love' yearning. In the social scenario of that time, the opportunities for sex were limited. Moreover the complications of possible pregnancy often made it necessary for the lovers to withhold sex. In a sexually liberated society this distinction in the behaviour of lovers might not be necessary.

This is also part of the Eastern tendency to deride anything that comes out of bodily needs. Anything coming out of higher emotions, intellect etc. is praised. (This also explains why in countries like India, bodily sickness or unattractiveness is considered tolerable. After all, the body is *worthless*. On the other hand, even an iota of doubt about mental health is considered a heavy stigma.). Thus 'pure love' is extolled as the emotional meeting of hearts. However, passion or '*vaasna*' is the craving for each other's body, and condemned as something inferior and undesirable. In fact, the sexual liberalism of the civilizations which have given the world erotic sculptures like Khajuraho and detailed sexual treatises like the *Kamasutra* should have been celebrated. But centuries of Mughal rule in India, with its Islamist Puritanism, have caused sexuality to be considered forbidden. The colonial rule of Europeans with their church-led chastity drive has also strengthened this hypocrisy.

Typologies of 'Love'

Let us focus a little more on our discussion related to love. In the spiritual context, 'love' exists in different forms. At a very selfless level there is universal love. The love of Christ or the compassion of Buddha lies in this category. This love originates from a very enlightened mind. Then there is a platonic love between opposite sexes or between same sexes. One often refers to this love as affection. Then, as mentioned earlier, there is the *non-platonic* category of emotional love, without the compulsory requirement of sexual contact. For the traditional Indian therefore, the love of Romeo and Juliet would fall under the non-platonic love high in emotional intensity but which is not purely driven by sex. This nuance is often considered of negligible importance by the average Westerner, where falling in love at an emotional level and making love at a physical level would be natural extensions of each other, if not entirely synonymous. The figure given below depicts it holistically. For a conservative Indian mind-set, it would not be an inconceivable scenario for two people

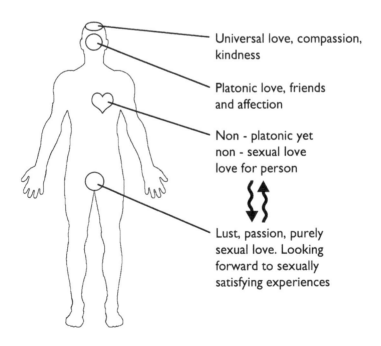

Universal love, compassion, kindness

Platonic love, friends and affection

Non - platonic yet non - sexual love love for person

Lust, passion, purely sexual love. Looking forward to sexually satisfying experiences who are intensely in love at an emotional level to wait for the sexual experience only after marriage. That would be categorised as non-platonic, but yet 'pure' love. The love of Heer and Ranjha (in the South Asian cultural context) could also fall in this category. Here the feeling originates strongly from the heart, and driven by love, affection – not driven purely by lust. Theoretically at least, this form of emotional love is satiated without sexual acts.

And then we could mention pure sexual love. During the early decades and centuries, many (especially in countries like India) have come to look down upon this last category of love as inferior. As the wriggly arrows in the figure show, there is a close connection between the love coming from heart and lust. Some cultures do not waste too much time trying to understand the finer nuances between non-platonic love from the heart and one that translates *easily* into sexual pleasure. They believe that the end result of all non-platonic love is sexual pleasure, which may or may not lead to creation of family.

Having said all this, pure sexual need without any minimum feeling of affection or desire for a long-term company is clearly different from 'love'. This overriding sexual need often means treating a person like a living sex toy. As long as this treatment of the other, almost like a living sex toy, is mutual and does not involve deception or breach of trust, this book will unequivocally state that there is nothing karmically wrong with it. The following figure can depict these various types of non-platonic love. It might also be a good idea to refer to Chapter 5 of this book to develop a more holistic perspective on romantic love.

Pure Romantic	Sexual Romantic	Pure Sexual (Lust)
Non - platonic love. Purely romantic. Only the emotional bond which is powerful and strong. Bond of feelings. No sexual activities involved.	Non - platonic love, but involves romance and deepest feelings of the heart. This is coupled with sexual enjoyment and sexual activities.	Pure sexual enjoyment. No real emotional feelings for the person. Sexual enjoyment and fun is the objective in this kind of non - platonic lusty love.

In much of South Asia, sexual activity by unmarried, even if they are consenting adults, is looked down upon as grossly immoral. It seems to be considered animal-like, genital-based, pleasure-seeking behaviour, devoid of 'affection'. Since marriage was considered the surest route to stable affection, anyone who indulges in sexual activity other than marital sex would be considered debased. Even after marriage, sensual activities must be limited to bedroom and that too, in darkness. After all, this dark act would best be completed in the cover of darkness. The same allusion to darkness is made when a woman has sexual relations before marriage. This strongly disapproved of act is often referred to as '*mooh kala karna*' (blackening the face). This expression also denotes that the act has brought great shame on the family.

Impact of "Avoidance" on Overall Health

At the risk of digressing from our main topic of karmic impact, it might be worthwhile to note the importance of yearnings or avoidance on our physical health. It is rather well-known that creatures like tortoises live much longer. Many yoga teachers attribute this to the fact that tortoises breathe only three to five times in a minute. On the other hand, animals like dogs and rabbits breathe much more rapidly. Adult humans breathe between 12-20 times every minute. The link of breathing with longevity and well-being is considered vital in most Eastern systems of well-being like Ayurveda and Reiki. Most schools teaching yoga also teach '*pranayama*', the science of breathing correctly.

Very fast breathing leads to over-oxidation and consequent damage. On the other hand, if enough oxygen is not made available to different parts of the body it leads to damage. Simply put, if breathing is tampered with, health is disturbed. Having said this, let us look at the relationship of breathing and various sub-categories and manifestations of yearnings and avoidance, which we mentioned earlier. We are all aware that when we are scared or angry, we tend to breathe at a faster rate. Similarly, an intimate and lustful situation also often causes laboured and quick breathing. This imbalance or breathing anomaly is caused by the excess intake or shortage in the exhalation of air from the left or right nostril. This, in turn, is caused due to the emotions arising in the left or right side of the brain.

Sometimes this change in breathing is very observable. At other times, this change in breathing pattern is subtle and not easily discernible. This happens when the breathing irregularity almost becomes a habit. This long-term habit could be a result of guilt, suppressed anger or stress. The resulting damage to the health is also of a chronic nature. When anger or stress gets its grip on the breathing rate, this oxygen-altered condition often causes problems like high blood pressure, migraine or heart trouble in the long term.

The organ that could be damaged also depends on genetic proclivities. Each human being is born with some internal and external organs being weaker or stronger than others. Some people inherit strong hearts or bones or lungs as a result of their genetic or racial backgrounds. Still others inherit strong livers or pancreases or brains. Some have weak hearts, sensitive lungs or sensitive skin or nasal cavities. There is a simple saying that the strength of a chain is equal to its weakest link. The same applies to health. When the breathing is impaired by continuous anger, guilt or fear there is a continuous breathing anomaly that puts pressure on the 'chain'. This relentless pressure leads to the breakdown of its 'weakest link' (generally the weakest internal organ). Hence the person with a weaker heart suffers from heart disease as a result of stress, whereas another person might suffer from high blood pressure or diabetes (weak pancreas), as a result of a similar situation. (Another term for a long-term fear situation could be stress. In stress too, many of the body's hormonal/breathing responses are the same as in a moderate 'fear/anxiety' situation.)

Another analogy to understand the link between breathing pattern and health is the car. In manually driven cars, there are three pedals operated by the feet, namely accelerator, brake and clutch. If one is driving the car at a good speed it is definitely not advisable to keep the foot on the pedals of the brake or clutch. If the clutch or brake is kept half pressed without any reason while the car is in full motion, then the wear and tear of different mechanical parts and tyres is likely to increase. Similarly, the amount of petrol consumption for a given distance tends to increase. The impact of breath-anomalies due to avoidance-based guilt, shame, anger or fear is similar to this impact of a half-pressed clutch on the smoothly moving health of an individual.

Other literature also proffer seemingly varied explanations of the mechanism of breathing. Although all these are consistent explanations, they sometimes differ in terms of which part of the mechanism they highlight. Let us dwell a while on the other versions and explanations. It must be remembered that there are many layers or fields surrounding the body. This is different from the **overself**. While the overself is the actual entity that goes from life to life, there are other magnetic and electrically charged fields surrounding the body. These are invisible sheaths and one of the outer ones is often referred to as *aura* in English. In Hinduism, these sheaths are often referred to as **koshas**. These *koshas*, in particular the aura, often protect our body and mind from illnesses and psychic attacks (as we see in later chapters). All these layers are also influenced by any changes in our breathing pattern – in fact they are nourished by our breathing. Hence when the breathing pattern is impacted by guilt, fear or negativity, holes or vulnerable points develop in these protective sheaths. This can also lead to diseases, depression and so on. Both the above explanations are consistent and only differ in the nomenclature and focus. It is up to us whether we use the aura and sheaths approach to understand the negative impact of guilt, fear etc. or the metaphor of clutch and gears in cars to understand the problems resulting from change in breathing.

Hence when Christ exhorts people to forgive each other, it is not just for the karmic reasons but also for the temporal benefit of good health. Many healing therapists and retreat programmes these days insist upon deep and sincere forgiveness, because that releases the breath impairment or the 'pressed clutch' effect. Stored anger towards a person, object or even towards fate can be referred to as 'a grudge'. Many people have a grudge against their parents, friends or relatives. Some even have a grudge against themselves or against fate. That might be the reason why former pope, John Paul II, talked about the necessity of accepting oneself first. People who do not love and accept themselves first and foremost often keep a long-term grudge towards themselves. Sometimes this grudge is expressed as an inferiority complex, which has been discussed earlier as one form of avoidance.

Hence those who harbour long-term anger often irreparably damage some slightly weak organs in their body. Some results of other avoidance reactions on health are given below:

- Guilt: Guilt held for a long time starts pressing upon the breath. It often creates common aches, pains, migraines etc.
- Shame/Inferiority complex: Severe shame and its long-term memory create breathing anomalies similar to guilt. The manifestations of shame are skin disorders, pimples, acnes and such. Inferiority complex, which is also a form of 'grudge' against oneself produces results similar to anger and shame.

From this health point of view, avoidance-based and yearning-based manifestations should be treated differently. In terms of long-term breathing impact, the *avoidance-based* manifestations of guilt, fear, anger, shame etc. cause more damage. *Yearning-based* manifestations like greed, lust, romantic love and pleasant shame (as in 'blushing') do have some karmic implications due to the pull of desire. However, their detrimental health impact due to breath tampering is minimal. It is for the same reason that despite an athlete's exercises creating heavy-breathing patterns, there is no damage to his health. In fact, physically created and temporary acceleration of breathing often brings benefits.

One could argue that all hot-tempered men do not suffer from many of the above-mentioned diseases. There are two points to remember. Firstly, while it is generally agreed that cigarette smoking is injurious to health, all cigarette smokers do not necessarily die early. In other words, cigarette smoking only increases the existing probability of that person dying. The same situation is applicable to those who are hot-tempered. (The important phrase to be noted here is *'assuming other things are the same'*. In real life *'other things'* are rarely the same for all individuals.) Secondly, anger that explodes like a small volcano and dissipates the emotional energy is always better from the health perspective. People who are blunt in their manner of speaking often dissipate this energy. It is the person who retains the simmering grudge but is unable to unleash it periodically who causes the most damage to the breathing pattern (and to health).

Christ himself knew the health impact of these twin banes of guilt and anger. The well-known sacrament of confession in the Catholic Church is similar to the Freudian method of psychoanalytic counselling to get rid of guilt. Similarly Christianity emphasises sincere forgiveness of those against whom there is a long-term grudge. If applied, it immediately clears some of the subtler breathing anomalies.

Krishna, the Hindu god, also talks about operating without guilt or anger in his advice to Arjuna in the Bhagavad Gita. Arjuna, the warrior prince was depressed about the possible results of the fratricidal Mahabharata war. Despite being his rightful duty, Arjuna did not want to fight some of his beloved relatives. His possible fear and guilt at being responsible for their bloodshed and the love or attachment ('yearning') for his loved ones prompts Krishna to give this advice. Krishna exhorts for actions without 'attachment', namely, without undue 'yearning' or 'avoidance' of the results.[7] Of course, Krishna's philosophical oration is not limited to concern about Arjuna's temporal health but also aids his karmic deliverance. People all over the world faced with the dilemmas of attachment can use this advice.

Introduction to the Concept of CSB

There are other noteworthy karmic angles. An innocent human being, just born, has a direct link with the forces of the universe. This is pretty much an actual connection. It is like an invisible thread that connects the upper region of the brain to the rest of the universe. It covers the area of the brain that receives and transmits signals from the universe. But as the human being grows, he utters falsehoods, indulges in complicated manipulations, deceives and generally speaks things that he does not mean in thought and action. Slowly this dichotomy starts creating a sort of additional film (or if it is simpler to understand, a blockage) of this area that is meant to make the connection with the universe. Changes in breathing pattern and negativity also increase the layer of blockages in this connection area.

This is similar to our understanding of how arteries get clogged with fat or cholesterol. If the blood is full of undesirable fat and cholesterol, it impacts the blood circulation. The heart has to work harder. These fats block certain arteries and those areas of the body stop getting the benefit of full blood circulation. The agility of the body is lost, impurities are not flushed from the system and the nourishment slowly decreases. Let us use another analogy. Imagine the roots of a tree slowly getting coated with plastic film that prevent it from absorbing nutrients from the soil. Yet another metaphor is that of the flute – a musical instrument. The efficacy of the flute depends on the flow of air through the various finger holes and the fact that it is hollow. If the holes on the flute start getting blocked a little with every passing day, the quality of music comes down slowly. Interestingly, the most common depictions of Krishna in Hinduism show him playing the flute.

Thus, it is not without reason that Christ said that 'the meek shall inherit the earth'. Although most Christians understand this to mean that those who lead good lives go to heaven, this also has the technical meaning mentioned above. Within this book, we could refer to this invisible, intangible coating (or blockage) of the special area of the brain as 'Cosmic Sensitivity Barrier' or CSB. The greater the thickness of the CSB, the lesser our connectivity and communication with the universe.

The advantages of a very low CSB and high connectivity to the universe can be summarized thus:

- Low CSB permits us to connect to the universe and communicate with our overself for answers about our past lives etc.
- Almost zero CSB permits us to freely interact with the universe and increases our awareness to other invisible cosmic entities. These entities vibrate at different frequencies. Our mind is born with a great capacity for subtler vibrations when the CSB is almost non-existent. In the present age, due to CSB thickness, we have lost the ability to perceive a certain bandwidth of vibrations. That is why infants are able to perceive 'ghosts' or 'angels' (entities existing at different vibration levels), which a normal adult is unable to see. (Unfortunately young babies cannot translate their sightings into clear and intelligent words, due to which this world of angels and friendly ghosts

often remains a private joy for these infants. Besides, most children lose their memory of these incidents when they grow up. That explains why these entities still remain in the domain of magic and fantasy). A very low CSB sharpens this awareness to a very high degree.

- When there is almost no CSB, we are able to ask wishes of the universe and the universe grants us our wishes almost immediately. In other words, the time lag between a strongly held desire and its fulfilment decreases drastically. Christ curses the fig tree that does not give fruit and it dies within a day.[8] This aspect has also been elaborated under 'Curses' in Chapter 3.

- Less accumulation of karmic load, since the direct communication between the universe and overself help us to do things with a long-term vision and knowledge. Our intuitional abilities increase drastically.

How to Reduce the Thickness of CSB?

Feelings of shame, guilt, all forms of manipulation, lies, violence and coercion increase the thickness of the CSB. Simply put, the greater the incongruence between our words, our thoughts and/or our actions, the thicker the CSB becomes. To avoid formation of CSB, there should be absolute congruence between thought, word and action. What a person says should be similar to what he thinks. Language should not be a tool for masking real intentions but only a means to proclaim existing thoughts. That is the real meaning of 'meekness', shown below using the mathematical symbol for congruence.

$$\text{THOUGHT} \cong \text{SPEECH} \cong \text{ACTION}$$

It is worth noting here that sex done in its purity with joy, without coercion, deception or guilt, does not increase the thickness of the CSB. That is why sex within marriage does not impact the CSB thickness in any manner, whereas, concealed sexual activity and secret affairs increase the CSB thickness. Needless to say, acts of coercion that create negative karma and guilt definitely increase CSB thickness.

Therefore, it is important that we create a free society where individuals who love sexuality are able to do so without increasing their CSB thickness through deception and hypocrisy. Most well-brought-up people in today's average middle-class generation rarely indulge in violence and terrible crimes. But even then, CSB continues to thicken as the 'innocent child' slowly transforms into the person 'of the world', skilled in social lies and manipulation. Sometimes, even when we have no intention of seeing another person again, we still say, "See you later," or "We shall keep in touch.' At other times, we praise people when our real thoughts are different. We smile and act friendly with a boss whom we hate and tolerate insults from people who are more powerful than us. We pretend to nod approvingly at the comments of those whose favour we seek. We pretend to be amused at the jokes of those who we are trying to please. The more intelligent and sophisticated the person, the more skilled and diplomatic he/she gets; these are the people skilled in being politically correct. The demands of modern life and good form often make us say things we do not mean and do things which we do not want to do. All these dichotomous actions increase the thickness of our Cosmic Sensitivity Barrier and slowly sever our connection with the universe.

More about the Cosmic Sensitivity Barrier

Even among babies, despite their innocence, the range of cosmic vibrations they can perceive vary. As the CSB thickens, a person starts losing the ability to perceive different vibrations. Gradually, their overall sensitivity starts dulling. Besides the reasons mentioned earlier, high use of alcohol, smoking and other impurities like drugs also increase CSB thickness and leads to the blunting of senses. The mind starts perceiving only bigger stimuli. Music needs to be louder to be heard, and even smells and tastes need to be stronger to be perceived. This is indeed a tragic loss of the subtle mental system with which the human being is blessed. The ability and finesse of the intelligent mind is the one great gift to the human species. Most other animals only have the cruder senses.

Can we prevent and undo the damage to our CSB and reduce the thickness? Fortunately, yes. At the simplest level, intake of soft poisons like alcohol, tobacco and other drugs should be reduced. Leading transparent lives, without hidden agendas, lying and manipulation, also keep the CSB thin. If a workplace requires constant deception, probably it is not the right workplace. Simple country folk, farmers, labourers and even prostitutes can have thinner CSB coatings. (Having said this, prostitutes might often have other addictions like cigarettes, drugs, alcohol etc., which increase CSB thickness. Similarly, more sophisticated call girls in bigger cities tend to have thicker CSBs, because they often lead double lives.)

Some time for regularly silencing the mind sharpens our sensitivity further. Meditation is the easiest way to achieve this. Over the course of time, disciplined meditators manage to increase the range of vibrations that the mind can perceive by clearing away the clogged surface of CSB and reducing the thickness bit by bit. A good session of meditation also prevents further damage. Just like exercise reduces body fat, meditation reduces fat CSB. With longer periods of meditation, the sensitivity keeps improving. Eventually it reaches the level that we become capable of interactions with higher cosmic beings and entities. These entities exist in their natural states at certain higher vibration levels only.

Do Higher-Order Beings Manifest Themselves to Just Anyone?

Some clarifications may be needed here. Sometimes people wonder why divine entities and gods have sometimes appeared to sinners or otherwise unfit people? Well, the answer is, there are times when a higher cosmic entity seeks to initiate contact. This may be due to the person's good karma in the past or forms a part of the mission on earth for which the person was selected before birth. It must be noted that a higher entity can manifest itself any time. For instance if the spiritual being of Christ wants to appear before any human being, it is easy. A higher cosmic entity can always tune in to the vibrational range of humans if they choose to. However, if we want to initiate contact or communication from *our* side, in their natural states, we can only perceive their presence if our CSB is thin enough to accept the subtle vibrations of their level. Maybe an analogy is needed here. Imagine a lowly citizen of a far-off nation wanting to talk directly to the President of the USA. It will be almost impossible to get past the barriers of the President's staff. But if the President decides to talk to such a citizen, it is very easy for him to reach the person concerned. After all, the President has so many resources to do so. In practice, in most cases, Christ or even the Virgin Mary, have made appearances to people whose CSB is thin. For instance the apparitions of Mary in Fatima, Portugal were revealed to peasant children. However, even when the CSB is thick, the higher beings can always bring themselves to the sensitivity levels of the recipients. In Christianity, this is often referred to as **divine grace**.

If an individual wants to do this on his own, it is generally only possible with several years of spiritual or meditative practice. These spiritual practices can increase his sensitivity to the vibrational levels of certain higher beings. Let us continue with the analogy of the President. Let us say that a person works hard and becomes a great business leader, a great celebrity etc. In this case, he/she will often become a part of the President's network of people who have direct access to him. In other words, he/she will earn the right to enter the President's presence. He may also become part of the President's list of guests and invitees. This is what meditation and spiritual merit do to us.

Again it must be noted that just like here on earth, there is a protocol and cosmic hierarchy amongst the higher beings. For instance the President of the USA is at a much higher level than the US Secretary of State. In turn the US Secretary of State will be at a level higher than the Deputy Secretary of State and so on. Similarly, more powerful and higher spiritual entities exist at higher and higher energy bands. Interestingly a great amount of the collected spiritual-merit passes through the death barrier. That is the reason why some people seem to accomplish more within a short time of starting their spiritual practices. (In another words, they have gained from their accumulated spiritual merit from previous lives.)

If one reads the Bible and looks at the kind of people that Christ surrounded himself with, we see that all his disciples and friends were people with thinner CSB coating. Prostitutes, tax collectors and fishermen may not be perfect examples of sinless people, in the conventional sense. However, they were perfect examples of meekness and simplicity. They did not lead double lives. The ones that Christ rebuked the most were the hypocritical Pharisees (the thick-CSB people).

Some Assumptions Made in This Book

Marriage: In Eastern societies and in Islamic countries, marriage continues to be an institution. (Is it a coincidence that in most cases, the word 'institution' refers to prisons, schools, colleges, mental health organisations, hospitals etc.? In all these places, freedom of some form is taken away and regimentation applied. Is the word 'institution' indicative of what marriage really stands for?) As modernity, development and 'Western' values creep into most parts of the world, this situation is changing. These days, the urban youth often decide to live together in sexual relationships without marriage. This is happening in countries as widespread and geographically and culturally dissimilar as India, Japan, Oman, China and Morocco. This is more prevalent in urban areas because here the long tentacles of society cannot easily discover and chastise them. Semi-urban and rural areas are seeing and partaking in only a reduced level of this change. Here the local community still holds the role of moral guardian. The local community often involves itself in areas considered to be 'personal freedoms' in much of the developed, democratic world.

Hence, for our culturally conservative readers, marriage has been used as the template (this and issues of marital fidelity are discussed in Chapter 5). However, the same analysis would apply to those living in long-term, monogamous, stable sexual relationships with another person of any gender. In the case of same gender relationships, the words 'husband' or 'wife' would have little relevance; they could be read as partner 1 and partner 2.

Use of Male Nouns and Pronouns: This book is about creating a world of sexual liberties, free of gender, religious or other prejudices. However, a mixture of habit and literary conditioning has resulted in the occasional usage of male noun or pronoun forms. Wherever this usage is seen, it must be understood as applying to both genders. Again, in the chapters that discuss karmic issues related to prostitutes, it might seem there is an assumption that the prostitute is a female. Although male prostitutes (or gigolos) are increasingly common, it is easier to find an organised female-prostitution industry in many parts of the world. This is especially true for developing countries. However, wherever 'prostitute' is mentioned, the analysis applies to commercial adult sex workers of both genders.

Use of Stories and Examples from India: It may be seen that several examples in this book come from the Indian subcontinent. There are two major reasons for this. Firstly the author's own Indian background, which makes it more convenient to pluck examples and anecdotes from India's almost infinite treasure trove of folklore and mythology. In a country that worships literally thousands of gods in different forms, there is little shortage of fables, myths and tales. The other reason is more objective. The Indian subcontinent is the birthplace of most Eastern religions, namely Buddhism, Hinduism, Sikhism and Jainism. The concept and entire idea of karma is integral to many of these spiritual traditions. Therefore, since this book attempts to set a karmic template and standard in human sexual experience, it feels right to bring in that flavour of India. After all, India is the ancient fountainhead of non-organised, non-religious individual quest for spirituality.

Reasons for Some Significant Omissions

Although major trends have been covered, all possible variations and sexual practices have not been covered in this book. A significant omission is the lack of any exclusive chapter on 'masturbation' despite the heavy punishment of God in the Bible for those who 'spill their seeds'. The most important reason for the omission is the increased acceptance of masturbation in most parts of the world today. Even in the strictest Islamic countries, it is accepted in practice, simply because there are no practical ways to curtail masturbation done in private. Most religious scholars accept that, in private, masturbation is an acceptable outlet for sexuality. In karmic terms, masturbation without any guilt is a harmless pleasure.

2

Karma and Marriage

The concept of marriage comes from the idea of a socially acceptable, structured outlet for human sexuality. Another aim would have been to provide a stable, loving and rooted system for the upbringing of progeny. Some of the religiously inclined might argue that sexuality itself is only a biological ploy. It makes the whole process of procreation a tolerably pleasing one. And perhaps therefore, the primary object of marriage itself is to create a home for the next generation.

Karma and the Choice of Spouse: Arranged Marriages

Does previous karma have any role to play in the choice of a spouse? In many parts of the world, such as parts of Asia and the Middle East, where marriages are still arranged by the parents or elders in the family, it is easy to understand why the spouse is said to be chosen by fate. But since we also understand this 'fate' to be the accumulated fruits of karma, we can simply say that karma leads us to the choice of spouse. This explanation is accepted by those who belong to Eastern civilizations. In some of these regions, the first time a lady speaks to her man is only after the marriage. All that is left for the couple is to figure out how best to live harmoniously with each other. Often, in these cultures, it is the wife who adjusts to her man and bears his idiosyncrasies while loving him. The husband might also have to make some adjustments to his idea of a spouse.

It is only possible to appreciate the tremendous implication of this fact when one remembers that divorces are highly frowned upon by these societies. Knowing this, partners in marriages, but very often the women, make unimaginable compromises. For instance, some women in rural Asia and the Middle East live with their drunkard husbands without any thoughts of divorcing him. These drunkard husbands think nothing of occasionally 'disciplining' their wives with some corporal punishment. Others tolerate their philandering husbands while still others bear their hot-tempered 'lords and masters'. An oft-quoted ancient Hindu law from 'Manusmriti' states that 'women when young should be under the protection and guidance of their fathers; when older under their husbands and in their old age, live under the protection of their sons.'[1] Many followers of this otherwise laudable document refuse to believe that this must have been written for the social context of that era. In reality, the writer must have kept in mind pragmatic difficulties like bad policing, the socio-cultural situation or governance of that time. As mentioned in Chapter 1, the same problem of inability to read things in context beset the die-hard believers of Quran and Bible.

One might argue that if arranged marriage is indeed a mere man-made social convention, where is the question of karma? Marriage, especially in societies like India or Middle East, might indeed be arranged. Despite the nature of this 'arrangement', a spouse plays a pivotal role in a person's life since, once married, divorce is extremely difficult. In societies like India and Nepal, divorcees (especially if they are women) are often treated like social outcastes. In the lottery of finding a spouse in arranged marriages, a person can have a peaceful existence or a stressed, worried life. In many parts of India and Asia, life-transforming decisions of the wife such as the ability to work after marriage, the ability to pursue further studies and the number of children to have are decided by the husband. (There is little choice on whether to have children or not. It is often assumed that married couples not having children have some medical inability to produce any.)

In the case of the men too, wives have subtle but strong influence in matters related to finance, choice of house, choice of location, choice of servants, condition of interiors etc. As the marriage grows older, the influence of the wife increases. By the time of the silver wedding anniversary, the wife (who is now a mother and sometimes a mother-in-law in many regions of the world) plays a major role in choice of bride (or groom) for the son (or daughter). The choice of the colour of cars, the choice of jewellery, clothing, home management, etc. are also often decided by such older wives. The queen-mother-wife starts to enjoy veto powers in all these matters.

In cases of 'hen-pecked' husbands, the situation is graver. The wife virtually takes all the non-financial decisions related to the family. The husband merely performs the rubber-stamp function of giving assent, with little veto powers. Hence it is easy to see the influence of the spouse in the overall direction that life takes. In most Asian countries, it is understood that a wife can make or break a man. Hence it is easy to see why, like the choice of a birth family, the spouse choice is an important karmic junction in life. Based on the karmic destiny of a person, he/she will be given an appropriate life partner. This karmic influence is acknowledged in Eastern cultures. Hindu marriage arrangements are often preceded by the careful study of astrological horoscopes of the proposed couple. If the expert study of astrological charts shows grave incompatibility or danger, the marriage proposal is killed immediately. Doting

Hindu couples often express their desire to be with each other with the phrase, 'together for the next seven lives'. In Western societies too, very often, despite our own best efforts to secure the love of a specific person, the relationship never works for some or the other reason. Those who are playing the dating game for some time know this reality well.

Destiny versus Choice: Understanding 'Hard' and 'Soft' Karma

When we speak of karmic destiny, many people get into the old debate of whether man's life is predestined. If yes, then why is man given a free will at all? When a man jumps in front of a moving train and ends his life, is he merely fulfiling his destiny? Or merely exercising his will to do what he wants? If we take this argument further, if people are not responsible for their actions at all, why should criminal laws exist to punish anyone? After all, is it not merely the unfolding of their pre-written destiny?

It is necessary to get a clearer grip on this debate for a better appreciation of this book. Is man's total life predestined as per the cosmic karmic system? Without getting into many complications, a simple answer to this oft-repeated question is that karma is of two main types in terms of its effect on humans. (A more detailed classification may be found in various karma philosophy books and some articles published by the followers of the Hare Krishna movement.[2]) Eschewing the Sanskrit names for these types, we can simply classify them into 'hard' and 'soft' karma. While the hard karma is often inviolable and predestined, the softer areas of karma can be changed drastically with human willpower and endeavour.

The hard karma of our previous lives decides many irrevocable things in life: the country of one's birth or the type of family that one might be born into etc. For instance, if in a past life, one has committed a murder, there is a possibility that in the present life, this person may be killed, quite by surprise. This could be his inviolable hard karma. 'An innocent boy walking on the street is stabbed to death by a drunken drug addict' – this type of a newspaper heading reminds us of previous hard karma being brought to its fruition. Another result of hard karma might be seen in a person born blind or without limbs. (One must remember however, that this might not be the only cause of a person being born blind. There are other possibilities. Refer to the last part of Chapter 3 for a discussion related to this.)

What constitutes a 'hard' karma could be the next question? A good analogy for understanding 'hard' and 'soft' karma is to think of skin injuries. There are some injuries like rashes, scratches and even falls which result in the tearing of the skin, or some bleeding etc. Most active kids suffer from these injuries. However, over a period of time (say in a span of 1-2 years) there is no marked scar, or perceptible depression, swelling or change in the texture or shape of the skin at that location. These are similar to soft karma because they leave no permanent marks on the overself. Soft karma sprinkles the seeds of softer actions and interactions in our present or future lives, but do little permanent damage.

On the other hand, there are some injuries that result in a permanent and life-long scar, mark, discolouration, bulge or depression on the body. These are similar to hard karma, which leaves powerful karmic scars and must be cleared. Hard karma (just like scarring skin injuries) inflict permanent and deep scars on the overself and are etched powerfully on the karmic record of an individual. Usually hard karma will not go or melt away by a cleaning of some of the outer sheaths of the self (what some books refer to as 'aura'). A murder, suicide, extreme violence, powerful curses of people hurt at our hands etc. fall into this category and the karmic fruits cannot be wished away or easily diluted. (Again technically, there are some rare exceptions to this general rule that hard karma cannot be wished away or erased. Let us remember that when even the tax laws of most nations are so complicated and have hundreds of caveats and exceptions, how much more exhaustive will the universal karmic system be? Please refer to the section 'Mid-course Corrections' in Chapter 11 for further discussions related to this.)

Karma and the Choice of Spouse: Western Societies

Reverting to our topic of marriage, there are other relevant questions. What about strong-willed people who choose their own spouse without any parental influence? What of the Western style of independent dating and marriages, where parents play only a very marginal role if at all? The Western readers will agree that many of those who are in marriage or a long-term relationship with a self-chosen partner would have been hard-pressed to have known the name of that spouse, about ten years before the actual marriage. In other words, Mr. X in 1999 would not have known that he would marry Ms. Y in 2009. That answer itself would seal the argument of those who proclaim that they chose their spouse themselves. Very clearly it was fate/karma which produced circumstances in which they met.

'Mr. X met Ms. Y at a party, which he was not supposed to attend because of some other engagement. At the last minute the other engagement got cancelled and he went to the party.'

Or

'Mr. X got up a little late, unusually, and ended up missing the usual bus for his journey to work. He waited for the next bus in which he sat next to the unusually beautiful Ms. Y, with whom he had a conversation. This conversation bloomed into an interest and over a period of time into a beautiful friendship and relationship.'

Or

'Mr. X met Ms. Y on an internet dating site. They exchanged a few emails and found they got on well. Eventually they did meet in person and found they were compatible. Today they are married.'

These stories are common enough to pulp the myth of couples who claim that fate had no hand in their meeting. It is certainly not implied that the two lovers in arms do not have any choice before saying 'I do' in front of the altar. As most young people in the Western world know, merely being in a relationship does not necessarily mean that it will end up in marriage. All lovers are not *meant to be* blissful husbands and all women that one sleeps with do not make it to the altar. This truth is also being discovered by the youth in developing countries (much to the dismay of the older generation and religious leaders).

Having a 'Wife' and Karma

What of people who live together only as partners for a long
time? As mentioned under the section 'Some Assumptions
Made in this Book', the analysis remains the same. We should
remember that the karmic system is also based on intentions.
The karmic system is not dependent on the marriage certificate
or signing of the church register. When a person lives with
another for a sizeable period of time, the treatment in terms
of karmic records is that of wife/husband. Even in the case of
same-gender couples, the karmic treatment of a long-term
sexual relationship is the same. In the karmic/spiritual world,
what is important is the long-term deep bond which results
out of initial sexual involvement. Whether two people have sex
before they sign the marriage register or *after* is hardly noteworthy.
This is also highlighted by Christ when he implies that in the
spiritual realm 'marriages' are not as relevant as on earth.[3]

In Eastern cultures, simply living together is frowned upon. In
such cases, the deep-seated guilt and/or shame of not having
'legally' married could remain. (Guilt and its impact upon the
breath have been explored earlier at length in Chapter 1). In
stricter parts of the Islamic world, living together could lead to
similar punishments to those who commit adultery.

Any long-term companionship is in keeping with a person's
hard karma. For instance, someone might be born a king
out of his previous good hard karma. In this case, even the
concubines would exert a positive influence on him. Very
clearly, the title of 'wife' does not have much relevance in the
karmic or spiritual realm. A long-term relationship lasting
for several years is better recorded in karmic records than an
arranged, short-lived 'marriage' in front of a registrar. That

is another reason why many Eastern cultures have a long marriage ceremony often lasting hours. The purpose of such elaborate ceremony and chanting of mantras or prayers is to strongly mark the event in karmic records. Chanting certain *mantras* also uses sound vibrations to etch the event in karmic records and inform the overself.

Christ's generous treatment of prostitutes also highlights his conviction that larger numbers of sexual partners do not close the doors of spiritual well-being. In fact, Christ reserves his strongest vitriol for pride, hypocrisy and intolerance. What better pointer to the biggest hurdles on the path to spirituality? Considering oneself superior owing to sexual abstinence or monogamy is quite common. It comes from our Christian or Islamic religious roots. However, this thinking is similar to the assumption that a constipated man is healthier since he is holding back the food. In Hinduism too, the influence of these Abrahamic religions on the original sexually liberated ethos has resulted in much unwarranted orthodoxy.

With this abridged, yet technically nuanced understanding of karma, we can proceed to the next chapters. Important concepts to remember since they will keep recurring in this book are the **Overself**, **CSB**, **breath and its impact**, **yearning** and **avoidance**, **hard** and **soft karma** and the interplay between all of these.

PART II

CONSENSUAL SEXUALITY

3

Want Pleasing Harlot on an Empty Pocket

Prostitution

Gautama Buddha, the great teacher, talked about freedom or *'moksha'*. Unlike the Christian paradigm, which talked about doing good deeds, helping the neighbour and involving oneself in noble deeds, the Buddha talked about freedom from desires. There is more emphasis on avoiding bad karma than accumulating good karma. Buddha wanted to lay stress on freedom from the karmic cycle of births and deaths. When there is positive karma the person has to be born again in some better world to enjoy the fruits of that karma. Maybe that better world is in a different galaxy and is so scientifically and spiritually advanced that it will be heaven for the inhabitants of our earth. A world free of violence, crime, deception and other evils would be heaven indeed. However, such a birth does not free a person from the cycle of karma. If he does something impure in that world, there are chances that he might be born again in another inferior world (the 'world' here referring to another planet or celestial body) where the conditions are worse.

Curbing Karma to find 'moksha'

Completing a disproportionate amount of good deeds is not desirable if one wants freedom from the cycle, the 'moksha'.

We could think of an interesting analogy of a boxer fighting for money. Every time he wins a big fight, he gets his big money. Then he is expected to fight a stronger and meaner opponent the next time. If he beats that opponent, then he has to fight an even fiercer opponent. If he loses the fight, he comes down in the rating again. At the end of the day, it is still like a rat race. The wiser man wants to get out of this cycle. Winning bigger and better fights that only take him to a higher level but do not grant him freedom is not the wisest of choices.

This happens because the karmic system is a perfect system of accounting. If a person has a lot of positive balance in his karmic account, he cannot escape the system unless he has made it zero. The positive balance in the karmic account has to be spent in some way by the person's overself. The overself can decide to take a physical body and birth in a family of nobles or kings on the same planet and spend one lifetime in complete luxury, thus spending the accumulated good karmas. Or the overself could decide to be born on a superior planet or celestial body. The overself could also decide to suddenly make the person win a multi-million lottery jackpot. Anything can be done to clear the extra karma. But in the case of most people, by the time the positive karma is cleared, the person born in that lifetime of luxury may accumulate additional positive or negative karma, thus unbalancing the system again. It is like the funny story of a man wanting to spend a million pounds or dollars, as part of some challenge. Eager to spend all his money, he bets on a horse, only to find out at the end of the race that the horse has won. Instead of decreasing his money his bet has only increased his funds.

Another interesting metaphor would be the person burning calories on the treadmill. If he is running on the treadmill while simultaneously eating high-calorie sweets, there is little chance that there will be a net loss of calories. In the end, the person eating sweets while taking long walks or doing his exercise on the treadmill may end up gaining more weight if what he is gaining in calories is more than what he is consuming in energy. The same happens with the person born lucky as the crown prince of a rich kingdom. Due to his previous inclinations, he may accumulate further good karma in the present life and by the end of this life, instead of spending previously accumulated good karma, he may end up adding to that account.

A similar thing happens to the guy with lots of bad karma. Let us look at a fictional example. A guy with a negative karmic backlog is born in an extremely poor part of the world. His parents die at a very young age and, due to this karma, bad luck continues to dog him. He loses his money and belongings in some natural calamity and so on. Now if this guy is smart and knows why all this is happening he will let the accumulated bad karma spend itself out in this lifetime. But what actually happens is the opposite. Driven by circumstances, this man falls into bad company and starts out on a path of crime and degeneration. By the end of this lifetime, instead of merely spending all his previous negative karma, he ends up accumulating an additional load of bad karma, which takes him another two or three lifetimes to dissipate.

Both bad and good karma can create vicious self-replicating circles. What then is the solution? The solution is to have equanimity. Equanimity means being aware of what is happening but not accumulating additional bad or good karma while allowing the previous karma to release itself. When a person is in a state of equanimity and balance, he does not allow the creation of additional karma. Another way to look at this state of equanimity is to do what is one's duty under a particular circumstance and not do it out of anger or love for the result of the action. This is the essence of the Hindu scripture, the Bhagavad Gita (advice given by Krishna to the warrior Arjun, who was vacillating from his duty of war). The soldier who fights for his country because that is his duty and not out of personal animosity hardly incurs any karma. The butcher who slaughters animals out of a sense of duty incurs no karma. When there is no guilt or no yearning, generally karmic accumulation is very negligible.

The difference between Karma-free action and repressed guilt

Some people may start noticing a contradiction here. Does it mean that the serial killer who can get a good night's sleep or the thief who sleeps peacefully in the day with robbed possessions under his bed is accumulating no karma?

Although we as human beings may not easily understand this distinction, there is a clear distinction between a **karma-free action** and **suppression** of the actual knowledge of a wrong-doing. Most of us like to believe that when we do something wrong our conscience pricks us with guilt. We also like to believe that sometimes this guilt can be very terrible and won't let us sleep peacefully at night. It is this view of guilt that gives currency to the Shakespearean tale of Macbeth where the guilty have no peace of mind.

But we know that sometimes even intelligent people directly or indirectly responsible for crimes manage to sleep peacefully. To say that all the perpetrators of the Rwandan genocide, drug lords of Latin America, warlords, murderers, rapists and serial killers are sleep-deprived people would be false. Similarly, it is hard to believe that corrupt politicians are literally unable to get a wink of peaceful sleep. If that was the case, most of the politicians in the world would be sleep-deprived people. (As we probably know, lack of sleep can kill people faster than lack of food. Would that not be an easy way to rid our earth of all wrongdoers?)

How Do Some People Deal with Guilt?

Most people with some degree of intelligence manage to push guilt to the side through rationalised analyses. Terrorists who kill innocents in America or Israel rationalise that it is revenge for the killing of their countrymen in Arab countries. Robin Hood justified himself for robbing the rich by giving part of it to the poor. Rapists often say that the victim asked for it through her provocative behaviour. Robbers and muggers rationalise that they needed the money more than the victim, or that the rich victim would not miss the money as badly as he (the robber) needed it for his survival.

But this form of rationalising is not the only method of dealing with guilt. Lots of others bury their guilt so deep in their minds that they may even forget about it. Still others try to do some good deeds to compensate for this guilt and try to rationalise it. A man guilty of killing a baby may in later years, donate a lot to a charity dealing with children's causes.

Whatever the form that a person's treatment of guilt takes, it remains in some corner of the brain. In fact, it increases the thickness of the Cosmic Sensitivity Barrier and disrupts the communication of the individual mind with the universe and receipt of cosmic knowledge. In fact, that is the reason why they say that children can see angels. Their Cosmic Sensitivity Barrier is so thin that there is almost one hundred per cent transparent communications with the universe. A child is able to communicate easily with various spiritual entities and interact with some entities called 'angels' in Christianity. There are other interesting aspects. Abiding by the universal principle that similar objects, forces and persons tend to get attracted to each other, a child born with heavy negativity from its previous life or lives, also tends to attract lot of negative spiritual entities. (That is one of the reasons that some children seem to be happy a lot, when they are alone, while other kids remain nervous, scared or crying when they are alone. They are probably seeing and encountering different types of entities.)

Guilt and Negative Karma

Wherever there is guilt – repressed or rationalised, the CSB starts thickening in various degrees. However, the presence of guilt does not automatically mean that the deed is a strongly negative karma. Let me elaborate further. A motorist who killed a cyclist by mistake suffers from heavy guilt. Actually it was the mistake of the cyclist who was riding without adequate lights and little protection. The court has exonerated the motorist. However, the motorist feels terribly guilty of killing a young person. In this case too there will be some build up of sadness and an increase in the thickness of CSB. However, if we look at this case carefully, the motorist in question is only bearing the fruits of some previous bad karma. He is not incurring any fresh negative karma out of his actions. Despite this, there is a heavy guilt that must be flushed out of his system. As probably mentioned elsewhere in this book, guilt is like a dark cloud that will result in rain somewhere. Guilt sometimes produces outcomes independent of the karmic consequences of the action. Guilt can create psychosomatic disorders, depression, lack of concentration and poor health.

Hence one could say that while guilt can exist without any negative karma being responsible for it, no negative karma can really be created without guilt being present either in its pure form or in a repressed, suppressed or rationalised form. An interesting analogy for guilt is a snake. The bite of any snake is a tension-filled and nightmare scenario for most people. Now while any snake is bad, the venomous snake is much worse because it adds to the terror of the snake bite with a potentially lethal venom. So while any guilt is bad enough, the guilt associated with an actual negative karma is doubly so because it also incurs consequences beyond the short-term.

Supposedly 'remorseless criminals' such as serial killers are often people who have succeeded in repressing or rationalising their guilt. Hence they are different from those who haven't incurred any karma while merely fulfilling their duty. A soldier of mediocre intelligence who shoots an enemy combatant while on duty, without personal hatred, incurs only very little negative karma, if at all. On the other hand, the politician who orders the bombing of innocent civilians to avenge the killing of his countrymen incurs more negative karma. The political leader may also try to completely rationalise his guilt away. He might defend himself by saying that he only fulfilled 'his duty' to avenge the deaths of his countrymen. But the politician did not do things under direct orders and had made a conscious choice in his decision-making.

How does one get this finely tuned balance between 'non-karmic action' and 'action which incurs karma' right? As mentioned earlier the simplest way is to maintain equanimity. Another way to have this equanimity is to be introspective about oneself. Some call it the ability to poke fun and laugh at oneself; the ability not to take offence even when someone makes fun of our height, weight, colour or religious belief, is a sign of equanimity. The ability not to take oneself very seriously is another requirement for not having unnecessary karma. That might be the reason why it is impossible for a devout Muslim who takes offence from others making fun of the prophet not to incur karma. Similarly, a Christian conqueror who believes that Jesus Christ is the only way to salvation and hence forcibly converts people to Christianity, will incur terrible negative karma.

Keeping Non-karma Transactions with a Prostitute

This aspect is also highlighted in the Hindu scripture, the Bhagavad Gita. Krishna advises Arjuna that only those whose minds are not disturbed by sadness, fear, anger, attachment or become unduly elated by happiness can be called sages.[1] Although the passage is not explicit in terms of the relationship with breathing pattern, Krishna has highlighted all those aspects which create any disturbance in the normal breathing pattern of the individual.

By now we know that based on intentions and use of free will, both good deeds and bad deeds have repercussions. The theme of this chapter further refines this conclusion. We know that prostitution and sexual coercion (even when subtle) is not desirable. Yet, if one is a regular customer of a prostitute, how does one make it a zero-balance karma action? The simplest way is to make sure that the prostitute or call girl is paid as per the agreement and there is no breach of trust. Firstly it is good business sense to maintain a smooth relationship between the provider of service and the customer. After all, who other than a masochist service provider will ever like an abusive, miserly and grumpy customer? Secondly, it is also the best way to avoid creating karma. Paying unusually large amounts to the prostitute out of sympathy will incur a positive karmic balance, which is not desirable. Heavy positive karmic balance here creates the possibility of being in a situation in the future where one could receive sexual benefits quite unexpectedly. In other words, one could expect and get some sort of sexual windfalls, in this life or in a future lifetime. To neutralize the positive balance, one may even be forced to take another birth.

On the other hand, cheating a prostitute incurs bad karma. Besides that, if the prostitute is really wretched, in the sense that she is doing the job as a result of her own volition but due to some bondage that she is unable to get out of, she could curse this customer. Although we live in the era where people think of 'curses', 'spells' etc. as pure fantasies only happening in Harry Potter movies, it is important to understand how curses and other malevolent psychic acts work in terms of karma.

The Mechanism of the Curse

Let us understand the concept of the curse in a little more detail. Generally, as mentioned earlier in this book, the human being in his purest form with a highly sensitive CSB was destined to have complete communication with the universe. When he is in this mode, he would be able to ask the universe for anything and be able to obtain it almost instantly. Similarly, since his words, thoughts and actions are totally consistent with his purity, his thoughts would immediately convert into words and the universe would bring forth the results almost instantly. What would be needed for it to happen is:

a) purity and
b) absolute faith.

Purity is needed because only then the CSB is thin enough to create the communication between the human being and the cosmic system. Similarly faith is needed because the moment there is a shred of doubt the total congruence between thought and word is lost. For instance, if a person says, let there be rain and he himself deep inside does not believe it is going to happen, then the universe cannot make it happen. In fact, Christ himself says it very clearly when he says that even a mountain will move if there is faith.[2] Similarly, if the man due to the thickness of CSB is not able to communicate with the universe then it will not happen. Christ does not speak in the passage about the second requirement of purity and thin CSB, because if the disciples were to follow his teachings, most probably this requirement would take care of itself. But this aspect is highlighted separately when Christ says that the 'meek shall inherit the earth' and 'blessed are the pure in heart, for they will see god'.[3]

When a person high in purity and faith asks for something from the universe, it is generally provided to him. This is what we would call a curse (or a spell). It must be noted that the mechanism of spells are slightly different from that of curses.

Some curses would work instantly, while others would come to fruition only after several years, depending upon the words. This ability to utter a powerful curse was shown by Christ when he cursed the fig tree and it withered right from its roots within a day.[4] In Hindu mythology, Durvasa was a sage who was famous for cursing humans, gods and even demi-gods. Supposedly an offspring of the Hindu God Shiva, he had an irrepressible temper and cursed many gods and humans at the slightest provocation.

Sometimes people are born in extremely sad situations merely to pay back the karma from a previous life. For example a person born congenitally blind or terribly handicapped *may* be one such case. If such persons are not incurring any fresh negative karma, then we can call them 'wretched'. Such 'wretched' persons, whether a prostitute living and working in conditions of bondage or an innocently jailed convict, carry with them some power due to the purity of their CSB. If they utter a curse from the depth of their hearts, it is most likely to come to fruition. This is also somewhat in keeping with the old Christian wisdom that the gods listen to the poor and suffering. In the Eastern traditions, many curses uttered by holy men would be uttered while touching their hands to the forehead and/or using the water from the *kamandal*. The *kamandal* is an oblong water pot used by Vedic/ Hindu ascetics or holy men, made of coconut shell, wood or metal which stores charged water. These ritualistic actions while uttering the curse transmit a confirmatory signal to the universe that the curse has been uttered and mechanisms to fulfil it can be initiated. For this reason, generally, the curses uttered by nuns, mendicants etc. who lead a simple and pure life free of falsehood, have stronger impacts because of their communicability with the cosmos (again as a result of their thin CSBs). Sometimes curses uttered by less pure persons may also bear fruit simply because the recipient of the curse keeps repeating the curse in his mind. In these cases, these curses often work on principles similar to self-hypnosis.

What about the person who pronounces a curse? Of course, this person too incurs a negative karma, depending on whether the curse is uttered out of instant anger or well thought out. That is simply because like any negative action using a physical weapon, curses use psychic/spiritual resources available with the person. The deed is still negative, only the weapon is different. This karma has to be cleared in this or some other lifetime through meditative practices or other means. Verbally spoken curses are generally more effective than mental curses, because thought curses are generally weak. However, if a person is focussed on this curse and meditates on this every day, then this thought-curse also becomes very potent. That is because, by constant meditation upon the thought, people actually tend to initiate a thought-based chain of action in the universe which harms the other person, especially if the other person is eligible for harm through his karmic records. The word 'pre-meditated' is apt for describing this form of curse.

Other Malevolent Psychic Acts: Creating Thought Forms

A more potent way of harming another person psychically than curses is by creating a supernatural invisible entity or a 'thought form'. This 'thought form' is a pure energy entity created from the mind of the meditator. This 'thought entity' can then be sent to do the bidding of the creator. Of course in practice it does not happen so easily but takes years of practice and spiritual merit, but it can be done, an example of which is mentioned in the next paragraph. *Mantras* and incantations can also be used to accelerate the development of this thought entity.

If a metaphor can be used, it is somewhat like cloning. Cloning happens at the physical level through the use of genes. A similar mental creation of a pure energy entity is possible. Just like how a physical baby is created through cloning cells and may be given tonics, better energy rich food etc. for aiding growth and development, *mantras* and chants can be used to build up this energy thought form. In fact, ancient Egyptians seemed to have potently used this technique to guard the tombs of their kings. That is one reason for the mysterious jinxed deaths of many archaeologists who worked in Egypt and opened or tampered with the burial chambers of famous kings. A detailed discussion of this phenomenon is provided by Nowicki and Brennan in their book.[5]

Of course there is severe karmic negativity in the creation of a special 'thought form' entity to do evil things. In contrast, natural, spontaneous cursing as a result of circumstances and frustration has lower karmic negativity. In some ways, it is the difference similar to that between manslaughter (due to sudden and intense passion arising from some severe provocation) and pre-meditated murder.

Other Malevolent Psychic Acts: Taking Help from Dark Forces

An even more hazardous way of creating harm is by taking the help from certain darker forces. In Hindu terminology, these forces might be called Asuric forces or Rakshasa forces, while Christian literature might term them evil spirits, satanic forces, demons or devils etc. These darker forces can be invoked in special ways and asked to do the bidding of the person wanting harm to be done against someone. Since these dark or evil entities look for opportunities to get involved in karmically darker deeds (as a result of their nature, just like forces of goodness look forward to doing good), they often accept such assignments if approached. The devastation that these dark entities can bring is often far greater and more lethal. Metaphorically the difference in the earlier methods and this method of taking assistance of evil entities is the difference between a man fighting with his own bare hands versus hiring a mob of well-armed goons and thugs to harm another. Naturally the latter method is more devastating and powerful. This sort of assistance is the one given by black magicians, voodoo practitioners and sometimes by Hindu tantrics in return for money. (*In much of the Western world, the Hindu word 'tantric' is associated only with tantric sex, but it is much more than that.*) Besides severe karmic negativity, there are real dangers of using this method of invoking these evil entities to harm others. Some of the dangers are:

- Rebound: Person X invites a dark force entity to harm another person Y. The dark forces try to attack the person Y and implement X's bidding. But unfortunately for X, Y has a strong spiritual guardian who not only protects Y from harm, but also powerfully commands the darker forces to go back and harm X himself. So the dark forces come back angry and humiliated, to attack the person X himself. It is like a bullet returning back to kill the shooter.
- Unpleasant Retention: Another danger of this method is the danger that the darker forces once invoked (especially

when the invocation is done by amateurs), refuse to go back even after completing the malevolent deed. Sometimes it is even worse and these forces refuse to do the bidding of the invoker, but continue to linger around the invoker and create all sorts of troubles, noises and nuisances in and around the area. It is similar to inviting a monkey to climb your shoulder and then finding that it cannot be easily got rid of. Young people with little knowledge who sometimes use Ouija boards to invoke spirits for 'fun' often find themselves in this position.

Can curses be withdrawn or changed? Generally, if a spontaneous curse is uttered by a spiritually realised person with a low CSB, it cannot be withdrawn. It is like an arrow shot from the bow. However, some modifications can be made. For instance if the curse is that a person will become penniless soon, the pronouncer of the curse can also make a special provision about when the curse will end. It is almost like the addition of a clause in the main contract. As long as this addition does not attempt to completely undo the main provision of this curse, it is possible. In pre-meditated curses, repairs can be done by changing the pattern of thinking and sending good vibrations to the cursed person. In a case where a thought form entity has been created, it can be asked to repair the damage, but only if it was not created by too much malevolent mental energy.

However, in the last case where assistance is taken from darker, severely negative forces, things are complicated. A darker negative entity cannot be involved in doing any good deeds. Just like a professional contract killer can only be hired to do killings and not for good deeds, darker forces will only implement negative karma and obey instructions to do only harm to others. Once the instructions are given to them, only a skilled and powerful occult practitioner can stop or modify the instructions. Needless to say, this is another reason why the use of external dark negative forces to aid malevolent deeds should always be avoided.

Curses and the Wretched Prostitute

Reverting to the discussion on breach of trust, cheating a wretched person (like the unhappy prostitute mentioned in an earlier paragraph), will have negative karma. Besides this, there is the possibility of their curse. Having said this, curses of such a wretched person (mentioned above) act like a big expenditure from their own karmic savings bank account. But despite this, they may be aggrieved and depressed enough to spend from their karmic savings or incur fresh karmic debts by cursing. Hence the more wretched the condition of the prostitute that one sleeps with, the more careful one has to be to make sure that obligations in terms of remuneration have been fully met. Similarly a politician or government official in a third-world country who asks a poor lady to sleep with him in return for obtaining a job must under all circumstances fulfil his obligation once she has accepted his condition. Of course this act of coercion is in itself very bad karma, coming under the category of explicit coercion. Most probably such a government official will have to be at the receiving end of a similar situation in this or another lifetime. This is in addition to the real danger of a powerful curse. There is a possibility that he could be born in the future on another planet as a woman in similar or worse circumstances. People who cheat wretched prostitutes also face similar karmic paybacks, besides the danger of a curse.

A man simply visiting a prostitute does not incur the same kind of negativity as the government official mentioned in the previous paragraph. Unlike that government official, this man is not fully responsible for this prostitute's situation or adding to the wretchedness. However, there is a slight possibility of indirect responsibility. If all men stopped visiting prostitutes like her, the business interest of people pushing her into sex slavery might vanish. They might even find her some other work. Faced with danger, she might be forced to venture out on her own and find other suitable occupations. Forced or near-forced prostitution only functions when there is steady demand for newer women brought into business from men who could not care less. Of course, educated women working as upscale independent escorts in developed countries rarely fall into this category, because they do so out of their own free will.

Should Wretched People be Given Additional Remuneration?

The same wretchedness holds true for the prostitute who is in the business not out of her full free will but due to a combination of unfair circumstances. These might be lack of education, destitute poverty or terrible social conditions. Her birth in such familial conditions could probably be the result of her previous karma. So if she is merely bearing the cross of the previous karma in this life while avoiding accumulation of fresh negative karma, then her curses will have enhanced potency. Even while enjoying such a prostitute, it must be done with empathy and understanding. Such a prostitute is also likely to respond well to a shower of understanding and love. Of course as noted earlier, too many good deeds done to people in 'wretched' circumstances will add positive karma in our balance. There is also the danger that powerful blessings may be sent to us in a mechanism similar to the curse. If one is thinking of accumulating positive karmic balance, it might be desirable. For those who are seeking liberation from the cycle of births and deaths, this would be like another stone tied to their ankles. Prostitutes who seek and accept any undeserved additional remuneration may develop low self-esteem. Part of this might be due to blunt refusals from some other customers since additional remuneration was not agreed upon *a priori*. Of course if the additional remuneration is for extra services provided by the prostitute, then it is a just and deserved reward. However, if it was not agreed upon at the time of providing the service, the customer cannot be held liable to pay additional charges. Since karmic laws can see the intention, it is different from how a human law court would look at it. In a human law court, the man would be simply free to not pay any additional charges since it was not agreed upon. In karma, any man who enjoys an additional service but refuses to pay, despite knowing well that he should have paid, accumulates some negative karma. However, a man who was genuinely not aware of the need to make additional payments and was under the impression that the additional services were part of the normal service does not accumulate any negative karma for refusing to pay.

Imagine a situation where the prostitute has only agreed to provide simple penetrative sex. However, once in the room she also gives a man an enjoyable kiss and a sensual massage. In this situation, it is only more exalted behaviour karmically if the man compensates her additionally although it was not agreed upon. However, the prostitute cannot curse the man with any high potency (causing future ill effect). The curse will have little impact, since there is no real breach of promise and the grievance felt by the prostitute is largely of her own making. The prostitute might have given additional services in the first place with the ulterior motive of extracting additional money out of the client. This in turn suggests a level of cunning and a poor sign of CSB purity (thinness), which is essential for the curse to fructify.

How the Karmic System Balances Positivity

Let us also look at some peripheral issues. Let us assume that the genteel prostitute who showered her client with additional favours does not ask him for any additional remuneration and never shows any change of facial expression or unpleasantness. In her mind too, she does not have any expectation of additional payment. Despite the fact that the man in question does not incur any serious negative karma for not paying additionally (as mentioned in the last paragraph), there is positivity generated within him. Everyone who gets something extra for nothing is usually delighted. What is notable is that unlike many win-lose situations, the prostitute has not built up any negativity equivalent to the positivity generated by the man. If the man felt positive and this level of positive feeling was balanced by the negative feeling or bitterness by the prostitute at being 'duped of extra money', then there is no net positivity created at the cosmic level.

Now comes the exciting part. Since the prostitute did not have any negativity that balanced out the positivity felt by her client, the cosmic system has to provide some other form of positive reward in the future *to the prostitute* so as to balance the additional reward obtained by the man. Now this is the exciting part. No unrewarded act goes truly unrewarded by the karmic system.

In fact this takes us to some very important lessons, which are shared by books on positive thinking and many religious scriptures. All such literature tells us that we should not be bitter when we have some bitter experience through no fault of our own. If a person takes advantage of us and we know it, we should not feel very bitter about it. Most of the time we relate this advice to the principle of being good human beings. But the fact of the matter is that it is also a very pragmatic principle. Whenever we are negative about being taken advantage of, our high negativity and anger might cancel out our cosmic rewards, which the karmic system was supposed to give us. Most books of success and self-help available in the market today talk of this principle.

Returning Positivity: The Story of the Sage

There is an ancient Indian tale worth narrating in this context. Once, a Hindu *rishi* (holy man or seer) was standing on the bank of a river. Finding no boat to take him across, he decided to swim. Suddenly he heard the voice of a black scorpion nearby. Since this *rishi* was a great soul, he could instantly communicate with the scorpion. The scorpion told him that it wanted to cross the river also. Would the sage kindly take it across? The scorpion suggested that it would sit on the back of the sage and the sage could swim across the river while making sure his back was on the surface of the water, so that the scorpion would not flow away in the strong current. The great sage agreed to transport the scorpion on his back. While still halfway in the river, the black scorpion, sitting on the back of the sage started stinging him, injecting full poison. The sage writhed in pain but still continued to carry the scorpion on his back. After some time the scorpion repeated its action. By this time the sage had started turning blue due to the effect of the poison but he continued to swim across. When the sage reached the other bank, the people waiting there saw him swimming with a black scorpion on his back and were stunned.

They were even more stunned to see the scorpion merrily stinging the sage on his back every few minutes. "Is the sage such a fool?" some of them could not help remarking. "Why couldn't he just take a deep dip in the river and then the scorpion would have been swept away from his back in a jiffy?" When they reached the river a crowd had gathered around the sage. The scorpion promptly jumped off the back of the sage, thanked the sage for the transport and scampered away. People asked the sage instantly why he did not take a dip and dump the ungrateful scorpion in the river while it was relentlessly stinging him.

The reply of the sage is a powerful lesson in understanding goodness and bearing negative circumstances. The sage said, "When the scorpion did not change its nature despite knowing the consequences that it could face, how can I change my nature for fear of consequences?" In other words, the sage was pointing to the fact that while it is the nature of a scorpion to sting, it was the nature of a sage to do good and return positivity for negativity. This is also a powerful lesson in the concept of being proactive (a concept which has gained much currency after the popularity of Stephen Covey's powerful book *Seven Habits of Highly Effective People*). While the sage could have been reactive to the actions of the scorpion, he chose not to react but to respond.

Karmic Template for Fair Business Practices

Coming back to the question of the prostitute, is the customer expected to do favours by showering extra money on the prostitute? As explained in the earlier paragraphs, that will yield unhealthy results in the future. The prostitute who takes that money given as charity knows that she has not done anything to deserve it. Therefore there is every possibility that she might be born in some life as a servant to serve the customer. Maybe on a not-so-advanced planet, the customer might be born as a landlord and she might be born as a slave serving him all the time. In fact, one reason why many good masters of *Reiki* (a system of healing which originated from Japan) charge their customers, is that free healing energy supplied to a person may create avoidable karmic debt for the patient. The same will happen to a doctor who treats a patient totally free. The patient should try to pay something to the doctor if he is satisfied with the treatment. For instance in a poverty-stricken situation like in Africa or parts of Asia or Latin America, the doctor could be paid for his/her services in kind, in vegetables, fruits, food grains or livestock. Doctors should accept some form of remuneration, even in poor countries, in order to clear the karmic obligation of the poor patient. Sometimes people who are treated for free, leave the office of the doctor stating that they will pray for him. However, on reaching their homes, they forget all about it and do not utter a single prayer consciously for the doctor. This puts these patients in karmic obligation to the doctor.

Now if a Reiki expert is charging money, how does one know whether the price is right or excessive? After all, the expert does not want to give his service free, since by doing so, he himself accumulates positive karma and puts the receiver in an obligation forever. We could apply this dilemma to businesses also. How does a manufacturer or supplier of services know whether the price he is charging is karmically right? A simple test would be to gauge the reaction of the buyer or the customer. If the patient of the Reiki expert tenses up or has a totally unfavourable reaction after seeing the bill, most probably, the Reiki expert has crossed the limit of karmic balance. He is now operating in the area of greed. Another rule of thumb is to find the average price of such service in the local area and then price it a little lower than the average price. However, when calculating such a simple average price, one should apply common sense and ignore data outliers.

The Case for Compassionate Capitalism

If the customer is not expecting to be charged so much for the product in a situation like this, even if he/she pays up the money, the feeling that it was a terrible 'rip-off' generates some future consequence for the seller. Let us elaborate with an example. A traveller moving around in a desert on his camel finds to his dismay that his water bag has fallen off somewhere. Since he has no idea where it might have happened on his journey of fifty miles, he cannot go back. Moreover, he still has to travel thirty miles north to reach his destination. So this thirsty traveller moves on. To his luck he meets another traveller coming from the opposite direction. This traveller has a lot of water bags hanging from his camel. Our thirsty traveller is immediately excited and asks the other traveller whether he is open to selling one water bag. Now both the travellers know that the cost of such a water bag would be say, the equivalent of thirty dollars in the cities just before or after the desert. The second traveller sees that his prospective customer is almost parched and completely fatigued due to thirst. So he immediately quotes a price of $300 (approx. £208) for the bag of water. The first traveller requests him to reduce the price. "Well, I am not forcing you to buy it…" is the answer of the seller. The buyer is keen on pressing his terrific advantage and making the maximum money of this situation. This is exactly where our capitalist system loses out on ethics. If your product is reasonably good and you know you have an advantage in making customers buy them, there is no cap on the greed. After all, the argument is that they are not forcing anyone to buy. Now let us look at what actually happens in the desert when the second traveller hears this price. He, in his desperate state, pays $300 to the seller. In economics we often refer to this as an act on the part of the seller as price discrimination. Taking full advantage of a situation is a good method to maximize the revenue for the business. An airline might charge an extraordinarily high price for the last minute passenger who wants to visit his dying relative in another city.

But if we understand the karmic system we will better appreciate the consequence of getting into this kind of greedy price discrimination. Let us continue with the example of the desperate traveller. After buying the product and drinking his water while on the move, he will curse himself (for losing the bag) and the unfair, greedy seller. The satisfaction and contentedness that he receives for being able to quench his raging thirst is not enough to balance his negativity for the seller and for the loss of money. This strongly projected negativity has the potential to seep into the karmic system of the seller of the goods, such that in this lifetime or any future lives, that seller will also have to face a rapacious vendor of goods and bear the same feeling of being ripped off. That would be the karmic pay back.

Hence if we are producers of goods or services, it might be a good idea to adopt a more compassionate version of capitalism. Price discrimination is not bad, but it should not be so much that it generates terrible negativity in the mind of the buyer. For instance, if the water bag is normally selling for thirty dollars, this seller could have sold it for fifty dollars without suffering too much negativity. The buyer would have probably understood that the extra twenty dollars would be able to motivate this seller to take the trouble to carry all the additional water bags. Sometimes a buyer is not aware of all the costs, risks etc. and so expects a much lower price. For instance the customer might not be aware that the government charges a heavier tax on some inputs used by the seller or that the rent for the premises is high. The buyer could be made to feel comfortable by engaging him/her in a dialogue and explaining why the extra twenty dollars are being charged for the bag (elaborating on the cost of time, risk and the trouble taken). This practice of 'compassionate capitalism' creates a more friendly and receptive customer, which is not only good for repeat business, but also a good strategy for karmic harmony.

Karmic Rules for Refund

With respect to the question of the prostitute, there are other scenarios. What if, after the booking is over and the payment made, the client visits the prostitute only to mention that he does not want the service today. Should she not refund him the money? Or does the client have the right to expect the money back? As we all know in business dealings, time is money. Therefore the prostitute is well within her rights to keep full payment for the hour, even if no service was provided. There is nothing inappropriate in this. However, there are interesting karmic situations where variations could be expected. What if the prostitute knew very well that either way she would not have had any other work or appointment? If she is aware that she never actually had to refuse any other client who wanted the same hour and there was never any question of lost earnings, karmically the right thing to do in such a scenario would be to refund some part of the money (especially if it is a large amount). Retaining the whole amount knowing fully well that there was no actual service and no lost earnings would accumulate a bit of negative karma, which would have to be repaid to the client in some form in this lifetime or the next.

Karmic impact of ill treatment towards prostitutes is generally worse than the impact of ill treatment of women generally enjoying sexuality. In general, the karmic ill effects of an act are more pronounced when the victim is in an underdog position merely paying back his/her previous negative account. For instance violence against a man born blind has greater karmic consequences than violence against a normal able-bodied guy. Any act of abuse of power against a disadvantaged person has more severe consequences. Violence against children, handicapped and vulnerable others, would fall in this category.

Are People Born in Poor or Disadvantaged Situations Always Bearing their Past Karma?

Seeing people suffering or in disadvantaged circumstances should not automatically lead us to assume that they are suffering due to previous bad karma. This may not always be the correct assumption. Let us look at an example. A person may be put in prison for a couple of weeks as a punishment for some petty crime. Another person may confine himself in a retreat centre for a couple of weeks in order to achieve some spiritual milestone through meditation. (In fact some good prisons in countries like Sweden or Norway may be better in terms of facilities and conveniences than some of the meditation and retreat centres.) For a layperson, both of these may look like confinement situations, but the wise would be able to discriminate between the two situations.

The same is true for those who are seen to be bearing unfortunate circumstances. Some suffer as a result of previous karma. On the other hand, it is also true that some of the great spiritual entities deliberately choose a painful experience for their spiritual advancement. Certain higher beings might be consciously trying to accrue some spiritual merit through a difficult life while also accomplishing some other earthly mission or purpose. For instance a great soul like Christ may choose to be crucified for certain purposes. Similarly, another great soul may choose to be born as an African slave and suffer for some mission, which could be either spiritual or worldly.

Sometimes when intelligent life forms on a particular planet in a particular galaxy are stuck at some point in their advancement and need to go to the next level, a great soul sometimes decides to help the civilization on that planet, by being born on that planet and providing the necessary push in some area of science, literature, philosophy or religion, which can take that planet to the next level. It is like a terrible traffic jam on a busy crossroad, where the services of some outsider, such as police personnel, are needed to restore order. For instance, when mankind was stuck at Newtonian levels of physics, which considered time-space as absolute and unchangeable dimensions, another paradigm of thinking was needed for science on this planet to move further. Based on this need, Albert Einstein was born to bridge this gap and take humanity to the level of relativity in time and space. There is every probability that the next level of paradigm shift in thinking will further bridge the gap between certain spiritual phenomenon and science. After all, in the highly evolved worlds, there is no gap between what is classified as science and spirituality.

Only those with a shallow understanding of karma think that those who are seen as suffering are necessarily paying for their past negative karma. The wise know this is not a comprehensive and general explanation in all cases. Hence, based on our incomplete knowledge of a person's entire karmic records, we should never try to judge anyone who is suffering.

4

Movie Stars Without Clothes Act the Best

Pornography

One of the most unintentional impacts of the internet revolution is the explosion of the pornographic industry. It is very difficult for a person using the internet regularly to avoid being exposed to some form of pornography without some specialized protective software. Even when pornography is prevented by use of complicated firewalls and preventative settings, one may be exposed to different forms of sexuality through online chats, sharing of pictures using email etc. In fact, an article from 2006 suggests that eighty-seven per cent of university students in Canada have sex using the webcam, instant messenger or even the telephone.[1] Millions more worldwide have access to the internet today than in 2006, so we can only imagine the expansion. Some figures of internet pornography are staggering. For instance some statistics portals mention that close to $3000 (approx. £2070) are being spent *every second* in the world for pornography.[2] $3000 is the yearly salary of many people in developing and poorer countries. The same article also states that the revenues of the porn industry are bigger than the combined revenues of the biggest names of the internet world (Microsoft, Yahoo, Amazon, E-bay and Google). Around 2001, the total revenues of the smut industry were pegged at around

$4 (approx. £2.76) billion.[3] Even if the second estimate is considered, it is still larger than the GDP of many countries in the world. There are other sources which emphasise that increasing usage of internet porn in the office is resulting in losses of astronomical amounts due to lost productivity.[4] Several UK newspapers reported the story of an Australian banker caught red-handed watching pornography in his office as another analyst spoke into a live camera about business matters.[5]

Those who pretend pornography does not exist often live an ostrich-like existence. A good example of such an organisation is the Catholic Church, which acknowledges that religious workers including priests and nuns must have access to internet technology in order to spread their message and work efficiently. Yet, in an ostrich-like manner the Church believes that these workers will somehow be miraculously insulated from the temptations of a sexualized internet. It is like sending a person without any medication or vaccination to live among smallpox patients and hoping that he/she will be miraculously protected from the disease. Even without the omnipresent challenge of the internet, sexual chastity is a challenge to all Catholic priests and nuns. After all, the young, well-developed body does have a sexual need, at least on occasions. Only after reaching a state of meditative bliss (a rough equivalent of the physical orgasm) can a person hope to reach a position of sexual conquest. Even a near-saint like Gandhi failed in some of his sexual experiments when he found that he woke up one night with an erection.[6,7] This was a humiliating experience for Gandhi who had tremendous pride in his ability to 'conquer sex'.

Karmic Implications of Pornography

If we go by religious books such as the Quran and the Bible, we find some verses that condemn pornography indirectly. What are the karmic issues related to pornography? One needs to go into some of these arguments before we talk about the karmic implications. For instance, one of the bedrocks of the Catholic teaching against pornography is based on the idea that sex itself, if used for anything other than procreation purposes, is wrong. It is this central objection that appears again in their views against the use of the condom. When sex is not meant for pleasure, anything that deals with the idea of sex as a pleasurable activity cannot be ethical. For this reason alone pornography is condemned by the Catholic Church as a sin. An extension of this argument is that even a husband who looks at an erotic homemade video of he and his wife making love is committing the sin of injecting sinful pleasure into what should be a strictly procreative function.

Adultery? Or a Foundation for Sexually Permissive Marriages?

We all probably know that most of those who enjoy pornography do not always watch their own videos. After all, if one goes to the effort to watch pornography, why not watch someone other than their partners. It is this prospect that worries the religious sticklers more. They contend that even when one is not physically doing it, the act of getting involved in the pleasure of others is almost a direct violation of the sixth commandment on adultery.[8] Interestingly, the internet is in many ways, one of the many nails in the coffin of sexual exclusivity in marriages and relationships.

Islam and Pornography

There are other interesting non-Christian secular arguments
against pornography. But before we go into these, it might be
worthwhile to know the Islamic perspective on pornography.
An oft-quoted verse of the Quran against pornography in
Chapter 16, verse 90, forbids injustice and 'shameful deeds.'[9]
Some versions use the word 'indecency' or 'lewdness' instead
of 'shameful deeds'.[10] This verse is quite general and states
nothing explicitly about pornography. Some books and articles
speak of the Prophet's views against pornography using the
verses in Hadiths, rather than the Quran.[11] Hadiths are based
on reports/traditions/narratives from the time of the Prophet,
considered sacred text by Muslims.

The author Abdul Malik mentions that *'fuhsha'* used in 16:90
is the word for shameful, and is a word used (among others),
for 'un-Islamic sexual behaviour.'[12] This, read with the earlier
paragraph, is somewhat like a paradoxical cycle. Pornography
is *un-Islamic* because it is *shameful*. It is *shameful* because it is
un-Islamic. This leaves no one the wiser. Most of these Islamic
verses refer to the indecency and shamefulness of sexual
behaviour. Aren't these subjective terms based on the realities
of that time period in medieval Arabia? The argument that
the Prophet remained silent on the subject of pornography
because pornography as an industry did not exist at that time
might be a noteworthy one. During Prophet Muhammad's
time, a pornographic industry didn't really exist, let alone an
exponentially growing global pornographic industry as is the
case today. Wealthy men of his time, who felt the need for
sexual variety, probably took on concubines who took care
of their sexual needs.[13] Even if one accepts this argument,
it merely means we do not know the mind of Prophet

Muhammad on this matter. If such a well-developed industry existed at that time, where women could freely choose to become pornographic stars as easily as choosing to become a hairdresser, the Quranic views might have been different. Probably Prophet Muhammad would have made some injunctions to ensure the safety and consent of the women who became part of the pornographic industry. This is similar to his interventions to ensure more respect for women in the society that existed during his time. Perhaps it might be useful here to delve slightly deeper into sexuality, women and Islam.

Prophet Muhammad, Sexuality and Women

Despite perceptions to the contrary, anyone who reads about Prophet Muhammad can see what a great liberal he was *for his time* (as mentioned in Chapter 1 of this book under the section on Prophet Muhammad and karma theory). However, like many other religions, Islamic rituals and symbolisms often end up being more important than the actual spiritual guidance and experience. In Islam, purely contextual teachings relevant only to that period's social, political and economic conditions are too many. Unfortunately many Muslims continue to believe in them as universal teachings, often without thinking deeply about whether all other religious scriptures are wrong. They often believe that the words of the Quran were given directly by God to the Prophet Muhammad. This erroneous perception of greatness (since words of the Quran supposedly come directly from God) often makes Islam a bit intolerant to the voices of spirituality coming from other religions. But if one dispassionately reads the Islamic holy texts, we can discern the imprint of Prophet Muhammad's lifestyle and background on these texts. Similarly, one often forgets that

Muhammad was also a tough, pragmatic ruler and many of the ironclad 'rules' mentioned in the Quran (or ascribed to him in the Hadiths) are derived from his desire to be an exemplary administrator.

When one looks closely at Prophet Muhammad's choices in life, his liberal views on sexuality become more apparent. For instance, historical records say that the prophet married a widow named Khadija when he was merely twenty-five and she was around forty.[14] Again there are various sources that mention that he also married a girl of six but consummated that marriage when she was nine.[15] This in fact leads some of the Islam-baiters to say that the Prophet was a paedophile by today's standards. But applying today's standards on events that are several centuries old might not be ethically appropriate. In any case, there are Islamic scholars who dispute this and say that she was actually older than nine, despite what was mentioned in the Hadiths.[16] However, since most of the Islamic scholars also swear by the importance of the Hadiths[17], one can understand it as an event which might have happened but which is preferred not to be talked about by Islamic scholars. After all, in today's world we consider the idea of marriage or any sexual contact with minors quite abhorrent.

Considering the age difference between Muhammad's partners in his marriage, his views on marriages between partners with a wide-age gap would have been rather benevolent and liberal. It is relatively common to find older Muslim men marrying girls in their teens and twenties. For instance, the Quran permits men to marry up to four times[18]. It is quite possible that by the time the man reaches a stage of his life where he is able to take on a fourth wife, he is already quite middle-aged.

To Muslims who believe in the inviolability of every word in the Quran, can this number be a God-destined number for all humanity? No other religions specify such a precise number. Hence it is likely that Muhammad thought of this as a practical measure to create a more balanced society especially since the ratio of women to men during his time was much higher. One probable reason for this skewed ratio could be the internecine war in the Arab world, during Muhammad's time. Large numbers of soldiers were being killed, leaving behind several young, lonely widows. This permission to keep four wives could have been Muhammad's pragmatic solution to the problem.

Similarly the injunction to give women their *mehr* (bride money) made in the Quran[19], gives away the liberal outlook of Prophet Muhammad. In several other cultures there is the concept of dowry, which is given to the male's family at the time of marriage. This custom has often demeaned women in those cultures and is one reason for the preference of male children in those cultures. Bride money in Islam seems to send the message that a woman is precious. It is unlikely that *mehr* is the universal desire of a god almighty to make sure women got their 'bride money'. After all, the concept of bride money was more of a local custom rather than a universal practice. It is difficult to believe that a cosmic entity would issue precise instructions in a book destined for all humanity especially when the instructions were more suitable for one corner of the world. In general, wherever the Prophet Muhammad has dealt with sexuality or women, the verses in the Quran have talked about mercy and the forgiveness of Allah. It is a terrible pity that many Muslims do not really understand this liberal spirit of the Prophet.

But did the Quran not condemn women to an existence behind the terrible veil? In fact, quite the contrary; if one looks at the two most important Quranic verses which talk about the veil, one can see the error of extremist Muslims in making this an excuse for the suppression of women. Chapter 24, verse 31 of the Quran is the most extensive one that deals with this. In this verse, Muhammad says that women should lower their gaze and guard their modesty. However, what is interesting is that the immediate preceding verse says that men should do the same.[20] Moreover, verse 31 deals with women but is gentle, mentioning several groups of exceptions. It is almost like a gentle scolding that the pastor in a church might reserve for his highly fashionable congregation of young ladies. Moreover, since the prophet is clearly mentioning that the gaze should be lowered, it is clear that the face does not need to be covered. Quite obviously, in a face that is completely hidden and covered (as we see among Muslim women in some parts of the world), there is no meaningful reason for a lowering of the gaze. Similarly in the second part of the same verse, the prophet talks about not displaying the private parts. There is nothing surprising in this exhortation. Even the most liberal countries in the world rarely permit adults to walk around displaying their private parts.

Of course, some Muslim commentators and scholars have made this verse more contemporary by using the phrase 'guard modesty' instead of 'do not display private parts'.[21] The same liberal tone is reinforced in another verse which Muslims often quote with reference to women.[22] Here again, the prophet says that women who go abroad should preferably not show their face to prevent annoyance/harassment. This is certainly not a commandment from God, but clearly like a travel advisory for the safety of those women who travel in foreign lands. It can be that, the Prophet is making an assumption that women will be often travelling to other places without anyone accompanying them. If male(s) were accompanying a woman, naturally the fear of her being harassed or molested would not have perhaps crossed the Prophet's mind. If one looks at the whole verse, the concern that the prophet has for the safety of women travelling unaccompanied in unfamiliar territories is what shines through. Certainly the verse does not talk of godly punishments or great curses falling upon those who travel without covering their face. Also, if the first part of the verse is not good enough to convey the liberal and moderate world view of the Prophet, he has ended the verse clearly on a benevolent note, by stating that God is ever-forgiving and gentle. Although not explicitly stated, this is again a proof of the liberal nature of the Quran and Prophet Muhammad. Sometimes one observes today's orthodox Muslims implementing the exact opposite of these things in letter and spirit.

Today, unfortunately, some parts of the Islamic world are controlled by sadists and extremist fanatics who refuse to see reason. Thankfully, the majority of Muslims in the developed world enjoy modern life and do not swallow all the toxic prescriptions of the radicals. These extremist Islamic ideologists have converted what clearly was a benign advice into insidious and powerful moral injunctions, enforced often through ruthless coercion and violence using the power of the state in several Islamic countries such as Saudi Arabia or Iran. Besides, they also ignore the second part of the verse which talks about the forgiveness of Allah. The Prophet's appeal that men should lower their gaze has rarely been talked about by these fanatical hijackers of liberal Islam. These examples clearly show that even the most liberal sayings of Prophet

Muhammad have been usurped by poorly-educated religious fanatics who have not taken a broad and empathetic view of spirituality from different religions.

Secular Arguments against Pornography

Let us visit some other secular arguments against pornography. Some sociologists believe that pornography is another form of male domination and exploitation of women.[23] There are two interesting points which counter this outlook on pornography as a form of domination. To begin with, some statistics suggest that one in three visitors to adult-only websites are women.[24] Unless the argument is extended to state that only masochistic women visit adult-only websites to watch the 'exploitation' of one of their kind, the assertion of women as the exploited does not seem to be true. Almost all the women who work in the adult industry, at least in developed liberal democracies, are often those who do so out of their own choice. So definitely, there is more to the pornography industry, at least in developed countries, than the sad story of exploitation. Secondly there are other interesting variations of mainstream pornography like gay pornography and lesbian pornography where the interaction is confined to the same sex. The 'sexual power struggle' – the subject of sociologist debates – can hardly be the high point of these pornographic depictions.

Technologically-driven Dimensions to Pornography

Pornography today also has other dimensions, thanks to technology. If we look at internet-based pornography, the static pornographic model has also been supplemented in a

big way with the dynamic customized pornographic model.
For instance, pornographic magazines and internet websites
which post erotic pictures or even videos can be classified as
static pornography. Here, people whose images are shown
through the video or erotic pictures have little control over
who views the images. Of course the website itself can
have broad category-based controls. For example, by using
credit card details, they can verify the age of the viewer and
prevent others from viewing the images. Similarly, magazine
vendors can make sure the magazine is not sold to underage
customers. Beyond these one or two checkpoints they have
no control over who uses their product. On the other hand
the dynamic pornographic model is more challenging. Using
systems like PayPal to pay, it is possible today for a viewer to
arrange a lady to have a live pornographic show in the privacy
of his bedroom, without having the trouble to drag himself
to an actual stripping club, bar or brothel. Also, this is much
safer from the angle of hygiene and safety for the escort or
prostitute, besides saving energy and trouble. Interestingly,
technology often blurs the lines between action and various
issues. Would such a dynamic interaction between two players
using the internet come under the domain of sexuality with
a prostitute or should it be simply considered interactive
pornography?

If there is no payment involved, but merely two consenting
people who meet on the internet and have a wonderfully
stimulating sexual experience starting with harmless chatting,
should it come under the definition of dynamic pornography
or would it come under sexual experience with a stranger?
Would chatting on the internet culminating in an orgasm be
called virtual or 'cyber' sex or is it simply a case of online
interactive pornography? Some people might hesitate to call

it pornography if they find a sexy stranger in a chat room and chat to their heart's content, simply because there is no monetary exchange or because the people involved are not professionals. But there are other interesting angles to be considered. If transfer of money in some form is the only definition of pornography, then many free pornography websites should not be called pornographic at all, should they? There are also websites where the pornographic content like photographs and videos are uploaded by willing visitors to the websites, most of them being non-professionals. In fact these websites get more visitors because they welcome content from visitors.

Is Sex-Related Work a Negative Karma?

Sometimes an argument that pornography amounts to 'selling the body' is used. The same argument is often used against prostitution. People often look down on sex workers and others doing adult work (like pornography, webcam chats or phone chatting for money etc.) citing this argument. But those who say this forget that most average people sell their talents, their energy and skills to corporations in order to get their salary. Hence to an extent, every person who works for an organisation is like a prostitute, either selling their brains, or their education, or their skills. People who are engaged in purely manual work, which requires physical strength and energy, are also 'selling their body'. People who lift cartons or do other activities requiring physical strength are also 'selling their body'. The only difference is that a person who lifts a heavy box physically and puts it on a shelf brings his body only in touch with an inanimate object. The sex worker or the worker in the adult-movie industry brings his or her body in contact with another human being and at times, may even enjoy the work more than a carton-mover or a plumber. In terms of karma therefore, as long as there is no guilt about it, a good honest adult-industry worker who earns a good living is no farther or closer to spiritual realization than an average employee in a corporation.

From the karmic viewpoint, pornography itself would not have karmic negativity. It would be as bad as excessive eating, drinking or leisure activities, principally because in terms of karma, the argument of sex being not for pleasure is as pointless as the argument that eyes were not created by God for watching television, nor were the human fingers designed to type text messages on the mobile phone. The wrist was not designed by God to carry a watch nor the neck created to take the weight of a diamond necklace. The feet were not created to press the accelerator pedal of a car or change gears on a motorbike. This debate on the 'divine' purpose of organs could be endless. Therefore if eyes that were not originally created for television-viewing could watch television, why can't the sexual organs relay all the pleasurable sensations to the human mind without actually creating a baby? Hence if a husband watches nude pictures of his wife, and enjoys himself, there is little karmic negativity here.

Violations of Privacy: Pornography Without Consent

However, there are other issues that have more serious karmic implications. If one person is viewing the nude image of another person without having the permission to do so, it is a violation of that person's trust. This would be a case of voyeurism, which is dealt with in more detail in Chapter 7 along with the karmic consequences for this. However, an abridged understanding can be given below. For example, if Mr. A, after obtaining the permission of his wife, Mrs. A, has videotaped her in various sexual positions for their mutual enjoyment, there is nothing wrong. But if Mr. C, a friend or relative of Mr. A were to steal and view this tape, he is not only guilty of stealing someone else's property, which generates karmic negativity, but also commits a strong breach of trust against the lady whom he is watching through that tape. It is a violation of her right to privacy.

At the karmic and cosmic level, the procedure for privacy violation is very simple. We can compare it to the enterprise resource-planning software systems employed by corporations. In many marketing-driven companies, the moment a sales executive makes a sale and he punches the order into his hand-held computer system, instantly the message is passed to the production department asking them to produce that item. The moment the production department gets the message, another message goes to the inventory section and a parallel message might go to the accounting department about the value of that sales order. In other words, it is a completely automated system. The karmic system is a similarly automated, powerful cosmic system that functions with similar but completely error-free mechanisms. Of course the karmic system is a million times faster, because it is not bound by the constraints of time and physical barriers.

The moment Mr. C, the thief, starts watching the tape of Mrs. A, a karmic security/privacy violation alarm is conveyed to Mrs. A's overself (refer to the introductory chapters about the overself) and subconscious mind. Since Mr. C is not conducting this violation through astral or non-physical means, but acting within the time-space dimension, the subconscious system sends a message to Mr. C's overself stating that Mr. C has indulged in a karmic negativity which has to be repaid in some form. Mr. C's overself takes note of the karmic negativity from Mrs. A's overself and automatically debits Mr. C's karmic accounts further.

However, the karmic procedure is slightly different in a case where Mr. C is violating privacy through non-physical means. For instance, if Mr. C is blessed with some psychic powers of remote viewing and is merely abusing that power to view Mrs. A when she is making love with her husband. In such a case, Mrs. A's subconscious security/privacy system will simply rise up and give a powerful blow to the remote viewing capability of Mr. C (the psychic equivalent of a punch in the face) to stop the person watching.

In case the pictures of Mrs. A are published without her consent in a widely circulated magazine, the major part of the karmic negativity will rest on the shoulders of the editor who gave the go-ahead for publishing it. Even in third-world countries where laws protecting privacy are not well developed, karmic laws and procedures are very unambiguous. Similarly, if a video clip is widely available on the internet through a website, the responsibility of making sure that the persons depicted in the pornographic video have given their consent for wide and unrestricted viewing of the video rests on the person who originally posts that video.

If a pornographic video is not freely available on the internet and only available on payment of a specific amount of money, it probably also means that the persons exhibiting themselves on the video would not want people to see and enjoy their bodily charms without paying for it. Therefore those who pay for such videos must not make free copies or distribute it. If they did this would automatically cause them to accumulate karmic negativity for stealing and violation of privacy. Some people might argue that if a woman has already shown every inch of her body to one hundred admirers, would it make much difference if another five hundred admirers see it? Isn't her coy privacy act a big sham under these circumstances?

Well, privacy need not be a binary calculation where either one shows their body to nobody or they show it to everybody. For example, just because a woman had fifty partners does not mean that another fifty men can force themselves on her and say, "She is not a virgin anyway, what difference does it make?" That is a sick, inadmissible logic only used by rapists in some courts. Similarly, in the area of privacy, a woman might choose to display her body to one thousand people within a year and yet for the remaining part of her life guard her privacy zealously. That is her ultimate decision and choice. Therefore all those who are not authorised by her have no right to watch her body or sexual acts, and going against this decision would attract negative karma. However, if the lady is well aware that her videos are being uploaded on to a freely available, public website, then she cannot complain about her privacy 'being violated'. She also does not have reasonable grounds to feel bitter if she finds that her highly sexual video has been shared and has landed on the desks of her office colleagues a decade after she has all but forgotten about it.

The same holds true for sex using a webcam or the use of intimate self-portraits in sexual messaging (in a situation of dynamic pornography). If a person is exhibiting his/

her body through a webcam on the internet in return for a similar favour, the assumption made here on both sides is that there is an unwritten bond of confidentiality and privacy. However, if one of the partners has an intention of recording the webcam act for later viewing or sharing with his friends, he or she must clearly inform the other person, or this creates karmic negativity. Everyone who watches this video knowing that it was made in breach of trust also incurs karmic negativity. It is very clearly a breach of trust, mainly on the part of the first person who recorded what was only meant for mutual enjoyment during *that time only*. The easiest karmic implication of this kind of breach of trust is that the aggressor, in this case, may become the victim of such a situation some other time. As demonstrated in the famous teenage comedy *American Pie,* he/she might be the victim of a similar scam sometime later in life where someone records them in unpalatable circumstances.

There are also other concerns in pornography that could be of interest from a karmic angle. In this era of technology, movies are often embellished with special effects and enhancements that are unreal. As long as the audience is clearly informed about this, there is no danger. For instance people watching the Harry Potter movies know that it is fantasy and a lot of what is depicted in the movie is the creation of software. In the production of pornographic movies, if such additions or enhancements are used, the viewer must be informed, so that there is no deception or misrepresentation. Sometimes in some pornographic movies, the sizes of the breasts and the length of the male organ look so incredible that one wonders whether any digital software is responsible for these enviable physical attributes. The producer or uploader of such videos must make it clear whether any sort of embellishment has been used in the video. For these and other reasons, it is recommended that those who like to enjoy unreal sexual situations should consider pornographic writing or erotic fiction a karmically safer option because there are no real people involved here. Hence there is little chance of trampling on individual rights. Similarly the pornographic filming of children or any other disadvantaged and vulnerable groups incurs heavy karmic negativity because they are not in a position to give informed consent either due to mental inability or other reasons.

Consent is a key factor in the karmic justice system. Any action taken by another person, without the consent of the first person, is in most cases, a negative karma. The only exception to this would be in situations where the person is incapable of expressing consent and the action taken by the other person is **unequivocally good**. Unequivocally good actions are those where the good intentions of the doer are crystal clear and cannot be in any doubt. An example of this is parents getting a doctor to administer vaccinations to their children, who are unable to express consent because they are too young. No child will grow up to blame the parents for protecting him/her from a deadly disease. The *unequivocally good* intentions of the parents means there is no negative karma, even if the child is upset by this action at the time of the vaccination. Similarly, parents who sometimes trample upon the desires of growing children and discipline them do not get bad karma because of this principle. This is despite the fact that the worldly outcomes of unequivocally good actions may not always turn out as desired.

Digression Related to Consent: Suicide and Assisted Suicide

Consent and intention are the main reasons why suicide is not the same thing as being killed. A person might be poor and miserable, but another person cannot decide to end the life of this poor, miserable person without incurring some bad karma. It is for a similar reason that unless one is truly spiritually realised and able to connect and communicate with the overself the basic purpose of the present life and suffering, it is karmically wrong to extinguish one's own life, even if one is suffering from some terminal illness.

The logic is simple. Based on previous karmic history, if a person has been born with a firm karmic mandate of having to suffer from a terminal illness for three years, the act of a mercy killing cuts short the mandate and sends the person back without clearing the account. In such cases, the person has to be born again to complete the balance. It is similar to a person in a jail having to serve five years. Imagine that he manages to escape after two years. If such a person is re-caught, he will have to spend the three years balance plus another punishment for the act of jailbreak. Where policing and investigation is not very advanced, such as in underdeveloped and overpopulated countries, there is a chance that this convicted person may never be caught, but in the karmic system this is impossible. Hence a person committing suicide to escape suffering would still have to serve the remaining part of the sentence. This is *one* explanation for children being born and dying after some weeks or years or in childhood. Needless to say, this untimely death also causes terrible grief to the parents, but then the karmic system is always perfect. Most probably the karmic balance sheet also requires the parents to bear the loss of a loved one, due to some pending negative balance.

Similarly, helping someone terminally ill and in pain to die in order to 'end the suffering', in a situation where the person being so assisted has **not** consulted his/her overself or has not given the consent in a clear and calm state of mind, would not qualify as 'unequivocally good'. Sometimes people in unbearable pain say things that they do not mean. A person who must give consent for his life to be taken must be in a position to give a clear, well-contemplated decision, worked out over several weeks and not on impulse. Such a person should also be in a position to consult their overself through meditation or other means. Even when the person himself/herself expresses the wish to be killed, the first course of action to protect oneself karmically is to avoid acting on these instructions immediately. The person who expresses that wish should be dissuaded, because many people do feel suicidal at times due to severe pain fluctuations in mood, changing chemical balances in the brain etc. Some of these chemical imbalances might also be the result of medication taken by the person.

If one is the closest living relative or friend of a severely suffering, terminally ill patient who consistently and consciously requests to be put out of his/her terrible suffering, then it is a serious dilemma for this relative. If the patient is in a position to move around, the loving relative can flatly refuse to aid him. That way, even if the patient, after due consideration decides to end own life, the loving relative accumulates no negative karma.

Since the karmic system also takes intention into account, if anyone is enthusiastic about putting his aged relative to sleep forever, just to get hold of inheritance or to be relieved from the duty of looking after the relative, then this intention will itself be seen as enough to create negative karma. Karmic account management is holistic and is intention-based, not merely result-based. For example, if Ms. X is a close relative and care-provider of terminally ill patient Mr. Y, she cannot merely escape bad karma by verbally denying Mr. Y's request for assisting in the suicide, but keeping deadly poisons within the reach of Mr. Y. This kind of feigning and farce does not work in karmic calculations, because it is more intention-based and less result-based.

In an extreme case, if Ms. X decides to liberate her loved one of his/her terrible pain out of pity, she must have very clear instructions from the sufferer when they both are in a calm state of mind. She can also get a verbal acknowledgement from the sufferer that she will not be liable for any negative karma on account of this deed. This strong, verbal and specific acknowledgement will be recorded by the sufferer's overself and the loving friend, who has assisted him/her out of compassion, will not incur any negative karma. In many cases, the situation is one of sacrifice. Ms. X kills Mr. Y because she cannot bear the terrible suffering of Mr. Y. This is an act of love, for which Ms. X does not mind incurring the slight negative repercussions of karma. In other words, it is like going to prison for another person out of sheer love for that person.

Karma and Cybersex

Needless to say, in keeping with the overall karmic paradigm of 'there is nothing bad about sex per se', there is little that is negative in webcam-to-webcam sex or sex using Skype, messenger-based chats or other such voice software as long as the two people enjoying this sexual joy are consenting adults aware of the act. Similarly, sharing explicit photos of each other to enhance enjoyment also does not incur karmic negativity. Of course, like all good things, sometimes frequent enjoyment of online sexuality can lead to a habit, not easily broken. Some books might call it an addiction. When sex, leisure, social interactions and even work come together on the same computer, people can lose track of the time they spend in front of their computers or mobile devices. People can even forget to have food, bath and sleep. Of course besides the physical dangers of eyesight problems, problems with fingers, shoulders and back, lack of sleep and obesity, there could be other sociological side effects. A scenario where a son is so addicted to the internet that his parents have to send him an email to come downstairs for dinner is only a marginal exaggeration. Young children may prefer to play football, tennis and baseball on the computer while the real games with the physical exercise may lose their charm. Childhood obesity and other such lifestyle disorders are serious menaces to come out of the internet revolution.

Economic Reasons for the Growth of the Virtual Sex Industry

However, there are other economic principles at play causing the unbridled growth of the pornographic and interactive sex industry. People in all parts of the world find it difficult to get real sex without emotional and other such complications. Even in developed societies buying decent sexual services is by and large an expensive affair. Since the whole trade is to be carried out without proper marketing support and in a clandestine manner, the circulation of information about the market place is quite inefficient, as the economists would say. Hence given the shortage of information, consumers are unable to be relatively rational in executing the purchase decisions when it comes to sexual service purchases.

Due to the stigma surrounding sexuality, some of the best looking men or women in the world avoid getting into any sex-related work. To put things in perspective, when small children are asked what they want to be when they grow up, most of them might say that they want to be doctors, engineers or rocket scientists. Would a child ever say that he or she wants to be an escort or call girl or prostitute, despite the good money that a gorgeous call girl can make? A cursory search based on rates on escort websites will show that in the UK, the gorgeous and skilled call girls/escorts could make anything from £300 to £800 per hour and much more for the entire night.[25] This is much higher than the remuneration of most other jobs in UK. To put things in perspective, even the most qualified, top-rated freelance teachers working in the further education sector often make between £20 to £30 per hour, while those who work in the best supermarkets in London as counter sales staff earn between £8 to £12 pounds per hour.[26] In developed societies, some of the best-looking, independently working call girls often make as much, or even more money, than many other professionals and often have a delightful (no pun intended) work environment too. Despite this, the profession does not attract large numbers of people. The sophisticated and well-educated ones who work in this profession do it with guilt and often lead a double life of secrecy and nicknames. Hence, while the demand exists, the supply and information about the supply is very skewed and irregular. This, as the economists would say, leads to market imperfections and consequently the price for a good sexual service is often high.

In many parts of the world, there is also the fear of social ostracism, police harassment, loss of reputation and even criminal charges. The risk of taking up prostitution in these parts is no more limited to the financial risk of not having sufficient demand for the services. In some Islamic countries, if a lady is found having sex with a male other than her husband, she could even be stoned to death. All these make the intangible costs of the service much higher than the price of the service itself. The stigmatization of sex is the most important reason for the development of the brothel system, which has had a detrimental effect on working conditions and the status of the women. If this profession is freed from the purposeless shackles of religion and morality there will be much greater freedom for those who want to give physical enjoyment to others in return for some monetary arrangement.

Classification of the World Based on Sex-industry Freedoms

In terms of the freedom available to sex workers, especially women, the world can be somewhat roughly categorized into 3 blocks.

1. The *semi-liberal countries* like the USA, UK and much of Europe. If a person decides to give enjoyment to others for money, all that she has to do is to advertise in personal columns or online message boards on the internet using euphemistic messages such as 'sensual massage' etc. In the

UK, the law seems to be some sort of compromise to keep everyone happy. A person can decide to entertain clients in the privacy of her (or his) home. If she is discreet and does not make a nuisance of herself, no one will bother her and she can do it without expecting much trouble from the police or other government officials, as long as the work is not associated with brothels, pimps and does not involve soliciting on the streets. Hence, if one leaves aside the security concerns of prostitutes who work alone in flats, it is possible for a person in UK to take up prostitution work legally. This is possible in countries such as the UK because here one can choose to live for years in a crowded residential area without even making eye contact with the next-door neighbours. People expect to be given privacy and hate to poke their noses into other's affairs themselves. The weather also helps this attitude because the doors and windows in houses remain closed. For a large part of the year, the cold weather generally discourages people from unscheduled social jaunts and mingling. However, in the case of semi-liberal countries, the freedom of the individual is protected and guaranteed by law but there is often a lack of acceptance and a social attitude of abhorrence towards sexual philanderers and sex workers. Even in the heart of London or Paris, a 'good girl' from a respectable family background and working in a respectable office cannot easily gain acceptance in the local social circles if she proclaims that she is also a part-time escort or call girl.

2. The ***ambiguous poorly liberal countries*** such as India, China and many of the developing countries, exist in a milieu of social communities, which have a tendency to interfere and involve themselves within a person's life. It is difficult for a person to live a life without having

some form of contact with their neighbours. Since many of these countries in Asia and Africa are also tropical, it is no wonder that festivals in these countries become occasions for social revelry. The rights and freedoms of individuals have much less relevance compared to the perceptions of justice and morality of the public and social milieu. In such countries, it is common for the police and other government regulatory bodies to intervene on behalf of 'social grievances' of public and curb the rights of individuals. For example, if a woman is suspected of having too many boyfriends who keep staying the night with her, prying neighbours will surely step in and call the regulatory bodies to intervene, even if she is not interfering with anyone else and troubling no one. These countries, such as India, Pakistan and Sri Lanka might be referred to as 'ambiguous freedom' countries because while they may be democratic and freedom-loving in theory, the individual sexual freedoms are neither guaranteed nor meticulously protected. Similarly, in these countries, women can be charged, often whimsically, for prostitution and arrested by police even when there is no evidence of any wrong-doing other than consensual sex with many partners.

3. The *bondage countries* are those where sexuality, even when it is not for monetary gain, is severely controlled. Examples of bondage countries would be Saudi Arabia, many other Gulf countries and so-called Islamic countries. In many of these countries, a person can be easily put to death for consensual sex with anyone other than the spouse. Both societal and governmental structures go out of their way to try to stifle sexual expression of any type. At the minimum level, prostitution in Saudi Arabia can lead to heavy flogging. In terms of their legal and regulatory

framework, these countries are the worst of all for those
who seek a freer sexual climate

After the publication of this work and other similar ideas, and
with the idea of sexual freedoms within marriages becoming
more acceptable, it is hoped that most of the world will
slowly move towards the paradigm of *liberated countries,* the
characteristics of which are given below.

Liberated countries are countries where a person exchanging
her/his bodily pleasures for monetary or immediate non-
monetary considerations can do so without having to live a
life of social stigma or shame. She (or *he*) can be as proud
of her (or *his*) work as a chef working in a restaurant or a
doctor treating a patient. She can move, mix socially and
enjoy her life without being taunted, harassed or snubbed by
friends/relatives or others. She can even attend her chosen
place of worship without having to hide her profession and
without being lectured or treated condescendingly by those
who claim to be religious. She/he would not face pressure
from parents, relatives or even partners to change her/his
profession. If a banker, doctor, teacher or nurse does not
face constant pressure to change job, why should a call girl?
Of course, cities like Amsterdam and parts of countries like
Thailand could probably come under this category. Since
liberated countries are expected to be much better than semi-
liberal countries, it goes without saying that in a **liberated**
country, law enforcement or regulatory bodies will treat this
profession as equal, both in letter and spirit of the law to
that of a teacher, banker or a bus driver. One might argue
that this might be a little on the idealistic side. After all, in
the present-day developed world, the investment banker is
definitely treated better than an office janitor or a building

doorman. Similarly a school teacher will be rated lower in the social class hierarchy than a physician or a rocket scientist. Indeed that is true. However, it must be noted that the gap in social status between a school teacher and rocket scientist comes from the connotations of the educational sophistication and income which a rocket scientist is associated with. The status gap is certainly not due to any perceived dubious moral connotations in either profession. Even in sexually liberated countries there will be a social status difference between a top-earning, sophisticated call girl and a poor man's sex provider. This book is not about building a forced, semi-communist social order, where people of diverse income levels and diverse sophistications live together in forced harmony. However, what does happen in such a liberated country is that the highly paid, sensuous, sophisticated and educated escort can expect to be treated socially and otherwise with the same attention and respect given to a well-earning investment banker.

Impact of Skewed Economics of the Sex Industry on Online Pornography

It is in a skewed economic environment today that the pornographic industry thrives. Let us take another example. When many people around the world are forced to eat pizzas every day, albeit with different toppings, there is a chance that internet videos showing other types of foods will become immensely popular. This is despite the fact that in the case of food there are limitations. When I see someone eating a lobster on the TV, it is easy to imagine, but difficult to get that taste on my tongue. Neither is it easy for me to get even a small percentage of that same satisfaction by salivation. Why is it that people do not watch other people sleep on TV and get the same excitement (of sleeping themselves) or watch others have a Martini (and get the same enjoyment of drinking one) as watching others indulge in sexual acts? The answer is given below.

Why Pornography Will Continue to be Popular

In the case of pornography, it is much easier for someone to see a lovely lady having sexual pleasure with a well-endowed man and imagine the scenario as if it happens to him or her. It is also easy for the viewer to get a slice of that whole scenario and participate in it, when his/her arousal due to the whole viewing can culminate in a good self-given orgasm. All that is not possible if someone watches a person having a lobster on TV or a person having a good drink. Videos of a person having a good drink or good meal can rarely give the same level of satisfaction to a hungry person, because in the case of food there is no self-satisfying mechanism available. Moreover, in today's world, a person who has the technology and resources to see videos of enticing food, is also likely to have the money to buy it some time in his life. Additionally, in the case of food and drinks there are so many choices and varieties, all at a price within the reach of even the somewhat poorer sections of society. For example, it is easy to get a sandwich even at a modest price of £2 from a supermarket. Can a man get a disease-free, clean bout of quickie-sex for even double that price? Once various possibilities to satisfy sexual needs become easily available at prices close to the cost of internet connections and the electricity bills of watching internet porn, there is every likelihood that some of the action-oriented, resourceful people might prefer to have a piece of the real action rather than the actions of others in pornography. Of course, due to the possibility of self-satisfaction using pornography alone, this industry will always be more relevant than the food-video or the sleep-video industry.

5

With Maidens I Roam, When Wife is not Home

Marital Infidelity

Almost all religious ceremonies of marriage have the concept of fidelity. But what is this fidelity? From a dictionary perspective, fidelity merely means the act of 'remaining and being faithful'[1] but in marriage, this 'faithfulness' means primarily to have sexual intimacy only with the chosen partner. In the case of marriage, this written or verbal contract comes into existence in a church or some other religious place of worship usually in the presence of several witnesses. In other instances, the written contract is executed in a court of law or with some government organisation as the third party. Sexual exclusiveness is the key point of this contract.

Although the role played by karmic systems in the choice of spouse (or civil partner) is covered in Chapter 2 of this book, it might also be a good idea to critique this social arrangement from diverse perspectives. Like a dog walking on its hind legs, it is an arrangement far from perfect, yet considered one of the most viable arrangements in our structure of society. But it is important to note that this paradigm of sexual exclusivity is not based on any karmic ethical paradigm, but merely a structure created for social convenience and backed by some religious traditions.

The fundamental assumption that sex for pleasure alone is immoral is the basis of the argument against several sexual choices including pre-marital sex, homosexuality and contraception. Some of these arguments are dealt with below, while others have been discussed in Chapter 13 of the concluding part of this book.

Freer Sexuality Undermines Marriage

Argument that freer sexuality undermines the institution of marriage and increases widespread immorality is as fragile as connecting oversleeping or overeating to immorality. Let us imagine for a moment that our social norms were different and eating at home with the wife was considered the most sacred aspect of marriage. In such a society the food lover who dares to eat food outside his/her home would be considered the adulterer/ adulteress. Imagine women and men applying for divorce on the grounds that marital vows of 'always eating at home together' were broken. In such community, a husband visiting a nice restaurant and finding his wife finishing a juicy steak with her office colleague might file for divorce. ("And what were you doing with *your* friend inside the restaurant," the wife might ask. This would be similar to wives all over the world, bringing up the question of a husband's dubious fidelity when he dares to raise the flag of extra-marital suspicion.) Can we see the parallels here?

The Sanctity of Marriage

There are still hard-core believers in the 'sanctity of marriage'. What would be the shape of a so-called 'institution of marriage' if we remove the clause of sexual exclusivity, reflected in the symbolism of the ring and vows of fidelity. Probably, sexual exclusivity was a preventive system designed by ancient societies when they found males impregnating women and then moving on to more attractive companions, thus depriving the children of badly needed protection and nurture by both parents. Most developed societies have evolved much from that time. Today it is possible for single parents to bring up children in an environment of protection and care.

The search for this one great 'soul mate' is the result of this 'sacred marriage' idea, drummed into the minds of people, especially women, for a long time. In many parts of the world, the saying 'women give and forgive, men get and forget' gives an interesting insight into their understanding of distinctive sexual make-up of men and women. For most women sexuality is akin to giving. Hence a lovely woman by and large must be wooed before she 'gives more of herself'. There are studies which conclude that women continue to be extremely selective in their choice of sexual companions as compared to a man. In other words, sexuality is something like a reward to be 'given' for the winner of a woman's affections. By and large the man would not mind sleeping with several women even if some of them are less attractive to him. But with the world of sexuality opening up, these gender generalizations are being destroyed with each passing day.

Is Sexual Exclusivity Better for Women?

Some sceptics might argue that if sex with diverse partners is not such an important thing for a woman, isn't sexual exclusivity within marriage better for them? Even the spiratually-realized often agree that there are differences in feminine and masculine perspectives, just like the physical differences between them. Buddha, whose insights are relevant to the world today, seemed to have been opposed to the idea of female monks. To suggest that all the psychological differences between men and women are only a result of social conditioning might be being a bit miserly with the truth. Is it merely social conditioning that results in women (in general) seeking less aggressive sports? Or being less egoistic and more affectionate? Is it not true that the average young lady who travels in a mixed and crowded railway compartment is likely to encounter more male perverts than the reverse situation? Despite what feminists would say, we all intuitively know that a woman's way of thinking, perceiving and going through life is somewhat different than a man's. Even the sexual triggers, preferences and choices that women exhibit in sexuality might vary.

Despite all these arguments, to say that men would be the only beneficiaries of sexually free marriages is not necessarily accurate. As mentioned in the concluding chapters, the opening up of our sexual paradigm would eventually make women (including married women) more comfortable to freely give and take sexual enjoyment, without fear of crime, coercion, pregnancy or blackmail; especially when they are not looking for long-term commitments.

What Happens if Married People Start Falling in Love with Others?

So far so good, say the sceptics. But what if the man in question falls in love with his secretary and decides that he would prefer to leave his wife forever and stay with his secretary? Let us continue with the restaurant analogy. What if a man decides his wife's cooking is simply hopeless and decides to eat in the same restaurant every day rather than his home? This is an extremely rare situation. This analogy of the restaurant also gives us an insight into the real problem of marriage. The spouse does not mind his wife eating once in a while in another restaurant, because they know that no matter how many times a man eats out in a week, he always keeps coming back home. What if the situation were not so simple; let us imagine husbands frequently deciding to leave their houses for better food and friendship. In such a situation would the husband or wife be more worried if the spouse eats out? Or would the wife (or husband) try to improve her/his cooking skills?

From this example, can we comprehend that the real problem is not of a husband's or wife's preference for some sexual variety? The real problem is the insecurity and fear that the search for sexual diversity may lead to some emotional attachment to the sexual provider. But there are other angles to be explored. Is love merely a desire for sexual orgasm?

A person's need for food can be impersonally satisfied by any good provider of food. What about sex? Can an erotic service provider or an office colleague having sex with another person be able to do so without developing feelings of attachment? What about love? Is romantic love merely a desire for companionship fused with sexual fulfilment? It might be worthwhile revisiting the concept of love in Chapter 1, under section 'Typologies of Love'.

Understanding 'Love' Better

From the karmic angle, a strange affinity can come between
two people due to some connection in their past lives. A
wonderful comradeship between two people of the same
gender may also happen. In case they are of opposite genders,
then the social programming and expectations of opposite-sex
relationships help them 'fall in love'. 'Falling in love' happens
when a person's mental template of the desirable qualities in
a human being of the opposite gender (or same gender, if the
person is so inclined) starts aligning itself to the reality when
they meet such a person. In other words, every person who
falls in love often does so, not with the real person whom
they meet, but actually with the template of an ideal person
which was created in their minds. We do not 'fall in love' with
someone else. We get attached to the template of beauty and
desirable qualities created in our minds unconsciously. When
we come across such a person who somewhat closely fits that
template, we become attracted.

That is why a person of conservative mind-set born and
brought up in Africa could easily fall in love with a woman
(or man) of African origin. On the other hand, a conservative
person born and brought up in a country devoid of people
of African origin might not get attracted to anyone like that.
A Sikh woman brought up in a household of men wearing
turbans and beards would most likely find herself attracted
to a well-built, bearded Sikh wearing a turban. This
'attractiveness template' idea is vindicated when one looks
at dating advertisements and profiles, where normal people
who are not racists might still specify that they are looking
for other members of only a particular racial or national
origin. Having said this, sometimes genuine past life

karmic connections can complicate the situation. A woman from India may become attracted to a person of African origin, due to some really strong past life-history. The template creation for love is also a somewhat complicated process. The template is created by a mixture of what is considered socially acceptable in a man or woman, often reinforced by the media, movies, family and peer groups. For instance if the media starts projecting tall and fair men as desirable and if this is reinforced by peer groups and family, then it becomes a part of the 'love template'. In countries like India, long hair among women was part of the love template of many men. Also, qualities that were missing in a person's parents may become part of a person's love template. For instance, a girl whose childhood was devoid of close parental affection may add the quality of demonstrable affection in her love template. Sometimes this yearning becomes so strong in her template that she may even fall in love with the first person who gives her this affection. This love may or may not result out of sexual chemistry, although sexual enjoyment and pleasure could reinforce and enhance it. Hence, there are no easy solutions to these issues of strong emotional love with someone else after marriage. The alternative models of marriage offered in Chapter 14, could perhaps be a pointer to some possible solutions.

Karmic Obligations Within the Present Marriage System

First of all, when we look at marriage as some sort of contract which rests on the bedrock of fidelity, are we also aware that thousands of couples in all parts of the world, especially in the developed and developing world, live together without marriage? Are they also bound by this same condition of fidelity?

If a person living with his partner for years is also having an affair on the side with another woman, would this be considered infidelity, since there was no marriage? Yes of course, because although it was not specified in black and white, it is clearly something which is understood by two people who are intimate and exclusive in their sexual relations, from the moment they are 'committed'. Hence to begin with, in terms of karma, whether or not a person is married technically on paper is unimportant. As long as there was an understanding of exclusivity in sexual matters between two people and one person breaches this implicit/tacit agreement, the karmic accounting system registers it as a negative karma or a breach of contract for which the person is held accountable.

Karma and Tacit contracts

When does the tacit agreement start? For all practical purposes, in societies where physical love and sexual intimacy automatically means 'exclusive love' and 'exclusive intimacy', the very act of getting involved in either of them can be taken by both parties to be a tacit understanding of the start of the contract of fidelity. (Refer also the section on contracts in the next chapter.) However, it goes without saying that thought, word and action have three different levels of karmic consequences. An intimate action coupled with intimate words outlining fidelity is almost as good as a written contract for karmic purposes. Deliberately holding back words of intimacy while getting into unmistakable *acts* of intimacy cannot fool the karmic system, especially in a culture where intimate actions are considered love. In such cultures, since karmic accounting systems take into consideration the intentions of an action, acts of love-making and sexual intimacy, and later denial of 'any love' is already registered as a small breach of contract. To prevent this karmic negativity, a person can make a clear statement before things get too intimate that he/she is not thinking of any long-term relationship. After this statement is unambiguously made, even if the two people are going ahead to engage in sexual pleasure, then it is clear that one of the partners cannot claim later on that he or she was misled. Even if this prior declaration of intention was not meticulously followed, the karmic negativity is reduced by the simple action of informing within a short time after the coitus/sexual intimacy that there was no intention of long-term relationship.

On the other hand, if the person Mr X continues to have sexual intimacy quite regularly with person Ms Y for longer periods of time in such a conservative society, Y may rightly assume that X intends to have a full blown long-term relationship and possibly marriage. X can indignantly claim later on, "I never told you that I wanted an exclusive relationship with you," but this is karmically negative because, Mr X has already committed himself into a relationship of exclusivity or fidelity. Denying it later would not prevent negative karma due to breach of contract/trust. Even in countries like the UK, if one person expects a more long-term relationship while the other is treating the love-making as just good fun and nothing more, issues must be cleared up as soon as possible. The onus is on the person who does not have any interest in a long-term relationship. Even in countries where legally no action can be taken against those who close relationships after sex, there is a possibility of a curse from the aggrieved party, who feels used. If the aggrieved person has a thin CSB and decides to curse the person who is wriggling out of the commitment, then the curse may in fact take effect at some future point of time. (As mentioned in Chapter 3 under 'The Mechanism of the Curse'.)

Therefore, from a karma standpoint, whenever a person breaches a clear-cut commitment, negative karma is accrued, which is only cleared after that person himself/herself undergoes a similar situation in the present lifetime or future. Hence if a person would like to marry a girl while enjoying the fruits of sexual variety, the right karmic thing to do would be to inform his fiancée before the marriage itself about his intentions. It is then honourable to also offer the same freedom to the partner. If this is not a reciprocal arrangement, and one partner is expected to maintain complete fidelity while the other romps around seeking delectable variety in sexuality, it must be clearly mentioned to the partner before any marriage is contracted, so that the other partner has a real choice in deciding whether or not he/she would like to enter this unequal partnership. (In practice, it is difficult to make such an unequal arrangement work except under financial or other forms of coercion, because the human search for justice and fairness is a strong quest, often as strong as other basic instincts/emotions like jealousy, greed, anger, hunger and sexual desire.)

Ethical Options for the Philanderer

Presently, our marital paradigm bars decent men and women from searching for sexual variety, thus leading to a lot of cheating and breach of trust. This lying can lead to a build-up of the CSB barrier thus blocking one's spiritual progress and creating stress. Hence we must always strive to lead open lives which are reconciled and aligned with society.

What are the karmically ethical options after marriage? If a person decides that he/she would like to seek sexual variety after marriage, he/she must inform the partner of the changed terms of their agreement/vows. If one partner does not permit it, then divorce or breaking-up is the only option. Can it be pragmatic? Is it not a recipe to blow up even the most rock solid of families? Each family differs marginally in its internal dynamics and levels of communication, and a general prescription which fits all, would hardly be sufficient. However, some suggestions can be laid out. To begin with, instead of directly telling the wife about one's desire to have sexual intercourse with a sexy and willing office colleague, it might be better to reveal the flirtatious nature for some time and get the spouse gradually acclimatized to the sexual variety-seeking behaviour. Simultaneously the spouse can be encouraged to also mix with other members of the opposite gender. Taking the partner straightaway to a swinging/ swapping party may hardly be the best way since it might be too abrupt, but a more phased, gentle opening up of his/her mind to the joys of experimentation in sexuality is good. One will be surprised at how, with gentle love and regular persuasive communications, a person's perspective can be opened up to a paradigm of sexual liberalism.

This undoubtedly takes time and effort in a marriage, simply because re-programming centuries of religious and social programming about irrevocable sexual taboos is not easy. One must also accept that in many cases, despite one's best efforts, the desirable change may never happen in the spouse.

However, that is a pessimistic possibility. Human beings have tremendous capacity to continuously change, learn, adjust and re-orient themselves and this should not be underestimated.

There are also some minor issues here. As the saying goes, everyone wants a good spouse, but rarely want to be good themselves. The enthusiasm that a man shows in his sexual variety-seeking behaviour may instantly turn into rancour and bitterness if his wife shows the slightest inclination to follow suit. Polygamous Muslim men, often cover their desire for sexual variety under the umbrella of religion, citing their permission to have four wives, while denying the same freedom to their spouses. But Muslims are not the only ones using the cover of religion to advance their sexual quest. Patriotism may be the last resort of every scoundrel, but religion is often the last resort of 'perverts'. (The word 'pervert' being put under quotes to underline how today's definition of 'perverted actions' is often merely a result of society's denial of a legitimate human desire for sexual variety.) The scandals in Catholic church and the sexual tales of numerous Hindu swamis (present-day 'holy men')[2,3] all clearly point to how sexual variety-seekers risk negative karmic cycle and/or legal troubles by hiding under the umbrella of religious institutions to get their share of sexual conquests. For men to accept that women must also have the same freedoms that they enjoy, men must be taught to accept the sexuality of women. There are many parts of the world where they still believe that women do not fully enjoy sex. Men must understand that although there are biological and hormonal differences which make the sexual arousal, experience and gratification mechanisms different in women, what is good for the goose is also good for the gander.

Etiquette for Free Marriage

Once the parameters of sexual exclusivity in marriage are removed, the partners must avoid playing the number game. If the husband has seven sexual experiences with others in a year, it does not necessarily mean the wife must follow suit and sleep around with seven men just to compensate. That would become a stressful experience. In other words, just because your partner is trying seven different types of foods, does not mean you have to keep doing likewise, if you mostly prefer the Chinese food. In somewhat rarer cases, it might be the wife who seeks wider variety, while the husband might be happy with only one or two different partners.

It is wise to presume that society might take some decades before it adjusts and becomes comfortable with this new paradigm of relationships. The etiquette for sexual variety-seeking behaviour within marriages and other stable relationships will take more time to be established and well respected. The association of sexuality with power, domination or self-esteem which is presently common among men, must be eliminated. It must be accepted by society that just like some people love food or books or movies more than others, some men or women may love and appreciate sexual enjoyment more than others. Men who love sex less than others must not be made to feel worthless, incompetent or inadequate. This must not be related to or confused with gender. For instance, if we carefully look at our society today, much of the folklore, mythology and other parts of the world's cultural heritage has symbolisms of male sexual power, dominance and the submissive sexuality of women. This kind of imagery must be erased gradually from human consciousness and social programming, if we are to progress truly in the area of sexual liberty. Impotence among men, which leads men in most parts of the world to have a very low self-esteem or suffer depression, must be erased from our world social programming as something to be ashamed of. It must become a simple and mundane physical disorder similar to a stomach ulcer, acidity or mild hypertension for which there are simple and adequate treatments.

6

Seduced to My Bed, You Will Never Be Wed

Breach of Trust

Magazines like *Cosmopolitan* often have articles with titles such as 'Sizzling Sex Tips'[1] and 'Get Yourself Party Sexy'[2]. Some articles such as 'Your sexual health: The STD 80% of women now get'[3] talk about postcoital hygiene and health issues. Most other magazines like *Marie Claire* have followed up with articles in a similar vein. In the last few decades almost all such magazines with a large female readership have made it a point to have a few such articles on sexuality in every issue. These articles are not just concealed within its pages, but are given enough point-of-purchase publicity by being boldly mentioned on the cover.

The underlying assumption behind these articles is that the 'liberated women' must be engaging in quite a lot of casual sex, enjoying and experimenting with the exotic and esoteric. Behind this assumption lies the feminist agenda for equality in sexual behaviour amongst men and women. When feminists want to make their point on the need for equality for women they often feel that this quest will remain incomplete without building up a credible paradigm on sexual equality. One implication of this has been to create the theory that women and men have similar sexual drives and motivations for sex. A corollary of this created paradigm is the theory that women are capable of and willing to enjoy casual no-strings-attached sex as much as men. This assumption must be explored in a bit more depth.

Large bodies of magazines, popular TV serials and books have almost given it an air of normality and mundaneness, as if to say, for women (as in the case of men), it is no big deal to have just fun sex with any guy without issues of commitment or love weighing them down. But the reality, as highlighted in some recent books and studies, is vastly different.[4]

Recently, a more academic, blue-blooded team of professors from reputed universities like Florida State University and Midwestern College, worked on this question of different sex drives and came out with largely conclusive results.[5] This team consisted of professors who personally held diverse views about the sex drive, with one professor believing that men have higher drives and another member holding a very feminist viewpoint that there are no differences in sex drives. But their end conclusion was unambiguous and based on substantial evidence. Men definitely had more 'sex drive' than women. In terms of the number of times they masturbate, the number of times they have sexual fantasies and in terms of the risk and cost they often incur for sex, men were definitely more motivated towards sexual behaviours than women. Put bluntly, generally speaking, men wanted more sex than women, despite what feminists kept asserting.

In many parts of Asia, mothers often advise daughters to be careful in friendships with men, because men are sometimes known to lose interest in a woman after a sexual encounter. There are expressions like 'knock her up', 'shag her' and so on, which imply that men have to take the initiative. Even when we talk of rape, we generally understand it to mean that a man had forced sexual intercourse with a woman. How many cases of women forcing themselves upon men have we heard of (even if we ignore the biological technicalities of such an incident)? Would a man be as regretful if a woman puts a gun on his head and forces him to have sex with her, assuming that she suffers from no venereal disease and is able and healthy? And if such a woman 'rapist' were to look gorgeous, is it inconceivable that some men would volunteer to be 'raped'?

One important theme of this book is that despite the differences in the way women love and enjoy romantic sensuality, it is wrong to say that women are not capable of sexual enjoyment for its own sake. It is also a completely wrong perception in some parts of the world that women always think of long-term commitment. To have a perspective that only men are capable of being like aimless bulls and hump anything that moves, is only the result of bad social and religious conditioning in some parts of the world. However, due to a strange combination of hormones, emotional and sexual triggers which are different, it is also possible that large numbers of women might prefer to explore sexual variety with fewer partners, that too in an environment of all enveloping emotional trust and security.

Emotional Breach of Trust

Why is this discussion so relevant for this chapter on breach of trust? As mentioned before, despite the genuine sexual liberalisation which this book advocates, there will be a lot of good-looking women (and men) in the world who will continue to enjoy full penetrative sex and beautiful orgasms only in an environment of emotional security, rather than through sexual escapades. Despite this, it is not difficult for us to believe that there are more **men** who would happily enjoy sex with *any* interested woman. Sometimes in order to get sex, they even lead her to believe that there is a strong love and prospect for future relationship perhaps ending in a marriage (with all the trappings of a lovely wedding ceremony). In developed, individualistic societies that pride themselves on the rule of law, paradoxically, this sort of intellectual and sexual breach of trust has become more common, because it is easy for a man to walk out of a relationship after his sexual enjoyment of the woman is over.

Of course, having said this, such a breach of trust can happen even from the side of the female. Imagine the situation where a beautiful Caucasian girl dates a well-built man of African origin. Despite the splendid sex, she prefers to dump him after the rather discreet and intense relationship, without any thought of a long-term relationship simply because her socially elite family would frown upon her marriage with a 'black' man. The poor guy in love, in this case, is left to lick his wounds alone.

In many Eastern societies, where sexual contact is forbidden before marriage, when a man changes his mind about marrying a woman after sexual enjoyment, he can face very daunting consequences. In the Middle East and parts of Central Asia where Islam holds sway, a man enjoying sexual relations with a woman and then trying to flee may be killed without a second thought by the clansmen/tribes/relatives of the girl. Sometimes, it can be worse and the couple is killed for bringing dishonour to the family. In South Asia, especially India, the man who has violated a girl (the question of her consent is unimportant) is expected to marry her. If he refuses to do the 'honourable thing', the society, in rural areas often consisting of village elders and other respected residents, will 'force' the person to marry the girl. This may not be merely a South Asian phenomenon with similar actions being quite common in Mexico, parts of Latin America and even Europe. In such circumstances, the responsibility is laid squarely on the man's shoulders. It is assumed that the woman, on her own volition, will not jump to have a sexual romp. It must be the 'evil' man who must have seduced her with promises of marriage and a long-term relationship.

The Suppression of Women's Sexuality

The situation can become more serious if a married woman would like to enjoy sexual relations with a man other than her husband. Most frequently, if such an 'aberration' happens, it will be presumed that it is because her husband is not able to satisfy her due to his own physical problems like impotency. In many such Asian 'offbeat' movies, married women who seek sex outside marriage are depicted as those who happen to be married to much older men. The implication clearly is that the older husband, is either impotent or has lost his interest in sex due to advancing age. The possibility that a sexually active woman who has an active and fully potent partner can also look for sex elsewhere in a quest for sexual variety is a subject meant only for pornographic movies, not to be taken seriously, even in a non-commercial movie. In fact, perhaps this non-conforming behaviour of women in pornographic movies (where women often take the initiative and 'act like sluts') only add to the popularity and novelty of the pornographic flick, among Asian males. In reality, if women had to take the initiative for sex, such women would risk being ostracised at best and face unspeakable violence at worst, in much of South Asia's social communities. To escape these drastic consequences in their search for sexual variety, these women, if caught, would simply blame the men for making 'advances'. In case they are caught red-handed, they might even accuse the man of rape.

The Karma of 'Just for Sex' Relationships

Even in sexually liberated, high-income Western societies, those who end the relationship immediately after sex rarely say 'it was only about sex'. They often have to go through a less direct, roundabout way of getting out of this situation. The argument that the other, 'dumped' person also enjoyed the sex is not considered relevant.

The karmic problem arises because in several ways, one person has dangled the prospect of a secure long-term relationship in front of another, perhaps in subtle or implicit ways. Sometimes a sexually aroused man is faced with the choice of either saying, "I love you," and getting sex *or* not saying, "I love you," and being denied sex. Quite unsurprisingly, he often chooses to just blurt out "I love you," and get his orgasm. In this case, it is not easy for the man to wriggle out of the relationship after sex without acknowledging in some way that he had lied. Sometimes the situation is not so black and white. All that the woman might want is an implicit assurance that they have something more than sex going on. The man might transmit implicit assurance by non-verbal gestures and body language. Later on, this person moves out of the relationship orbit after the sex is over, taking advantage of the clear confusion/ ambiguity about his expressed intentions.

Examples of Implicit Contracts in Karma

This use of ambiguity to escape commitments can also happen from the side of a lady. Let us consider an example of a beautiful college-going lady in an Eastern urban society, for example in a city like Mumbai. This beautiful college-going girl has a beau. She knows well that he is in love with her. As happens in many Eastern societies, he aspires to marry her. Yet she has told him clearly, "You are only my friend." In terms of making her statement, she has said so clearly. Yet she accepts his gifts and accompanies him for shopping trips, often letting him pay for some of her expensive purchases including jewellery. He invites her for a movie and she pretends that she is busy. He requests her again and she demurely accepts. Since he has made the request, she 'lets him' pay for her. When he drops her home she allows him to kiss her on the cheeks, when no one is looking. In countries like India, adult males do not usually have any physical contact with any adult woman and kissing, even on the cheeks, is something that must be done between lovers or spouses. Despite receiving the kisses, every once in a while she reminds him that they are 'just friends'. Yet she takes in his appreciation, his warm comments and blushes dutifully.

After she graduates and starts working, she meets more attractive and sophisticated men and does not feel the need to go out of her way to meet him. This lady can clearly argue that since there was no clear commitment between them, she has no obligation towards him. She can also argue that she had clearly stated on several occasions that they are 'just friends' and nothing more. While this is a perfectly acceptable argument in a human court of law, in terms of karma, it can be said that there was an implicit understanding of a long-term relationship made here. Karmic laws know clearly that she had deliberately maintained an ambiguous situation to make sure she could take financial advantage of the man and 'use' him as a diversion in her otherwise dull life.

A similar situation can exist when a boy carries on with a girl, as if he is going to marry her and then finds another beautiful woman and dumps this girl like a hot potato. Similar to how breaking a real legal contract has consequences, breaking an implicit contract that existed only in terms of intentions in the hearts of both people has karmic consequences. The simplest consequence is that a person indulging in this kind of foul play will have to bear the brunt of such a game sometime in this life or in the future.

There are people who live as law-abiding citizens. But that is not enough. Those who want to live karmically right lives must also observe their own intentions all the time. In the case of the college-going lady above, she should have clearly told the man that a marriage between them is not possible and probably insisted on paying for her own shopping and paying for her own cinema tickets etc., if they wanted to go out together at all. When a person deliberately avoids saying no unambiguously and creates expectations by continued demure acceptance of love rituals which create an impression of relationship, an expectation is generated which can create karmic cycles.

The Mechanism of Karmic Contract by Intention and Implication

What is the specific point where contract by intention and implication becomes valid, thus kick-starting karmic consequences? Let us take an example of two people, Ms. A and Mr. B. When A *feels* that she is being promised something although it was not written or stated clearly and B is aware of this, then it is like an implicit contract. It is B's responsibility to clearly state the truth and, of course, back it up with appropriate actions. Sometimes when B says something but his actions run contrary to this, it again strengthens the implicit contract. This behaviour is called *deliberate-ambiguous* behaviour. For instance, despite maintaining that Ms. A is just a platonic friend, whenever he drops her home, if Mr. B kisses her, even on the cheeks, to say goodbye, this is an example of deliberate-ambiguous behaviour. In such cases, although nothing is said or written, there is clearly an implicit contract (or 'understanding', if one prefers that term). This feeling of Ms. A that she has got an implicit understanding may also result from Mr. B's style and communication, perhaps a nod, a nudge or even the way B shares his personal space. Similarly if – despite being 'just a friend' – B makes efforts to present A to his parents or other relatives, it may strengthen A's understanding of the implicit contract.

Later on, if Mr. B drops Ms. A completely on the pretext that he never had 'any such feelings or intentions' towards Ms. A, it is not right in terms of karma. Technically, the karmic part of breach of implicit contract will kick-start when the grudge of Ms. A against B is sent to the karmic exchange. Then the karmic justice system checks for traces of the same intention in B's mind at that time. Since time and space are no constraint for the karmic exchange system, it can check person B's frame of mind at the time the action or implicit contract was said to have been created. If person B did deliberately create the impression of an understanding by his action, non-verbal language etc. the karmic system will kick-start the negative consequences for person B. (Of course the word 'negative' is our classification, but for the karmic system it is just a matter of actions and results, nothing being 'positive' or 'negative'.)

There are also cases where one person feels aggrieved despite an absence of reasonable grounds. This may happen for example if Ms. A feels Mr. B had entered an understanding simply because B's innocent gestures have been misinterpreted by A. Even in such cases, person A could hold a malevolent grudge. But the difference between this and the earlier situation is that there are no automatic karmic consequences for person B for any 'implicit contract' violation. Of course person A can, based on her perception of injustice still send a curse to person B, but the impact of this curse will be limited by factors like the purity of CSB, the faith of person B etc. (refer to the part related to 'curses' in chapter 3). Moreover, sending out a virulent curse amounts to starting a fresh karmic cycle on the part of Ms. A. Figure given below gives us a better understanding of this karmic paradigm of contracts.

THE KARMIC IMPLICATIONS OF CONTRACT

	IMPLICATIONS
MISUNDERSTOOD CONTRACT (One person presuming it is an implicit contract or understanding. The other person never intended it to be so. The first person feels 'injustice' has been done.)	**NO KARMIC CONSEQUENCES.** (Possibilities of curse exists)
IMPLICIT/UNSTATED CONTRACT (Merely given an 'understanding' by non-verbal communication, nods, actions etc. But nothing ever said verbally or in writing.)	MILDER BUT KARMIC CONSEQUENCES
UNPROVEABLE CONTRACT (Merely verbal but cannot be proven; or written but records are all lost. No witnesses.)	MAINLY KARMIC CONSEQUENCES
VERBAL OR WRITTEN PROVEABLE CONTRACT (Presence of witnesses, records, paper)	LEGAL AND/OR KARMIC CONSEQUENCES

Of course a curse can be sent even if the contract violator has borne his share of legal or karmic consequences for breaking the contract. In situations and countries where the legal system is corrupt or inefficient, this is likely to happen. Similarly in the case of legally 'unprovable' contracts, the only recourse often open to the law-abiding victim is cursing the offender and sending some malevolent psychic attacks. This is in addition to the karmic consequences for the offender.

In developed, high-income societies with guaranteed individual freedoms, implicit and unprovable contracts are often entered into by people willing to get round the system to enjoy sexual relations with emotionally vulnerable people, who are looking for long-term relationships. Due to the genetic, hormonal and societal conditioning and evolutionary make-up of the female psyche, it is often possible to interest a greater number of women if the other partner dangles the possibility of a long-term relationship. Another reason why some people opt to indulge in this kind of implicit expectation-building game is to retain with them the possibility of entering a long-term relationship if the situation later turns conducive. Keeping the options open is possible to a greater degree if there is an ambiguity shown in the intentions. A person who clearly outlines that he has no interest in a long-term relationship binds himself or herself to a short-term, purely carnal relationship with little room for change. In the case where one is looking for a female partner, this also immediately keeps out many serious, sober and well-brought up women (at least in the present era). The sad part for the short-term-minded, intelligent man who looks for a similar partner is often that the well-read, very intelligent woman who takes serious and meticulous interest in all aspects of the relationship is often the one who has never had too many sensual partners. Probably being busy with her intellectual/career pursuits, she might have neglected the glamourous aspects of personality which often attract sensual partners. Such a person is often looking for serious relationships. (It might also be a vicious circle in some cases: "*I don't have many sensual partners because I always look for long-term relationships and this puts them off. I also don't end up having many long-term relationships because my past lack of experiences makes me nervous about meeting people, dating and relationships.*") At times, the long-term-relationship-search situation becomes a cause for frustration when such a lady is good-looking. Having said this, the same situation can happen with a guy too, but since guys are often happier to sleep around without the possibility of a serious relationship, the probability is less (assuming both are attracted to each other) that men will reject opportunities for short-term sensual relationship, even if the other party clearly excludes any long-term relationship possibility.

Karmic consequences of a breach of trust lead one to be the victim of a similar situation in this or one of the future lives. When the breach of contract is incontrovertible and punished sufficiently through the legal system then the karmic consequence aligns itself with the legal consequence and often expires with the end of the legal punishment. However, when the legal system is inefficient and/or corrupt, then the karmic consequences continue beyond the minor legal price that the violator has had to pay. The technicalities and preconditions for this karmic-legal alignment can be the subject of a later book.

7

Peek and Be Peaked

Voyeurism and Exhibitionism

Kenneth Clark, the noted writer on art, mentions quite casually that despite the best intentions of the artists, every nude painting or artwork often brings up some vestige of erotic feeling. He calls it the 'fundamental desire (of human being) to be united with another human body'.[1] This is despite the efforts of puritans of all hues to consider the nude a sublime form of art alone. The human being is a holistic organism and therefore to attempt to separate the sublime from the basic urge of sexuality would be foolish. For example, a man deprived of a sexual outlet for long could find even a benign nude painting sufficiently arousing. In case of women too, this might work but since the normal biological sexual mechanism of women might kick in a bit slower, it might take more paintings or perhaps rehearsals of that image in the woman's mind for the arousal to take place. This is consistent with the view of some writers who believe that women visiting strip clubs often go there for bonding, unlike men who often go there for an arousal or even an actual orgasm.[2]

Nude art forms have survived over centuries. Nude paintings, sculptures and other arts and crafts have been made even in tenth century India where some of these have become part of temple art forms. Interestingly, it also shows the enlightened ancient Indian belief system that sexual appetite and spirituality do not run against each other. Just imagine sculptures of the most varied sexual poses in a church, a mosque or a synagogue and the liberal sexual paradigm of Hinduism becomes instantly clear. In the last few centuries, these ancient Indian, sexually liberated traditions have been severely damaged by the twin banes of Victorian hypocrisy and Islamic puritanism. The recent rise in Hindu right-wing thinking in India has also shown a typical hypocrisy when it comes to sexuality. On the one hand, the glorious achievements of ancient India are spoken of with great pride, while on the other hand the free-wheeling, liberated sexual traditions of ancient India which is apparent from the Hindu mythology is constantly downplayed. As mentioned in Chapter 1, many of the more extremist exponents of modern-day political Hindutva, in India try to completely ignore healthy sexuality in Hindu mythology. Since this sexual liberal paradigm embarrasses them, when ignoring does not work, they often try to push it under the carpet, pretending that the stories portraying sexuality are merely entertaining but purely fictional analogies to explain philosophical truths. This interpretation is certainly not how sexuality existed as a liberal paradigm in ancient India. Those who want to be true to the liberal traditions of genuine Hinduism must embrace this liberal sexual paradigm as something beneficial to the whole world, like Yoga or Vedanta, instead of shunning it.

Celebrating the Human Voyeuristic Instinct

This discussion is not about erotic art, but about how we humans have a voyeuristic instinct. Perhaps a tiny part of this voyeuristic instinct comes from our normal logical and intellectual curiosity which has also led us to progress scientifically. Since, in most cases, we only see others, especially of the opposite gender, in fully clothed conditions, the intellectual curiosity to see people without clothing can indeed be a strong one. Even children who are undeveloped sexually can have this normal healthy curiosity. The remaining part of this voyeuristic instinct might come from the sexual possibility of seeing enjoyable images to aid arousal or orgasm. Just like we salivate when seeing delectable food, this urge to enjoy and feast upon healthy images which would give us a lovely sexually gratifying experience is not unusual. Having said this, just like everyone does not get equally excited by the same food, it is unreasonable for everyone to have the same libidinous instincts.

In fact, Clark (cited earlier) points out that the English language sufficiently differentiates 'nakedness' from 'nudity'. Nakedness often signifies a mere absence of clothes and implies that a person is naked merely due to lack of clothes, implying chronic poverty, or some reason such as sickness. Nudity, on the other hand refers to a healthier, proud and even glorious exhibition of a body in all its splendour, without clothes. That is the reason why we have 'nudists' and not 'nakedists'.

Contours of Voyeurism

For the discussion in this chapter, every 'healthy' lover of nude art would not be classified as a voyeur. Voyeurism implies often that a person substitutes the mere act of observation for real sexual performance. Love of pornographic pictures or videos can be considered a part of our voyeuristic interest in the sexual activity of others. However, in karma, voyeurism also has a stronger, more negative connotation as opposed to regular pornography because very often the voyeur's victims are being observed surreptitiously, without prior permission.

Sometimes, the perfect voyeur meets the perfect exhibitionist. The voluntary webcam-based chat where one person bares all on the webcam, while the other person only shares his/ her appreciative comments, could be considered an example of this exhibitionist–voyeur exchange. In many cases, this webcam-based chatting on the internet leads to what we call cybersex. Cybersex often enables us to enjoy sex and meet diverse and multiple sexual partners while avoiding the triple-D problems of distance, disease and dinner-buying. Of course it might not be as satisfying as the real thing, but to have a real human being at the other end who arouses us for sexual adventure is certainly better than having no real-time human contact. We must not forget that the biggest sexual organ for arousal is our brain. Any arousing communication even using a computer can raise our sexual arousal to dizzying heights. Once the arousal is high, a good orgasm is often only seconds away. While earlier authors viewed cybersex as dark, depraved or even addictive behaviour[3], it is something which internet users are increasingly accepting as reasonably normal behaviour. After all, there are compulsive eaters of high-calorie food who end up overweight. But that does not make the whole eating process a dark, depraved or addictive behaviour. More recently, guide books have been written to advise people on cyber romance and sex without condemning it.[4]

The line between pornography and voyeurism is often thin. Is pornography merely a case when the voyeur meets the exhibitionist? The main difference in pornography and exhibitionism is that pornography is often done for commercial or other benefits and generally not merely for the orgasmic pleasure of the actors. In the case of exhibitionism, the orgasmic pleasure of the 'flasher' is derived from his/her act of 'showing'. Increasingly, the present era of abundant choice in pornography makes customers seek 'authentic' pornography requiring the actors to indulge in foreplay and real sex as if it is happening in real unscripted surroundings. This ring of authenticity often makes a particular video clip very popular. Understanding this mindset, pornography has found an attractive market using words like 'amateur' or 'hidden-camera'. Amateur or hidden-camera pornographic websites are the pornographic equivalent of 'organic' and 'natural' in case of food products.

Some theorists suggest that people who get excited by voyeurism also get the same pleasure by exhibitionism. This is also a view attributed to Freud.[5] If, for instance, a woman admires her own body while enjoying an orgasm, this would be a clear illustration of Freud's viewpoint. However, in terms of karma, a deeper discussion of the boundaries and contours of voyeurism and exhibitionism is relevant.

Karma and Exhibitionism

In terms of karmic implications, there are clearer guidelines. In the case of exhibitionism there is often a karmic negativity because the worst exhibitionists often get their pleasure by shocking people. When a person suddenly flips open his overcoat to reveal his erect penis to two women on the street, it is certainly not an act of love or affection. It is meant to deliver a shock and the ploy often succeeds. Some people may scream, while others may recoil in shock, shame or embarrassment. There are a minority who may take it sportingly and absorb the initial shock better, even laughing it off. Irrespective of the end result of the 'flashing', there is a clear transgression because no choice is offered to a victim whether he or she would like to see. This is quite unlike a stripper where the audience is already mentally prepared to see nudity. The strong reason for the lack of willingness on the side of both participants would be why exhibitionism will often be treated more negatively in terms of karma than a strip show, peep show or pornographic show. If the victim of the exhibitionist is a child, disabled or a vulnerable person, the karmic negativity is higher. The karmic result of such an activity could lead one to face similar unprovoked shocks in some area of life. In most countries, there are legal punishments for such activities, in which case there is a possibility of the alignment of karmic consequences with the legal punishment.

While exhibitionism involves 'forcing someone to see', there are practical constraints. The sudden exhibitionist who thrives on the shock of the victim knows that he could only expect the victim to have a momentary glance at his genitals. Only then is there an element of surprise in the whole act. The exhibitionist also often gets his thrill from the expression of profound horror on the face of people. Most normal people would prefer not to have a second glance when faced with the sight. In case a person's glance continues to enjoy the sights offered by the exhibitionist, one could possibly conclude that he/she is a voyeur. The exhibitionist however, might want to continue with this 'shock' treatment with different victims in order to continue deriving his pleasure. If he continues like this in a public square for some more time, there is the likelihood that the long arm of the law will catch up with him. In some countries, where sex is criminalized, he may face the wrath of a public mob and there is no saying what a violent mob may end up doing. On the other hand, an exhibitionist who takes his/her own time to disrobe is certainly likely to lose the audience, because in effect, he almost becomes an unpaid stripper. Another possibility is that some members of the prospective audience may restrain him from doing so. In some countries he might be beaten up or police called in. In terms of karma, the karmic negativity is lower in the case where the exhibitionist keeps disrobing at a leisurely pace because the time taken by the exhibitionist to disrobe ensures that only the most pruriently curious public remain behind to see his/her full glory. And if they do remain, they can no longer claim karmically that they were 'forced to view'. (Of course the exception here would be the case of children or vulnerable adults whose mental or physical lack of development prevent them from making an informed choice to view or not view, even when the act is done slowly.)

Karma and Voyeurism – Violation of Privacy

In the case of the exhibitionist, despite his best efforts, people only observe him for a few seconds. On the other hand, voyeurism has slightly more karmic negativity because the will of the victim is trespassed upon for a greater length of time. Since the voyeur is often doing his activity surreptitiously, there is little forced control over time. The voyeur often stops viewing his subject only when he has had his orgasm or there is some discontinuity in his ability to view, for example if the victim of his activities has closed the curtain of his/her window. Another probability is that the voyeur gets disturbed by a phone call or a knock on the door.

Subconscious Alarm System for Violations of Privacy

As clearly mentioned in the Chapter 4 on pornography (section on 'Violations of Privacy'), every possible victim of voyeurism has an inbuilt, subconscious security system. For example, the moment a person lays his eyes on a lady's private parts through a keyhole or some other electronic mechanism, the overself and subconscious mind are alerted. This is the reason why a woman often instinctively covers her legs or chest or even face when a strange man gives a glance over these parts. What is often amazing is that this happens even when the man in question is clearly not in the line of sight of the woman.

However, this alarm system works best for victims, whose Cosmic Sensitivity Barrier is thin. If the CSB is thicker, the alarm system is so faint that the woman may never feel it and the voyeur continues to watch her without causing her much discomfort. In the case of thin CSB, the victim of voyeurism would be able to instantly feel the gaze and violation of her privacy. The word 'her' is used for the victim, because most cases of aggressive voyeurs are men. But the basic principles mentioned above would apply to both men and women. As a result of this discomfort the victim would be able to protect herself immediately. But if this does not happen, because of high CSB thickness, the voyeur has a field day watching the woman. But clearly it is a violation of her karmic right not to be viewed (the right to privacy, in popular parlance).

The karmic punishment for this action is for the doer to face a similar embarrassment perhaps in the same or slightly different circumstances. For instance he may find that one of his private conversations has been published or disseminated through newspapers, websites etc. Something which he meant to be kept private would be known to others and cause embarrassment. The legend of Lady Godiva of Coventry where the voyeur known as Peeping Tom is struck blind while watching the nude Lady Godiva on horseback seems to be a case of instant karmic reaction.[6]

However, going blind or dropping dead would be a somewhat severe karmic reaction to voyeurism. If there is any truth in this legend, it is probably a reflection of how the subconscious mind of the victim can sometimes give a severe knock to the voyeur. In a case where the voyeurism happens psychically over a distance, this knock could be delivered to the astral self. (For the uninitiated, without going into too many technical details, it may be sufficient to understand that the astral body is also one of the important sheaths/*koshas* of the human body, similar to the outer sheath called aura. Also refer to 'Impact of "Avoidance" on Overall Health' in Chapter 1, for a better explanation.) For instance, a man who develops the psychic power of being able to astrally come out of his body may use this ability to watch his neighbour's wife while she is having a nice shower. In this case, there is no real keyhole or web camera, but the astral body of the voyeur, which can pass through physical barriers, enters the bathroom to view the neighbour's wife.

However, as mentioned in chapter 4 under 'violations of privacy', the subconscious alarm system of the victim will take independent action and give a 'psychic punch' to the astral visitor for interfering with the willpower of the victim. This 'psychic knock' can happen even when the victim's CSB is thick. For the sake of simplicity, this subconscious alarm system and its independent action mechanisms for protection are often referred to as the 'guardian angel' by some religious literature, because very often this subconscious entity can be almost independent and individualistic in their actions to protect the individual concerned. Of course, in reality, if the person has important karmic missions of a divine nature to achieve, there are other actual cosmic invisible entities to help and guide the person, these being the real 'guardian angels'.

Voyeurism in Hindu Mythology

Indian Hindu mythology also lists some well-known instances of voyeurism. For instance there is an interesting Himalayan legend of how a shepherd who had lost his sheep eventually stumbles upon a cave where the all-powerful Hindu god Shiva is 'entwined amorously' with his consort Parvati.[7] When these gods become aware of the voyeur, they immediately vanish to some other cave in the vast Himalayan range. What is notable is that unlike the legend of Lady Godiva, the Hindu gods in this instance, despite being highly powerful compared to the lowly shepherd are not recorded as punishing him for his impertinence or curiosity. This is despite the fact that Shiva is known generally as an angry god in the Hindu pantheon and the act witnessed was not a casual undressing or even a shower, but the final act of blissful intercourse. This is typical of the ancient Indian paradigm of tolerance and affectionate treatment of people and their sexual ways, irrespective of the power equations. This legend also points to the by and large sexually liberated and tolerant paradigm of sexual ethics prevalent in ancient India.

The young and naughty Hindu god Krishna is similarly known to have stolen the clothes of several young girls in his village while they were all taking a bath in the nude on a secluded part of the river. All the while, Krishna sits on a tree branch and gets a nice view, enjoying the beautiful scene of the lovely nude ladies taking a bath.[8] Later on, he only returns the clothes after they plead with him. These indigenous Indian traditions of friendly, bantering, loving sensuality were mauled, caged and ruined by the Islamic rulers of India, and later by the British (with their Victorian sexual paradigm) in India.

There are other mythological instances of this tolerance of minor sexual mischiefs like voyeurism. For instance, one mythological legend states that the great sage Dadichi, said to be the son of the ancient sage Bhrigu (who is credited with the creation of Bhrigu Samhita – an astrological treatise), was engaged in severe meditation and spiritual practices. This accumulation of spiritual merit worried the king of gods, Lord Indra, who sent a celestial nymph Alambusha to disturb the sage from his practices. It is said that Dadichi watched Alumbusha dancing (probably erotically) and had a seminal discharge (*a textbook case of voyeurism*), out of which a son was born.[9]

Another instance in the Hindu mythology is that of Renuka, the wife of Jamadagni – a spiritually accomplished sage. Jamadagni was the son of sage Richika. Richika was a *Brahmin* (highest priestly class among Hindus), whereas Richika's wife was of *Kshatriya* (second highest warrior class) family. The story of Jamadagni's birth is interesting. Richika, his father, had given a special potion to his wife and his mother-in-law since they both wanted children. The potion for the wife was meant to make a son with priestly, religious (Brahmin-like) qualities, whereas the potion meant for his mother-in-law was meant to create a son with warrior (Kshyatriya-like) qualities. However, the women swapped the potions by mistake. The result of this interchange was that Jamadagni was born a sage with the temperament of a warrior. He married Renuka who was a devoted wife and bore him brave sons. One day, while going to the river to fetch water, Renuka voyeuristically enjoyed the sight of a celestial couple cavorting erotically in the water. As a result it is said that she became aroused (some sources say 'became wet' or even reached an orgasm).[9,10] She was severely punished by her warrior-like husband and ordered to be killed. However, the background of this rather harsh sentence (the bit about Jamadagni's unusual warrior-like temperament) is mentioned in most Hindu mythological sources, probably to emphasise that this sort of punishment was not a 'norm' in the sexually tolerant ancient society. In fact, Jamadagni is said to have later restored her to life after his son, Parashurama, pleaded with him. Renuka is also worshipped in some forms in parts of India, with temples devoted to her. Similarly Jamadagni is still considered in the category of sages/seers.

Violations of Privacy and Karma

Both the above tales underline the fact that the karmic severity of voyeurism clearly depends on the depth of intention and pre-meditation. Similar to an accidental death due to negligence being different from a pre-planned murder, which again is different from a sudden crime of passion, the cases of voyeurism mentioned in the cases of spiritually exalted human beings is 'voyeurism by accident'. Both Renuka and sage Dadichi only happened to watch erotic sights which happened before them. It is almost like a scenario where the exhibitionist removes his clothes and the curious lady continues to watch the sight. In the case of Dadichi, others who wanted to disturb his attention probably meticulously planned the whole episode. However, in Renuka's case, she lingered on, enjoying the blissful sights of a cavorting couple. Perhaps, the celestial couple in Renuka's case should also have taken suitable care to ensure that the outdoors was sufficiently isolated and not used by the public.

Like any action which interferes with the will of another higher life-form, voyeurism or violation of privacy could be karmically negative. However, unlike the human courts of justice, the karmic cycles are fair because they often also take the intention of the 'victim' into consideration. If a 'victim' has left a big window open, knowing full well that she might easily be watched by a voyeur from a nearby rooftop, the human courts may still rule in favour of the victim, while the karmic system would take a very lenient view of this so-called violation. It would be treated as a pure, consenting sexual play with very little karmic consequence. In fact, the 'victim' may incur some karmic consequences for cheating and pretending, if she makes a big fuss about it. Celebrities who make perfunctory noises about violations of privacy while gloating secretly about their pictures in tabloids come into this category. The only negative consequence for the voyeur in such a situation is the slight thickening of the CSB due to the formation of guilt. The pretender victim also tends to have a thicker CSB in the long run.

8

Not Seeing the Face, Other Things Are the Same

Delights with Strangers

A well-known English idiom that clearly presents the danger of dealing with strangers, is 'better the devil you know than the devil you don't (know)'. In our lives however, it is often those who start as strangers who bring cataclysmic changes into our lives. A wonderful romantic liaison often starts with conversations with strangers in the bus, train or restaurant. The doors to spiritual growth often open through chance encounters with strangers. As noted by Sarah York in her book, it is through strangers that we often get our cherished gifts in life.[1]

The thrill of Sex with Strangers

Unsurprisingly, sexual experiences with utter strangers are also the mainstay of several novels, articles and erotic websites. The utter recklessness of sex involving a person you are never likely to meet again seems a great thrill. The mixture of danger and violation of our inbuilt caution is a strange aphrodisiac. Hundreds of books on erotic fantasies have sections devoted

to sexual experiences with strangers, giving detailed versions
of fantasies and 'real stories'. There are also books with titles
like 'Sex with Strangers', leaving nothing to the imagination
regarding its contents.[2] Some books even go as far as to
suggest that only the fear of disease, perception of immorality,
pregnancy and jealousy prevent complete strangers from
enjoying full sexual encounters with each other (assuming
they find each other desirable in other aspects).[3]

Casual sex encounters are different from prostitution
because prostitution involves exchange of money and is
often not based upon the mutual enjoyment of pure sensual
love. When one partner merely tolerates sexual activity for
some commercial advantage, it is clearly not a celebration of
sensuality. Having said this, it is also important to remember
that call girls and escorts also often enjoy sexuality while
making money ('doing enjoyable work'). It is important to
know this distinction between 'free choice' sensuality and
sensuality under some form of subtle coercion.

Sex with Strangers in Hindu Mythology

Interestingly most religious texts and mythologies have
interesting allusions to sexual trysts with strangers. Ancient
Hindu mythology, with its very tolerant attitude towards
sexual diversity, has a spiritual and ethical framework that is
often interspersed with sexual enjoyment with strangers. For
instance, in Ramayana, the god king Rama (an incarnation
or *avatara* of Vishnu, one of the most important Gods in the
Hindu trinity of Brahma, Vishnu and Shiva), is approached by
a *rakshasa* lady. *Rakshasa* is a term used for creatures somewhat
equivalent to the 'demons' found in Christian theology. But

more than a synonym for evil, which 'demons' have been in Christian theology, *rakshasas* in Hinduism denote more a type of sub-species, with an inclination to indulge in evil. However, the inclusiveness, tolerance and respect for diversity inherent in the great Hindu tradition can be better appreciated when we note that unlike the Christian treatment of demons (who are considered unequivocally evil), Hinduism treats *rakshasas* based on their actions. It accepts that despite the difficulties of being in the company of evil-doers, some *rakshasas* could be good and virtuous. There are numerous instances when the major gods in the Hindu trinity, especially Shiva, have granted boons to the *rakshasas*. It is also noted in the Hindu scriptures that many *rakshasas* undertake prolonged meditation and acquire spiritual, psychic and magical powers. There are also instances, where several *rakshasa* ladies have married gods, demi-gods and humans. Coming back to our story, this *rakshasa* lady proposes marriage to the Hindu god, Rama and bares her heart to him although he is a stranger. Since Rama is married, he teases her a little and suggests that she approach his younger brother Lakshmana (although he too is already married).[4]

There are numerous such episodes of gods enjoying their sensual side with strangers. For instance the Hindu god Shiva is often worshipped in India, in the form of the *lingam,* which is a representation of the phallus. It is symbolic of regenerative power and fertility. There are interesting mythological stories of how this great Hindu god came to be worshipped in the form of his *lingam* (phallus). One version states that this happened when the great sage Bhrigu reached the abode of Shiva and wanted to discuss some spiritual matters with him. However, Shiva was busy making love to his consort and did not open the door of his abode to this great sage. This upset the sage greatly and he cursed Shiva to be worshipped by people in the form of his sexual organ.[5] Another version, which is of relevance to this chapter, relates to how Shiva ventured through the Deodar forest area in Northern India, where several great hermits used to live with their wives. When the otherwise chaste and virtuous wives saw such a handsome, naked stranger amongst them, they shed their clothes along with their qualms and started embracing the naked stranger.[6,7] This version also states that somehow (either as a result of the wrath of the hermits or due to the frenzy of the wives) Shiva loses/sheds his penis here. Later on, devotees start worshipping him in this form. What is noteworthy in this episode is not merely the instance of sensual pleasure with a handsome stranger (since the wives had no clue about the identity of the good-looking stranger) but the tolerance of group sexual activity, since the *puranic* Hindu scriptures clearly talk of several virtuous ladies simultaneously indulging in sensual activities with a breathtakingly handsome stranger.

Islam and Sex with Strangers

What is Islam's history on this? Was the Prophet Muhammad, who was one of the greatest liberals in terms of sexuality, really against consensual encounters with strangers? One of the oft-quoted verses from the Quran (generally used as evidence by those who would like to show Islam as a degenerate religion) is the part related to admission to paradise, where it is mentioned that 'those who believe in Allah will have access to beautiful, pure virgins, river and shade'.[8] It is understandable that in a lonely desert with high temperatures, this would be the most basic of human requirements. Water, shade and a person to share company with would be indeed a paradise for a human being who is weary, tired, thirsty and lonely. This again points to the very pragmatic and contextual structure of the Quran, which is very empathetic to human needs of the time in Arabia.

Interestingly, the description of paradise does not include a mosque or prayers or old men and women saying beads of prayers, fasting or doing penance. This also shows the liberal mindset of Muhammad who understands the most fundamental human needs for rest, sex and leisure. Given the social mores and security situation of that era, it is understandable that most lone travellers across the desert during Muhammad's time must have been men. What is noteworthy from the angle of sexuality is that in most notable interpretations of the Quran, the plural form is used for company. The Quran does not say that a 'companion' or 'wife' will be provided. It clearly uses words like 'pure companions' or 'wives' or 'virgins', clearly empathizing with the human need for variety even in leisure and sexual activities. Quite obviously, these companions in paradise are likely to be beautiful strangers. The term 'virgin' or 'pure' might have been added to make it known that these sexual companions would be free of any disease. In the absence of major antibiotics and only long-drawn herbal cures available in those centuries, venereal and infectious diseases would have been a cause for concern amongst men (or women) loving sexual diversity.

In the contemporary strict Islamic world too, there are interesting uses of *burqa* (full body and face covering garment, banned recently in France) for sexually liberal behaviour. Many liberated Muslims from countries such as Saudi Arabia, argue in whispers, how the *burqa* has enabled women to meet strangers and have sexual encounters without being seen or identified in public. It has become possible for two lovers to meet even in crowded places using modern technology like Bluetooth phones. In fact, a Saudi national who bragged about his sexual exploits using technology, on live TV, is being punished by Saudi authorities.[9,10]

Even without technology the *burqa* has several advantages. Firstly, it becomes easier for people to conceal their genders within the *burqa*. For instance two lovers can easily meet, move around and be together in a train, shopping mall etc. by simply dressing up in *burqa*. It is much more easy for a male to move around in a loose-fitting *burqa* as a female, without being identified. The *burqa* can also be a useful accessory for gay couples who would like to remain unidentified. The *burqa* can help strangers meet up, have an enjoyable sensual experience and then depart their own ways without much ado, without facing the danger of being seen or recognized by others. Even when a strange male is with a lady in a *burqa*, the onlooking acquaintance or relative of the lady will never recognize her. It is almost like a permanent masquerade sex party. Did Muhammad foresee these interesting possibilities and uses of the *burqa*? Even if he did, his interest in pragmatism, a liberal attitude and the maintenance of social order would have prevented him from making a big fuss about it.

The Bible and Sex with Strangers

Despite the stringent Christian views against promiscuity, there are startling instances of Biblical heroes and their sexual adventures with almost strangers. For instance Judah, the son of Jacob has sexual intercourse with a prostitute who later turns out to be his daughter-in-law.[11] Similarly, the Biblical strongman Samson had sex with another stranger, who again, turns out to be a prostitute.[12] Probably in Biblical times it might not be easy to find strange women on the roads unless they were prostitutes. Most other women might be accompanied by male relatives. King David sees the beautiful Bathsheba taking a bath and finds no difficulty in bedding her, despite the fact that she is already a wife of one of his soldiers. For the diligent reader of the Bible there are numerous other instances of sexual adventures with strangers.

Practical Issues with Casual Sex

Despite the attractiveness of casual sex as compared to subtle coercion, there are some practical issues. In a sexually liberated society, it should be possible for a man or woman to meet up for sex as and when they feel like it without too many complications. Most of the complications that are mentioned about sex with strangers come into three broad categories and these arguments can be easily debunked. To begin with, there is the fear of disease, pregnancy or crime. Sexually perverted criminals often lurk in the guise of friendly hunks or ladies. Honey traps for money or for other motives often involve an attractive woman pretending to be attracted to the victim. Despite all these dangers and the high safety of sex with a devoted and regular partner, most sexually active people know the throbbing and thrilling effect of sexual encounters with strangers.

The third and the most important reason is often the 'ethical' and religious reason. If one keeps aside the convoluted debate about morality and religious views masquerading as pragmatism, we know that the objections to sexual experiences only come from our views of strongly protected sexual relationships, starting from marriage. In Western societies, we have expanded our outlook on permanent relationships to incorporate civil partnerships including same-gender relationships. Despite this, the walls of our understanding of sexual relationships are made of cemented layers of jealousy. The modern liberalised society has somehow learnt to *tolerate* variations in the gender of sexual partner, but our idea of a 'proper' stable consensual relationship is the one that is always guarded by thick layers of 'monosexuality' and 'jealousy'. Even gay or lesbian committed couples are expected to show a degree of faithfulness that simply means that he/she cannot enjoy sexual relationships as and when they tend to happen. While most of these 'religious' arguments against a freer sexuality have been debunked elsewhere in this book, it might be worthwhile looking at the other two 'practical' arguments against sex with strangers, and possible solutions.

The 'Safety' Argument: Disease/Unwanted Pregnancy and Possible solutions

An article in the *News of the World,* which talks about a bar girl finding strange men for sex using the internet (where she claims she bedded more than 200 men), ends with comments from relationship experts.[13] The first comment is a note of caution advising her to be 'careful'. This 'safety' argument in the case of sex with strangers can take various forms. Stripped of its unwarranted philosophizing, the issues surrounding sexual encounters are merely practical and implementation issues. It is simply the kind of choice faced by the traveller: "Should I have food at the roadside eatery or wait to reach home?" The question is of health and safety against all sorts of diseases which sexual intimacy can bring. Chlamydia, herpes and the dreaded AIDS are a case in point. The second question is the fear of an unwanted pregnancy.

These problems are not very difficult to solve. In the case of restaurants this problem was solved when strong government regulations and effective checks improved the sanitation and hygiene of all eateries and restaurants. This simple measure, wisely implemented, prevented outbreaks of disease among those who frequented cooked food vendors. In the case of sex, despite the lack of hundred per cent reliability of the condom, it continues to be a good first line of defence against diseases and pregnancy. The government can also take more steps to regulate hygiene and sanitation in this industry, but in order to do so, it is important for us to shed our layers of hypocrisy and demystify the sexual services workplace.

More education of people, better development of contraceptive devices that prevent germs and sperms from passing between partners, and easy availability of drugs to control the spread of sexual diseases could cause this fear to vanish. The present level of contraception technology among men is still primitively mechanical. The condom interferes with the full sensual contact of two people as much as a glove causes fingers to lose some amount of dexterity and tactility. The delay for the condom wearer also causes a loss in the spontaneity of love-making and is similar to pressing the pause button in a movie theatre at the height of suspense. Besides ruining the spontaneity of the moment, it does work like a sensory barrier and men who are already under pressure to keep their 'status symbol' standing, often face the prospect of losing a reasonably good erection when they come into contact with the wretched condom.

Coming to women's contraception, the present generation of contraceptive devices that women could use often provide them protection against pregnancy but offer little protection against diseases. Moreover, most of the contraceptive devices for women – whether pills or insertion devices – are definitely more complicated than putting on a condom. In the case of the female condom, it has had only limited acceptability worldwide till now.

Technology and research need to come together to provide a better contraception for men that does not interfere with the sensation and yet prevents sperms and disease-causing bugs from transferring. It is indeed astonishing that we live in a technological era where we are able to send pictures using mobile phones and decode gene sequences while our dominant contraception technology continues to be based on the old mechanical principle of building a thick rubber barrier between the sperm and the female body. To begin with, why are we not able to come up with a contraception device which can present a barrier for sperm, bacteria or viruses while being so thin that human beings may not even be able to feel that with their bare hands?

Even in the current climate, some improvements are happening. In fact, with innovations in female condoms in the coming years, there is a possibility that it might become the contraception of choice which women could wear much in advance without the male fearing the loss of his erection or loss in the spontaneity factor.[14] With improvements in design and the possibility of a tighter outer ring on the female condom it might prove a boon to women who have lost the tightness or elasticity in their vaginal muscles, thus enhancing pleasure for both partners and making sex more popular even among those who are past their prime.

In the future perhaps, there could be more sophisticated electronic contraception solutions. Just like there are germ-free sterile zones such as operation theatres in hospitals, there could be contraception zones in the future (similar to wi-fi areas). For example, an entire hotel could be a 'contracepted' zone where couples could enjoy sex without getting pregnant. Similarly just like a wi-fi router transmits internet connectivity to devices within an entire geographical area, these contraception routers, placed at strategic points should make the entire area 'contracepted', with no need for any other contraceptive device. The same device should also be able to destroy most of the sexually transmitted germs. Once this happens, it will revolutionise sexuality. Most big hotels and even large apartment complexes can be contracepted buildings. Similarly university premises and student halls of residences and other such places can be 'contracepted' with an option for individuals to temporarily disable it, if someone is looking to have a baby. Another solution is to have a common STD and sperm-exterminator oral vaccine, which can prevent all the common sexual diseases from developing and destroy sperm motility for a period of 6 months. The doses should be available with a one-month, six-month or five-year period validity.

Again all these increased technological breakthroughs would need research. Presently large parts of the world and religious groups are not interested in much research in the contraception area for fear of a further sexual explosion. This lack of funding could be remedied if this whole area of sexuality and reproduction is dealt with in a more open manner, creating enthusiasm and funds for research in this area. It is ultimately just a matter of time before contraceptive devices will be able to provide guaranteed prevention of both diseases and pregnancies. With some of these improvements in technology, this argument about safety from diseases and pregnancy is only going to wear thinner (like the condoms) and ultimately prove irrelevant to the debate.

The 'Safety' Argument: Sexual Crimes and Possible Solutions

That brings us to the next argument related to 'safety', namely, safety from criminals or other sexual predators. There is always the danger that the next stranger one meets for consensual pleasurable sex could be a psychotic serial killer or sadistic serial rapist. However, just like a good, sensible car driver always follows certain rules on the road, it will be expected that anyone wanting to meet strangers should follow some basic safety precautions. What is important in encountering such scenarios is to make sure that adequate checks are performed. Adhering to rules of safety should not be confused with being rude. A simple inviolable rule while meeting with a stranger from a dating website could be to insist on seeing an identification document like a driver's license or passport before allowing a guy or girl to step into our house or even while meeting for a coffee. This should be the first rule and order of business (actually *pleasure*) with every person one meets for a sexual adventure. This document could be checked for discrepancies in a person's age, name or other such details from what one has been told from the dating website. The second rule, which must always go with the first rule, is to always have the first meeting in a public place like a coffee shop, restaurant or even a busy shopping mall.

Having said this, just like even the best and most careful drivers can sometimes get dragged into motor accident scenarios due to the fault of other reckless drivers, there is some probability that one could eventually end up with a conniving fraud or criminal despite following sensible rules for being safe. Of course, in developed societies actual criminals are weeded out before they cause a lot of damage.

With technology it is possible for security forces to increase their effectiveness and ability to tackle crime. For instance, today the technology for viewing things from above is so good, it is said that some US satellites can focus in on objects and persons at a distance of ten to fifteen metres above the ground with very good resolution. If the same technology can be improved to get a street-side view of people on the streets and this can be linked to a search technology for pictures, all that the police will have to do is to put a picture search after uploading the picture of a criminal and the world wide satellites and cameras will be able to track this criminal down very soon. It might also be possible in the future using a special chip or tags with complicated software, to have a twenty-four seven behavioural check on existing people with sex crime records, with a provision for automatic alarm to the nearest police station once they start showing aggressive behaviour. It is just a matter of time before this sort of technology becomes easily available. Hence, as criminals are removed from mainstream society, our chances of meeting some serial sex killer keeps decreasing. Our fear of sexual crime will also decrease substantially.

There is also another aspect to the story of sex crime. The world today for people who love sex is murky and shadowy. As mentioned in Chapter 4, under the section on 'Economic Reasons for the Growth of the Virtual Sex Industry', as the situation stands today in most parts of the world, it is extremely difficult to ask a resident in a city, "Which are the places in this city where I can get good sex?" Hence this murkiness and shadiness makes it perfect for criminals to lurk in this world. Once the quest for sex becomes an acceptable search in our society, similar to the search for restaurants by a traveller, much of the crime surrounding the present murky world of sexual services demand would disappear.

We must also remember that despite there being more thrillers in the bookstores today about serial killers than about mundane road accidents, there are more people dying or getting injured in road accidents (at least in the developing world) than at the hands of sexual predators who enter houses with consent. And despite the higher number of road accident, the increasing number of cars on the roads tells us that people have not stopped driving.

The 'Safety' Argument: 'Psycho-emotional Complications' and Possible Solutions

The second comment to the *News of the World* article mentioned earlier seems more critical. One could, in some ways also call this an argument related to safety, but 'emotional and psychological' safety. This comment talks about how 'too much' sex with strangers could lead to an addiction with sex. This argument about 'sex addiction' is a hollow one and has also been dealt with in the concluding chapter. A brief discussion of this argument could throw light on its flaws.

No one denies that there are people with behavioural aberrations. There are alcoholics who consume very high quantities of alcoholic beverages and food lovers who go overboard. Similarly there are tobacco addicts and chain smokers. However, if a person has a small bottle of beer from a supermarket and a glass of beer at night with his dinner, is he normally called an alcoholic? Why is it then that a person who wants to have sex with a different person every week is labelled a sex addict without the slightest hesitation, with the imminent need for therapy?

Why are people reading a different book every day on the train not being called 'book addicts' with need for therapy? What about people viewing an hour of diverse TV programmes every day after work? Would they qualify for 'TV rehab' or 'movie rehab' or 'sports TV rehab' programmes? What about 'soft-drink addiction', 'bread addiction' or 'mineral-water addiction'? Can people who eat their lunch outside in a restaurant near their offices be called 'restaurant addicts'?

A clear distinction must be made between an 'addiction' and normal regular choices. People who have to compulsively consume some drugs at a certain time at sharply defined periodical intervals can be safely called 'drug addicts'. If a heroin addict does not get his dose, he experiences sharp withdrawal symptoms. Such an addict will steal or even kill others to get access directly or indirectly (through money) to drugs.

A person who has lunch every day at a restaurant would not qualify for this because this person presumably chooses to do so on his own. Similarly, a person who has consensual sex with another person clearly should not be classified in this category of 'addiction' just because he/she loves sex. Although the word 'sexual addiction' seems conveniently coined for media usage, religious sex bashing and sensationalism, it is certainly far from reality. Most of the so-called 'sex addicts' are a group of people with perhaps an above average sexual appetite and the ability and willingness to pursue their interest in enjoying consensual sexual experiences. Many times, it is simply that they are physically fitter people (for example, Tiger Woods, Arnold Schwarzenegger or our football players). In fact, their sexual-activity pursuit is often a far healthier option than slouching in front of the TV for an hour everyday while munching oily snacks. Yet these healthy sex-lovers are pilloried no end as the 'evil ones' with need for therapy!

Is It Good For the Future?

Another argument advanced by one agony aunt in response to the News of the World article is the very practical question of whether the future partner of the lady in the article will ever accept this chequered sexual history. In other words, do nice people always prefer sexual partners with *lesser* experience, although they might prefer employees or colleagues with *more* job experience?

Perhaps more empirical research is needed to let us know what the optimum number of previous sexual partners is, that we are able to accept our partners with. For example, if a person's prospective wife reveals that she had around seventy sexual partners (despite not being in the sex trade) before meeting him, would he be a bit upset? What about the prospective wife, if he tells her that he had ninety partners before her? Or would a much lower number like two partners before meeting her make her wonder whether he is lying? Intuitively, in today's world, it might seem that people are comfortable with partners who had a lesser number of sexual partners. Having said this, it would also depend on the social conditions, the country we are talking about, the age of people concerned, sometimes the type of job they do etc. For instance, in most Western countries with liberal attitudes, like the USA, Australia or the UK, an optimum number of sexual partners might be preferable to zero. A person in these countries, who is around thirty and has zero sexual experience may be considered a risky prospect rather than an attractive one, perhaps because this zero experience may be symptomatic of religious orthodoxy at best or some social adjustment or psycho-sexual problems at worst.

On the other hand, in many Eastern and Islamic cultures, the preferred option for a partner would still be zero sexual experience. The biggest numbers of prospects for hymen reconstruction surgeries come from people of these cultures, where zero experience is considered proof of 'purity' and 'innocence'. Husbands would take great pride in 'teaching' the whole act to his wife with delicacy and care. On the other hand, in some Western cultures, and as a message board comment states[15], men might find the whole 'teaching and making the women comfortable' part an avoidable distraction in the whole enjoyment process. Similarly other factors would also play a role. A person in the fashion industry, show biz, footballer or other 'glamorous' lines of work might be expected to have slightly more numbers of partner than people in mundane activities like a clerk or a teacher.

In general, it could be said that people's concern about their sexual partner's *golden number* may be more related to their own deepest sense of security. If the number is slightly less than or equal to their own, they would probably feel good and appropriate about it, whereas a disproportionately larger number than their own might create a sense of insecurity, at some level. The first might be an insecurity about themselves: "Am I so unattractive that I could only get two partners till now, whereas my partner (almost same age) has managed to bed fifteen." The other form of insecurity might be about the future: "Will this relationship last, if my partner has had so much sexual experience? Will he/she find me sexually good enough?"

In such situations, what would the coping mechanisms of the partner of an escort/call girl be? How do they manage to have long-term relationships? Are these partners the very model of how long-term relationships in sexually liberated societies of the future will be? Or do these people ignore the hundreds of sexual acts of their call-girl partners, simply because it is classified mentally as 'just work'? Will these people have a totally different mindset and behaviour if they know that their partners also *enjoy* sex with others? What if money alone is not the factor and the pleasure of diversity is also driving their call-girl partners to have sex with others? These are pertinent questions for deeper sociological research in Western societies also.

Even while commenting on the girl with 200 plus partners, the agony aunt takes great care to maintain the assumption that this girl would be happy to settle in a long-term monogamous relationship. This assumption may not be always true. Would a call girl who has enjoyed her work thoroughly not want the thrill of some enjoyable diversity, even while 'committed' in the bonds of 'holy matrimony' or 'long-term monogamy'? Does monogamy have to be so close to monotony? As mentioned in the concluding chapter, the time has come to challenge and shatter this paradigm of sexual monogamy.

The third argument related to psycho-emotional complication is more sophisticated. This argument is elucidated by Charles Johnson, in his paper on body language.[16] He quotes other authors to contend that just as in the case of conversations,

NOT SEEING THE FACE   181

deeper sexual communications can only result from knowing the person better. Further it is argued that two people who know each other can have almost a limitless range of sexual positions, nuances, etc., while with an unknown person the sexual communication will, at best, be basic.

To counter this argument we could perhaps use the metaphor of the pizza. If an Italian insists, "Why should people eat anything other than pizza, when the possible toppings on the pizza are almost limitless," we would find it laughable. While it is true that pizza can have much variety and so many possibilities because of the diversity in toppings, varieties of cheese and vegetables which are possible, the base remains the same. There is no reason why a person should not try rice or other wheat or corn products. Similarly, as long as the partner is the same, even with the range of possibilities, variations and nuances, there is a limit to the excitement that can be generated. Sexual trysts with strangers are always exciting even though the sexual process employed might still be basic. Does the cockerel mate with the same hen, experimenting with different poses, nuances and body language? Or does it prefer to stick to the more or less same sexual position while going with all the hens which are available in the proximity? That might give us a good clue about what is more preferable.

Making the Search for Sex a Mundane Activity

Making the search for sex as easy as a search for a neighbourhood restaurant also involves a whole change in our paradigm of understanding sexuality and the linguistic-semantic framework of sexuality. We can imagine the difference between a person saying, "I am going to the market," and a person saying, "I am going for sex." Or imagine a person saying, "I am going to the gym," versus "I am going for some sex." Is the sensation that is created in our mind when we use words like 'sex' merely the result of our curiosity and novelty in our minds, associated with sexual activity? Or is it partly the result of the kind of powerful sounds that those words emit? We might have to find a whole lot of mundane-sounding vocabulary to fit this paradigm of bringing sexuality from an 'exotic-morally relevant' to the 'mundane-morally irrelevant' category. For instance high-vibration, powerful words have traditionally been associated with sexuality. Words like 'fuck' and 'sex' will have to give way for milder sounding words which can be said without creating a sensation. More mundane words which could be mentioned without the eyebrows of people going up (mentally or physically) can be created.

Similarly, in this paradigm of sexual liberty, words cannot continue to be considered abusive merely because of their sexual nature. If words like 'shopping', 'eating', 'writing', etc. are not offensive why should 'enjoying sex' be so? Why has sexuality been converted through slang into a form of abuse? Why is there a 'fuck off' and not 'shop off' or 'eat off'? Why should 'suck my cock' be offensive when 'shake my hand' is not? If 'eater' or 'drinker' or 'preacher' is not an abusive word, why should 'fucker' be one? Perhaps the whole vocabulary of abuse is symptomatic of the framework of sexuality that we consciously and unconsciously subscribe to.

Karmic Repercussions

Are there serious karmic repercussions for sex with strangers? Karmic account-taking is only about keeping record of karma –

positive and negative. If sex with strangers is purely consensual and does not involve lies, broken promises and assurances of any kind, there is little karmic negativity. However, a breach of trust (for instance, saying that one is single while he/she is not) generates guilt to begin with and some bitterness, once the reality is known to the other partner, thus leading to karmic negativity. As a result, in a similar situation in the present or one of the future lives, this liar will experience similar hurt, due to the breach of trust by someone close. If a person – for example, a man – often lies to single women about his marital status in order to gain sexual advantage, this could result in a future female birth and this person could be made to experience the hurt and dejection of being *used* by someone for sex alone.

Having said this, a person constantly looking for sex most of the time could trigger a desire cycle within him creating a birth in his next life, in a situation where a lot of sex is available. Hence if the karmic balance is a highly positive one, due to this strong sexual desire the person could be born on a higher planet in surroundings where more sexual experiences are possible. Alternatively, even on a lower planet, a person could be born as a prince and thereafter ascend the throne while being the lord of a splendid harem. On the other hand, if sexual desire is coupled with an extremely negative karmic life, there is a real possibility that the person could be even born as a pig to fulfil his desires in the grimiest of circumstances. Of course, before we laugh at this as a fanciful joke, this rare arrangement can indeed happen, but as mentioned in earlier chapters, it would happen only with the full consent of the overself of the person concerned, as a measure to clear both his negative karma and sexual desire imbalance in one stroke.

Desire-load at the time of death in conjunction with the karmic load often decide the next destination for birth. That is the reason why the great Buddha often emphasised the need for destruction of desires (or cravings). In ancient Jainism and Hinduism, the concept of *aparigraha* is similar.[17,18] A simple illustration of this desire leading towards a destination can be found when we go to sleep. For instance, men who think or indulge in sexual activity (including masturbation) before going to sleep often wake up with a good erection (especially if their sleep has been sound). On the other hand, men who do not think of sex but meditate for at least ten minutes before dropping off to sleep often wake up without any erection. A life-long craving for something can lead one to be born in a situation where that craving would be fulfilled. Amba's story in Chapter 1 and her quest to kill Bhishma is a good example.

9

Do Not Covet Your Neighbour's Wife, Only Swap

Exchange of Spouse

When Moses came down from Mount Sinai with the Ten Commandments, it was clear that out of the thousands of possible major and minor sins which human beings could commit, God had chosen to include 'do not covet your neighbour's wife' as one among the big ten, almost giving it the same status as the commandment 'not to murder another human being'. If nothing else, this makes it clear that human behaviour was not much different at Moses' time in matters of sexuality. After all, there are few other things which are as primeval as the quest for sex. Hence, interestingly, it was found important enough to specifically mention that 'the neighbour's wife must not be coveted' despite there being a separate injunction 'not to commit adultery.' One must ignore the sexist connotation here which considers a wife as much a property of man as cattle and other assets. That is possibly the reason why there is no similar commandment not to 'covet a neighbour's husband'. Indeed, some of the original versions of this commandment include, as part of the same statement, an injunction not to covet any other goods such as the cattle, house, slaves or donkeys which belong to the 'neighbour'. If this commandment was written today,

185

it would have probably included the neighbour's car, house, mobile phone, shoes or clothes.

Deprived of the sexist aspects of the social context of the time, this commandment could probably read as 'do not covet thy neighbour's partner'. As we can see, this commandment then becomes in its contents, very similar to the injunction 'not to commit adultery'. The need for this special commandment probably arose because, at that time and probably even today, the typically testosterone-driven male would take the initiative to gain some variety in his sexual partners. That might be one reason why the likelihood of finding a male pervert in a crowded train would be higher than finding a female pervert. Of course, some authors do emphatically state that all these differences are a result of social and gender conditioning which has led to certain styles and patterns of typical gender behaviour. But this argument ignores the chemical and hormonal differences in the typical male and female physiology and the probable impact of these free-floating chemicals and hormones on behaviour and psyche.

In ancient society, a male who was coveting his neighbour's wife had only limited opportunities to bring his fantasies to fruition. Since the interaction between non-partner males and females in ancient society might not have been so free as in present-day liberal societies, there would be really fewer opportunities for love, friendship and relationships to develop. (Needless to say, there are many parts of the world where things in terms of male-female interactions are still almost the same as the society at the time of Moses.) There could be some simple reasons for this. Since the male would be busy generating income and the female would take care of home, hearth and children, the amount of leisure time for other pursuits would be very little. Taking care of home would also include labour-intensive, tiring tasks like drawing water, sewing, cooking, cleaning, maintaining the house, tending to the farm animals, etc. which would give little free time for the housewife woman of the time. In colder countries, foraging for fuel and keeping the house warm would have been additional tasks. In warmer agriculture-oriented societies, the woman would also take the food to her husband who would be busy working in the fields. All this would be compounded by the lack of technology permitting communication. Even writing a letter would require precious resources and considerable effort. Therefore assuming that the human nature was the same, certainly the possibilities of communication, interaction and enjoyment of the company of other human beings (especially of the opposite gender) would be somewhat rarer.

Biblical Instances of Coveting the Neighbour's Wife

Despite these handicaps, when there were brave men who aspired for sexual variety, they would either find women who were willing to indulge in some degree of sexual experimentation or if they had sufficient power and resources, would simply seduce or coerce the woman concerned. Examples of both these types of quests for sexual variety are found in mythology and scriptures. The biblical story of King David is a good example of a clear manipulation and coercion on the part of David when he sees Bathsheba, the wife of one of his soldiers.[1] Interestingly, no text mentions that the lady in question resists David or declines to have a consensual sexual relationship. Even when it is supposedly consensual, a subtle fear of the consequences could have led Bathsheba to consent. As modern organisational human-resource theorists would argue, whenever there is a very high degree of power difference between two individuals, even a consensual sexual encounter would probably be a case of sexual harassment. But King David did not merely stop at that. He wanted a proper possessive relationship with the lady and to that end, David abused his power to get the husband – who was a soldier in his army, killed in the battlefield.

Another interesting story related to the use of multiple sexual partners is the story of Jacob in the Bible. By no biblical account was Jacob considered a bad man. In fact, Jacob is considered an example of a righteous person. When he is working for Laban, Jacob fell in love with Laban's younger daughter Rachel. Jacob loves her so much that he prefers to work for Laban for no wages but on the condition that he will be given the hand of Rachel after the completion of seven years of work.[2] Laban agrees to this condition. At the end of the seven years, Laban makes a good wedding celebration and it seems the crafty man gives his first daughter Leah instead of Rachel to Jacob. When Jacob asks Laban the reason for this deception on the day after the wedding, Laban justifies it by saying that the younger daughter cannot be married off before the elder, as per the traditions of the country.[3] Interestingly, in many parts of the world, this tradition will find resonance. In countries like India and others nations where social conventions play an important role, marrying off a younger sibling before the elder one raises obvious questions in the mind of the community about the suitability of the elder one. Was the elder sibling not able to get a match due to lack of beauty, abilities, education or manners? Only in the rarest circumstances, would a younger sibling agree to or display alacrity to get married while the elder one remained unwed.

Anyway, Jacob is easily pacified when he is told that Laban is still open to giving him the hand of Rachel, provided he spends another seven years working with Laban. Neither Jacob nor Rachel seem to perceive this as extremely unjust, given that they have had to wait for a total of fourteen years. Interestingly, it seems Jacob did enjoy full sexuality with Leah before going to Laban with his complaint about breach of promise.[4] Was it because, after the feast, Jacob was too drunk to notice that he was enjoying the physical company of Leah instead of Rachel? Did lack of electricity and effective lighting play a significant role in this error? Or was Jacob too tired to make a fuss about it when he was in the mood to enjoy? We do not know the details of this 'error'. The next part of the Bible says that Jacob did finish his seven years and managed to get Rachel also for his wife. However, interestingly, his undesired-for wife, Leah, continued to bear him children, with surprising regularity.[5]

Considering that except in the case of Jesus Christ, there is no mention of virgin births in the Bible, it means in effect that Jacob continued to have regular physical intimacy with Leah, even after he got his first-love, Rachel. The details of the arrangement are not clearly outlined. What is clear, however, is that Rachel has a bout of jealousy about the children that Leah continues to produce for Jacob, while she is unable to produce any children. However, there is little evidence that Rachel has any jealousy about sharing her husband sexually with her sister Leah. Further evidence of this rather liberal outlook about sexual sharing is confirmed when Rachel asks her husband to have sexual intercourse with her personal maid, Bilhah, so that Rachel could enjoy the benefit of having children 'by proxy'.[6] Neither Bilhah nor Jacob (what more can a warm-blooded man ask for?) seem to have any objection to this arrangement. And this maid gave Jacob two children. Not to be outdone in this sibling rivalry for children, Leah, the elder sister, also offered her maid to Jacob, which Jacob accepted and the result of this

affair was two more children. The somewhat patriarchal bias of
the Bible is clear when one notices that a similar arrangement of
several sexual partners was not available to Rachel or Leah, and
the result of this union of 'god-fearing' Jacob with the various
ladies generally resulted in the birth of sons. Although there
is no specific mention of Jacob's views, there is no reason for
us to believe he was unhappy. This implies that the quest for
sexual variety is as ancient as the need for food, land, children,
clothing and shelter. However, when everything that happens
is consensual, without stress, jealousy or tensions and includes
fairness, it could be safely referred to as consensual **polyamory**.

Sexual Sharing in the Quran

Other religious scriptures are not far behind. In the case of
Islam, to begin with, the Prophet Muhammad allows men to
easily replace their wives.[7] The only injunction he makes is
that if some money has been given to the wife's family at the
time of marriage, it should not be demanded back. Notably,
Muhammad does not put any limits in terms of the maximum
number of times that a person can replace his wife. The Quran
also has a interesting allusions to what, in today's era, would
be regarded as a version of 'wife swapping', although an Islam-
friendly version might call it something done under the 'will
and supervision of Allah.' The story of Muhammad and Zaid,
his loyal adopted son is a notable one. Prophet Muhammad's
loyal adopted son Zaid has a wife called Zainab. Probably due
to severe incompatibility, Zaid finally divorces Zainab who
is promptly picked up by Prophet Muhammad as the sexual
partner. However, those who are more critical of Islam would
like to paint it differently as follows, quoting both Quranic and
non-Quranic (but reliable) sources. Prophet Muhammad went

out one day looking for Zaid. When he reached Zaid's house, due to the breeze and movement of curtains, Muhammad happened to see his adopted son's wife Zainab undressed in all her glory. Prophet Muhammad got immediately interested in the much younger Zainab, and his loyal adopted son Zaid, when he became aware of this, offered to divorce his wife and let the prophet take her, as a gesture of love and affection.[8]

Of course, since this version would certainly show Prophet Muhammad as a humane and normal person seeking some sexual variety like everyone else, the hawkish Islamic scholars promptly disagree with this version and incorporate 'Allah's will' into the whole context, to create the impression that Allah (God) wanted Prophet Muhammad to marry Zainab and that Zaid and Muhammad himself were merely 'honouring that wish'.[9] But the flaw in this Islamic argument is their inability to clearly articulate why exactly God would be interested in ensuring the marriage of a young lady to a rather older Muhammad. Or is this passage an indication of the more tolerant and liberal sexual paradigm that Prophet Muhammad wanted his followers to adopt?

Needless to say, the patriarchal Bible or the Quran does not mention many cases of polyandry and/or consensual and long-term spouse sharing. Interestingly, instead of spouse swapping, Prophet Muhammad does mention some interesting variations to the general long-term marriage, namely, the short-term temporary marriage, which has also been called *muta*. This is a marriage which is entered to by men purely for sexual enjoyment and gets dissolved by mutual consent after a fixed period of time. The woman is given money or property at the time of the dissolution of the marriage. Stripped of its trappings, ceremonies and rules, *muta* is nothing but a reasonably loving, relatively long-term relationship as opposed to pure casual sex

or a 'one night stand'.[10] Outside the marriage, there is also a
provision for engaging in sexual intercourse with a 'slave girl'
(*kaneez*).[11] Leaving aside the unethical aspects of slavery, one
could see that this is an interesting attempt to enjoy sexual
variety. Needless to say, the eagerness to show that everything
is holy, pure and spiritual in Islam has led to widespread yet
diverse interpretations of the Quranic verse which is the
basis for these facilities outside of permanent marriage.[12,13]
What is clear from these relevant injunctions in the Quran
is Allah's wisdom and all-forgiving nature (repeated time and
again after every second verse). It is highlighted that sexual
intercourse, especially within short-term relationships, must
be compensated for in money.

Sexual Sharing in Hindu Mythology

When one looks at the Hindu scriptures, true to their liberal
ethos, there are umpteen examples of a far more tolerant
approach towards sexual sharing than the one adopted
historically by other Abrahamic religions such as Islam or
Christianity. In Hinduism, Lord Krishna is considered one of the
most powerful incarnations of the supreme Hindu god Vishnu.
Being the incarnation of powerful Mahavishnu (or Vishnu), he
is known for his extraordinary powers, wisdom and capabilities.
The Bhagavad Gita, arguably the Hindu equivalent of the Bible
or Quran is a conversation between Krishna and Arjuna, one of
the princes. Besides his political wisdom and spiritual powers,
Krishna is also known for his tremendous capacity for love-
making and everything erotic. In the early years of youth, he is
often depicted as the charming cowherd. Radha, the cowgirl,
is one of his childhood friends and companions. As she gets
older, Radha is married to Ayana, but that does not stop Krishna

and Radha from enjoying the company of each other as lovers.[14] Whether Radha's husband did not mind it or this was an illicit affair is not very clear from most mythological readings. But we can assume that the entire village must have known and probably in the course of time, Radha's husband must have got wind of the adulterous affair. He would probably have ignored it or being a person of liberal mindset would have continued to love his wife, despite her passion for another man.

Interestingly in ancient India, the concept of divorce and closure of a relationship is an alien concept. Relationships, even with their inevitable fights, misunderstandings and probable complications resulting out of sexual variety-seeking continued to be maintained in time. This concept of love, harmony and the absence of an almost mathematically precise cut-off points in relationships (a common feature of relationship closures in the West) is very typically an empathetic Indian/Eastern concept. Tolerance, understanding, forgiveness and affection mark the flow of relationships. In contrast, the Western paradigms of relationships are marked by clear and well-defined beginnings, endings and closures. Of course, this is not to imply that the closures of all Western relationships are marked by bitter acrimony, but to draw attention to the fact that this concept of almost mathematical precision is largely absent in traditional Indian relationships. Even if the relationship is largely over, the passage of time is allowed to heal it gently and close the wounds, without any hurried display of an abruptly-stated and expressly-articulated 'break-up', as is often common when relationships are over in the Western paradigm of romantic relationships. This style of subtle and gentle closure of relationships through fading, is more in tune with the cosmic kindness of nature.

Reverting to Krishna and Radha, their erotic dalliances, music and fun activities are often referred to in India as *rasleela* (*leela* referring to act, dance or play and *ras* referring to enjoyment or delight). In fact, many mythical scriptures refer to it as a group activity, which many *gopis* (cow girls) participate in out of their own free will. Radha was, however, Krishna's favourite and most well-known lover and companion. Many famous temples in India are Radha-Krishna temples, depicting their great and holistic love which was emotional, intense, sexual and yet not tied down by strictures of matrimony and societal documentation. That people in India are willing to worship the god Krishna in his union with Radha without the social sanction of marriage is a clear pointer to the liberated ethos of ancient India.

Some of this ancient liberal sexual ethos is presently retained by some Indian tribes. These tribes live in a communal setting in the harmony with nature. Fortunately for some of these tribes, India's modern industrialization is still to uproot them fully. For instance among the Murias of Central India, teenagers are allowed to live in a group in some form of a dormitory, where they freely share and explore love with each other.[15] As they grow older they are helped by their parents in selecting compatible life partners. Cases of divorce or couples eloping are rarely seen[16], which points to the merits of a jealousy-free social community.

The Intolerance of Sexual Polyamory

Unfortunately, similar to the 'stricter' Muslim drive to purge most or all of Prophet Muhammad's liberal sexual mindset from the Quran and depict Islam as a 'morally upright' religion conforming to popular perceptions of 'sexual morality', Hindutva proponents have also, in recent years, been attempting to sweep this sexually liberal ancient Hindu heritage under the carpet. Movies on lesbianism are banned or attacked by so-called 'cultural organisations'[17] and many groups in India, at times aided by the state law enforcement machinery, keep trying to clamp down on consensual sex between unmarried adults.[18] A few years back, a so-called Hindu organisation assaulted women sitting in a pub in a south-Indian city and enjoying a drink.[19]

This system of mutually agreed barter of spouses for enjoyment of sexual variety, even in today's age, has several advantages over encounters with perfect strangers. To begin with, when a couple meets another couple there is some safety in being part of a slightly bigger group. If it is a group sexual venue with several couples, then it is even better from the angle of safety. When a single person meets another single person for a sexual encounter there is a fear lurking about the other person. What if the stranger is a serial rapist, conman or killer? Does he/she have intentions other than sex?

In conservative countries like India or Pakistan, people who seek sexual trysts with relative strangers and then get cheated by these fraudsters rarely report these crimes to the police due to shame. Fraudsters and criminals often take advantage of this. Women who might look for sex often lay themselves open to blackmail. In the shadowy world of spy craft and diplomacy, honey traps are often used to blackmail people into submission. The recent case of former International Monetary Fund (IMF) chief Strauss Kahn's sexual indiscretions was initially described as a honey trap.[20]

The lack of complete trust in strangers can also often create inhibitions in sexuality. Sometimes this mixture of fear and sexual desire creates an exhilarating experience. But there are also people who live to regret their impulsiveness. Besides criminal activity, the fear of diseases transmitted deliberately or otherwise continues to be a legitimate source of fear. The horrifying crime story of the Doncaster bouncer, Steve Robson in the UK, in the late 1990s, who had sexual encounters with countless women fully knowing that he was an HIV carrier is worth mentioning. Being a former nightclub bouncer he was endowed with a good physique and looks. Using his charms it is said that he had serial encounters with strange women, even in staircases and alleys.[21] His adventures in fact catapulted this small town of Doncaster to the top of Britain's areas with high HIV incidence.[22] Chlamydia, herpes and other diseases continue to be contracted often from sexual encounters with strangers. This is hardly surprising because the whole thrill of sexual encounters with strangers often hinges on unpredictability and spontaneity.

Getting Over the Distrust of the Stranger

This distrust of the stranger, while sexually enjoying diversity can also be partly overcome by using the regular services of professional sex workers including couples. Since the whole tryst is planned in detail, it usually does factor in the safety angle. Even if one person forgets safe sex, the professional, well-educated sex worker will certainly remember it. The more sophisticated the sex worker, the more hygienic and careful she/he is likely to be. In fact, dealing with a sophisticated adult sex worker/escort is often a pleasant experience both due to her skills of love-making and also for the social and conversational skills. Well-to-do business executives and others often use the services of these escorts while attending parties or social events in visiting cities. But despite these advantages of using escorts the fact that the sex is paid for removes all the pleasure of conquest. At the end of the day, it is still an 'impure' free choice. After all, removed of the pleasantries, it is merely some paid, but hopefully, enjoyable work for the escort. In fact, for every male, it might not be easy to know whether the escort woman is actually pleased or merely faking it in the interest of good customer relations. As Berlusconi, the notorious former Italian premier put it when the media queried him about his use of escorts for his famous *bunga bunga* parties: 'I never understood where the satisfaction is when you're missing the pleasure of conquest'.[23]

Genuine swinging parties amongst a trusted, known group of like-minded couples partly takes away the disadvantages of both the above methods. Mutually-consenting enjoyment of sexuality with an acquaintance or friend's attractive spouse can be a thrilling experience. In fact, in most parts of the developing world, including the Middle East and Asia, the constraints on sexuality could make this the safest method for enjoying sexual variety. In much of the Middle East or South Asia, prostitution is illegal or operates within heavy constraints. In India, for instance, it is impossible for call girls to advertise their phone numbers or publish details of their services, except under euphemistic and misleading headings like 'medical services' where they advertise for sports or ayurvedic massages. Even in such cases there is the ever-present danger of a police raid and front-page publicity in the next day's newspapers. In many countries, prostitutes can be imprisoned, deported or given corporal punishment. Under such circumstances, even for the clients, there is a grave risk of imprisonment, shame and/or entanglement in a legal mess. Other options for sexual experiences with strangers are also legally closed. In many of these parts, there are very few opportunities for real sexual contacts with strangers. In countries like Saudi Arabia, a misreading of signals to make an approach with a strange woman who did not have sex on her mind, could easily land one in prison for a long time, or worse.

Hence, in this scenario, a nice house party with a few willing, like-minded couples from similar social and income strata, in an atmosphere of affection, food, wine, laughter and intimacy is both secure and relaxing. As long as this is done with the willingness of every person concerned and to the level of their comfort, there is nothing more pleasing. Since this group would contain couples who do it for mutual enjoyment, there is little chance that anyone in the group would be indiscreet. After all, the slightest indiscretions could easily cause social and other problems for all concerned.

Complications in Spouse Swapping – Some Suggestions

However, these wife-swap situations are not totally free of complications. One of the common wedding vows is 'I take you for better or for worse, for richer, for poorer, in sickness and in health'. It is reasonable to expect that a wife/ husband may be ill at times or get to be very thin or very fat after marriage and sometimes may have lost some of her/his physical attractiveness. (Without going into the philosophical debate on what is attractive, let us just stick to conventional ideas of physical attractiveness.) What will be the karmically appropriate behaviour in such circumstances? If one partner is not preferred by others in such a spouse-swapping party, it could easily lead to a feeling of inferiority. One way to handle this possible situation is to ensure that all swaps take place in a mutual setting. Let us take two imaginary couples, John/Jane and David/Diana. In the swap situation, if John and Diana are looking forward to enjoying each other, while Jane and David want to do likewise, there is absolutely no problem. But if John, Jane and Diana are extremely attractive, while David is particularly unattractive, then there is a peculiar situation here. The mandatory rules of the game will mean Jane is forced to go with David, although she might not be attracted to him at all. Of course, David might have little problem with this arrangement, since he reckons that on his own, he would never have managed to get such a lovely partner. But obviously, this would violate the condition of free love, because considerations other than pure enjoyment of love-making have crept into the scenario. Jane is perhaps merely making a little compromise here, for the sake of her husband. But if Jane and John are a frequently swinging couple and meeting with different types of couples, this issue can be overcome because at some point or another, Jane might get an extremely attractive partner while John might be stuck with a very unattractive one, so this unfairness evens out. Another option is for each couple to take some time to discuss after meeting the other couple and only then to decide whether to go in for the swap or to not go ahead with the spouse exchange program if one of the partners does not feel the attraction. This can be done by prior exchange of pictures or by having an initial meeting at a public place between the two couples just to 'get a feel of each other'.

Another way to get over both these issues of unattractiveness as well as free love is to have a large number of couples in such parties, so that partner thought to be 'unattractive' by one is found attractive by someone else and in the whole group things are settled reasonably well. Again here, if the person is shunned by the opposite sex partners of all the other couples (*or same sex partners of other couples in case of a homosexual partner swapping scenario*), he/she could feel depressed or unwanted. One way to ensure that this does not happen is to make sure that there is some degree of homogeneity in all the couples who join this sort of arrangement. For instance a couple in early twenties might not find it interesting to have a swap with a couple in their late fifties. So there could be a mechanism to ensure that people of similar age groups and personalities join the group. Another way to leave the question of attractive/not attractive to luck would be to have some sort of randomising games. For example, all the women can be asked to write their names on a piece of paper, fold it and put it in a basket and men must be asked to go with the lady they get. In today's liberalised era, one also finds couples who have a vast difference in their ages. For instance a man in his late forties may marry someone in their mid-twenties. This arrangement would certainly work well till the man reaches his seventies. Despite attempts to remain fit and agile, his age may start taking a toll on him. His wife may yet remain fit, beautiful and attractive for another decade or more. In such cases, it is important to find a complimentary couple, so that there is no feeling of inequality. For example, in the above case, a couple where the lady is much older could be found. Of course, this is easier said than done.

Another problem which often happens to couples or one partner in a couple from a conservative culture is the roadblock of qualms. One partner might be an enthusiastic and willing partner in the whole enjoyment process while the other partner might be only doing it to follow the rules. Let us assume that

John and Jane are meeting with Ramesh and Sunita. While both the couples are attractive and seem friendly, Sunita is participating in the whole exercise only for the sake of Ramesh. She has no interest in sexual experimentation. In such a scenario, while Ramesh and Jane would enjoy enthusiastically, John might find that Sunita is a reluctant participant and behaves like a wet blanket. To prevent such scenarios, again the process of 'getting a feel of each other' through an informal meeting would be useful. If it is individually arranged, these things must be cleared beforehand through frank and fair discussions. Of course in our society these things happen often in an awkward and sometimes embarrassing style, which prevents detailed clarifications and communications between organisations, individuals and between couples. In many countries, since such activities are illegal, the communications between interested couples are in coded words, phrases and facial gestures. Obviously, the effectiveness and transparency of such coded communications, shrouded in shyness and fear of the law, would be partial at best. In terms of karma, as long as the arrangement is without guilt or coercion, it is like enjoying any service by mutual consent.

Most such partner-swap arrangements also tend to include safety considerations since swinging couples would not want to have children or pass on any diseases to each other. But as most contraceptive packs state clearly, the effectiveness of condoms is limited to ninety-eight per cent and the morning-after pill's effectiveness is less than this. Other contraceptive methods may prevent pregnancy, but might not prevent diseases. So what is the solution for the rare situation when a swap encounter results in pregnancy? Although this might be a rare accident, I think it is important that participating couples give a thought to this scenario especially when they are enjoying full, free sexuality. However, the spiritually enlightened thing to do in this scenario is not to abort a baby, but to accept it cheerfully as a karmic result without rancour. The couple who have got the baby must accept the baby cheerfully as their own. Aborting the baby is indeed a karmically black deed with consequences. Karmically, the situation is similar to the question of custody of a child, post-divorce. The swinger male may refuse to take responsibility for the pregnancy, but since the responsibility for preventing pregnancy in partner-swap situations is always a joint one, there is some karmic negativity generated when a man involved in the act just washes off his hands.

Unless it was clearly specified earlier that the female partner in a swap should bear responsibility for any pregnancy, the responsibility is always a joint one, although the mother's role, due to biological, hormonal and other reasons, is far more significant. One solution to prevent all these complications is to use double contraception, perhaps a condom and an intrauterine device. This will reduce the chances of pregnancy even further. (Using both a female and male condom is not recommended, since the chances of friction and tearing are higher.)[24]

Another way to reduce this possibility is to use sensual massage, kissing and the use of touch to stimulate, caress and ultimately bring each other to a lovely satisfaction. Sexual satisfaction by insertion of the penis is often overrated. After all, as some wise man has said, the brain is the biggest sex organ. With use of wonderful sex aids (many of them vibrational), hands and touch, it is often possible to get wonderful orgasms. All that is needed is sufficient gentleness and foreplay. Men often think of their penis as a substitute for foreplay. In fact if arousal is sufficient there is no reason why even a nice massage using creativity and different strokes and the use of sexual toys cannot bring a woman (or man) to a shuddering orgasm. Even the ancient text of *Kamasutra* advocates the use of sexual toys. For instance, *Kamasutra* advocates that when a man who has a smaller organ (referred to as a 'hare type' in the text) finds it difficult to bring a woman with a deeper, larger vagina (referred to as 'elephant type') to satisfaction[25], it is better to use sexual aids, rather than using weird remedies to increase the size of the organ. Dildos of various types, some meant to add to the length of the existing organ while others to be used instead of the organ itself and made of diverse materials like gold, silver, ivory or bull's horn are recommended.[26]

Karmically and spiritually, the whole issue has little negative consequence as long as everything is based on free will and does not end up hurting others. As long as there is no guilt associated with this, it is a pleasurable and joyful activity. Since marital vows talk of trust, it is important for both the partners to be willing. More than karmic worries, it is earthly issues of safety in practice that one must be most careful about. In developing countries such as India or China, which struggle with reconciling their traditional religious outlook with sexual liberties; issues of safety, law and order, and blackmail by criminals must be taken care of by couples venturing into swapping. As happens with anything that is considered taboo, criminals and people with dodgy agenda often get into the picture with intentions other than pure enjoyment. The taboo on sexuality in some of the developing countries has resulted in the proliferation of swap clubs, but often controlled by the mafia.

Hence it is quite possible that many of the couple-swap advertisements in countries like India, China or Pakistan are also inserted/run by unscrupulous people with an agenda of blackmail, abuse, extortion or even to run the pornography industry. Then there is also the constant fear of police and law enforcement agencies who think nothing of clubbing private sexual mores of people with national security issues. For instance, 'group licentiousness', a term used to cover orgies and swapping, was added into China's criminal law in 1997. Those arrested under this charge could face, on conviction, up to 5 years in prison.[27] More than black karma or spiritual worries, these are the pragmatic issues that one must really worry about.

10

My Brother is
My Greek God

Consenting Incest

The kind of taboo that incest has around the world is much more stringent than any other taboo known to mankind. For instance a cursory search on Google of a taboo subject like 'sexuality of Jesus' will reveal thousands of websites willing to discuss that proposition, despite a Christian population of more than two billion worldwide. On the other hand, there are extremely few websites (except the near pornographic ones) that are willing to have even a basic discussion about incest.

Similarly, movies have been made and books are available on every topic that was considered a taboo merely a few decades ago, except in the area of incest. Books and mainstream movies on homosexuality, lesbianism, transsexuality and on the real and imaginary sexual lives of religious or historical icons like Christ, Buddha, Muhammad, Alexander the Great and Napoleon are easily available now. However, it is still difficult, if not impossible, to find sensible books which debate and discuss incest at an intellectual level. Movies about homosexual love have even won Academy Awards, but to find a movie depicting incestual love in the present age is extremely difficult. When even books or movies carefully avoid this topic, what are the chances that it will ever enter the public arena as a topic of discussion?

And yet, there are probably thousands of families where growing teenagers and probably adults experiment, experience and guiltily enjoy incestual relationships. And in this era of advanced birth control and safety, what are the most severe repercussions of such a relationship? Perhaps the most severe disadvantage of an incestuous relationship would be the almost unbearable guilt, severe self-doubt of the appropriateness of such an experience and anxiety about the consequences should this relationship be known. For most people the burden of keeping such a tight lid on something they are taught is so terrible, is itself a severely constraining burden on their conscience.

Prohibition of Incest in the Bible

From time immemorial, incest has been condemned as a terrible crime in the Christian tradition. For instance, the Old Testament book of the Bible, Leviticus, condemns sexual activity with a stepmother, daughter-in-law, aunt and uncles.[1] Interestingly however, the punishment for sexual dalliance with all the relatives is not the same. For having sex with the stepmother, daughter-in-law, homosexuality, mother-in-law, any animal (bestiality), stepsister (or real sister), the punishment pronounced is death. However, the stringency of the punishment tapers off in the further passages which deal with having sex with an aunt (both uncle's wife and father's sister) and sister-in-law (brother's wife).[2] The punishment in these cases is to 'die childless', a somewhat milder punishment than being killed or stoned to death. The broad boundaries of those who fall within the parameters of incest are also somewhat unambiguously defined in the book of Leviticus, chapter 18.

Avoidance of Incest among Hindus

Among Hindus, marriage within the same family tree (referred to as *gotra* in the case of the priestly Brahmin class) is prohibited. The elder brother's wife is supposed to be treated with the same respect that is given to the mother. Some ancient Hindu Vedic teachings talk of seven kinds of mothers who need to be accorded the same status and respect as the real biological mother. These include, besides the real (biological) mother, the wife of the king, the wife of the *guru* (the teacher), the wife of the priest (the *Brahmin*), the cow, mother earth and the nurse (nursing mother, who is also the babysitter).[3] However, as we shall see in the later part of this chapter, there are very interesting instances of the highest echelons of gods in Hindu mythology indulging in incest. This only goes to re-emphasise the liberal outlook of ancient Hinduism.

Prohibition of Incest in Islam

The Quran also has a similar list of the relatives to be avoided sexually.[4] In chapter 4, verse 22 of the Quran, Muslims are asked not to marry those whom their fathers have married. Do most people need reminders not to marry their mother or stepmother? This is further proof of the great liberal that Muhammad was, and further proof that there is nothing greatly karmically negative about incest, except the terrible guilt, lies and hypocrisy. In fact regarding marriage between relatives, in most English translations the word used by Muhammad is that this is an 'abominable' custom. Of course some commentators have used the word 'evil' instead of abominable, probably because they wanted to emphasise the immorality of that act.[5] However, from the style of writing and the fact that Muhammad has provided some exceptions to this general rule, it is difficult to believe that this is a serious crime. Similarly in the next verse Muhammad mentions a list of relatives that a man should not marry. Here too, there are exceptions provided. Most notably, he also ends this verse benignly by noting that Allah is most merciful and often forgiving. Interestingly, as noted in the last chapter, Prophet Muhammad himself marries Zainab, the beautiful wife of his adopted son.

Notably, as is the case with most Quranic teachings, even the prohibitive verses end by talking about Allah who is forgiving, wise, all-knowing and merciful. Is this a hint that having a sexual relationship with someone from the prohibited list is forgivable and that Allah is willing to 'understand and forgive' this in light of circumstances? Compared to the biblical tone, the Islamic injunction seems mild and more liberal. In fact, one gets the feel that Prophet Muhammad's prohibition of incest was clearly for pragmatic reasons such as preventing the spread of diseases and possible proliferation of genetically damaged children resulting out of such unions, rather than karmic or spiritual reasons.

Incest in Biblical stories

Interestingly, the mythology of almost every religion has references to one or other form of incest. If one looks at the story of creation, Eve was created from a portion of Adam's body and yet Adam had sexual relations with Eve and had offspring, all under the watchful eyes of God, the father. Is it not a classic case of an incestual relationship? Similarly it might be reasonable to assume that Cain (after he killed

Abel as per the biblical accounts) had sister(s) with whom he had sexual relations and they produced further offspring. (Incest being a taboo from time immemorial, this aspect of the biblical myth of creation was not dwelt upon). Another option is that Cain slept with his mother, Eve, to give birth to offspring. How else did the human race continue, if one goes by the Bible alone? Since Islam also believes in the origin of the human race through this story of Adam and Eve, it can be surmised that they also accept the incestual relationships of the offspring of Adam. In fact, there are other clearer instances where incest was accepted. For instance, Abraham has married his half-sister.[6]

Again, the biblical story of Judah, the son of Jacob, throws some light on the actual treatment of incest in the Bible. Judah is the patriarch of the tribe of Judah into which David the King and, later on, Jesus himself was born. Judah gets a wife for his son, Er. Her name is Tamar. After the untimely death of Er, Judah exhorts Er's brother, Onan, to have sexual intercourse with his sister-in-law Tamar. Onan avoids impregnating his sister-in-law by practicing *coitus interruptus* (spilling the semen outside the woman's vagina by withdrawing the penis just before ejaculation).[7] This is an ancient method of birth control. As per the Bible, he is punished by God promptly for this form of birth control and put to death. Interestingly, the spilling of the semen was considered a more serious crime than incestual sexuality with his sister-in-law.

It does not stop here. After the death of Onan, Judah sends his daughter-in-law to her father's house. After some years, there was an occasion when Judah was travelling around that area, Tamar disguises herself as a prostitute and sleeps with her father-in-law. Judah is not aware of the lady's real identity and sleeps with her thinking of her only as a prostitute. Interestingly, the same God who was upset with Onan for spilling his sperm seems to be quite tolerant about Judah's sexual trysts with a prostitute. Later on, when Tamar is discovered to be pregnant there is some fuss about immorality. However, when Tamar is identified by the father-in-law and is called 'righteous', she peacefully goes into labour and gives birth to twins as a result of her sexual relations with the father-in-law.[8]

The story of Lot and his daughters in the Bible seems to be interesting too. Lot, the righteous survivor of God's anger in Sodom (a city said to be completely destroyed by God in a rage against rampant homosexuality), goes out and stays in a cave with his two daughters. One after another, the two daughters serve his father wine (probably to do away with any qualms that he might have), and sleep with him on two consecutive nights. Interestingly, the Bible does not record the two daughters needing any wine themselves. They had no need to forget that they were enjoying sex with their father. They merely rationalised it as a sublime activity for preserving the father's generation. Both of them duly became pregnant by their father.[9] In a very cavalier and almost dismissive manner, the Bible also tells us that one of Jacob's sons, Reuben went and slept with his father's concubine, Bilhah. It is also mentioned that Jacob is aware of this action. But there is no further mention of any fall-out or punishments. Does it mean that Jacob did not consider the action very serious?[10] We are only kept guessing about the mitigating circumstances in this case, when some people have been punished with death by God for merely letting their 'seed' fall to the ground.

Incest in Hindu mythology

In Hinduism, keeping with the liberal sensual background and liberal traditions, incest, like many other issues of ethical conduct has been left to the context and situation. The most striking aspect of Hinduism is its great appreciation of the concept of ethical relativism, of understanding that the world does not always consist of black and white concepts, far before the paradigm of relativity became a well-accepted line of thinking in the post-Einstein Western world. This compassionate idea of ethics and karmic laws, operating in a holistic manner, taking into consideration various possible mitigating circumstances even in so-called crimes, is often considered anathema by the Abrahamic faiths that believe in simple rules of dos and don'ts.

Hindu mythology also has several instances of incest, which can be found in *puranas* (the mythological part of the Hindu scriptures), the epic *Mahabharata* and other scriptural texts. For example, we have Arjuna, the warrior-god prince from the mythological *Mahabharata*. Arjuna's father was Indra, the king of gods. Indra had a wife but also had many exceeding beautiful *apsaras* (immortal nymphs), skilled in the art of love-making, dancing, etc. in his court. Indra, a cunning ruler of heaven, often used some of these nymphs as strategic weapons to disturb the powerful meditations of sages and others to prevent them from accruing extraordinary spiritual powers which could threaten his heavenly throne.

When Arjuna visited his father Indra on a particular occasion, Urvashi, one of Indra's nymphs propositioned him. Unlike the biblical Reuben, Arjuna politely declined to enjoy the sexual company of this exceedingly tempting beauty by pointing out that he considered her equivalent to his mother since she was once married to one of his ancestors[11]. Urvashi tried to convince him that the laws of earth do not apply to her and that in any case, many of Arjuna's other ancestors, cousins etc. have enjoyed 'sporting with her, without incurring any sin'. It was the cosmic equivalent of tax-free, on-the-house fun. But Arjuna refused to budge. Urvashi was quite upset at this snub and for his efforts for being the 'nice guy', Arjuna was rewarded with a curse by Urvashi which he had to undergo.

Another popular depiction of incest in Hinduism is that like Lot and his daughters in the Bible, the Hindu creator god Prajapati or Brahma seduces his own daughter Ushas to start the process of creation.[12] In fact, such was Brahma's sexual interest in his daughter that he constantly chased her and looked at her. Apparently, the four heads of Brahma (seen in most of the depictions of this deity) were created so that he could continuously gaze at his daughter while she moved around in the four directions of the world, without having to keep turning his head. One could surmise that Brahma's incestuous sexual affair, unlike that of biblical Lot and his daughters, was not a temporary, brief and liquor-induced sexual tryst, but a loving and sporting sexual union with prolonged flirting and foreplay.

In the case of Yama (the Hindu god of death), his twin sister Yami pronounces her love for Yama and invites him to her bed. The dialogue between Yama and Yami is interesting and romantic.[13] But Yama rejects her advances and leaves her heartbroken. Similarly, the deity Pushan (probably another form of the sun god) in Rig-veda is mentioned as his sister's lover.[14] The Hindu fire god Agni, the deity before whom most of the sacred Hindu rituals including marriage, worship rituals and even funeral is conducted, has also been shown as a lover of his sister.[15]All these clearly suggest that in the ancient liberated Hinduism, at least among the gods where the complications of genetically related offspring were non-existent, incest was not such a taboo.

Secular Arguments Against Incest

There are authors who believe that there could be genetic and evolutionary reasons why humans avoid incest.[16] After all, it is good science that inbreeding is bad, unless one is looking for children with deformities. Even first cousins who have got married have often ended up with children with abnormalities. Probably for this reason, many scholars believe that most mammals, especially humans, are given an internal aversion to mating within their family. Interestingly, although most religions prohibit incest explicitly among close family members, they are not so strict when it comes to marriages between cousins. Even Islam, which normally takes a rigid non-negotiable religious point of view on all matters sexual, is quite tolerant of marriages between cousins. In fact, while marriage between cousins is prohibited in many states of the United States (often mentioned as an example of a liberal society), it is allowed in Islam. Similarly, Hindus in South India, often encourage marriages between cousins born out of different sex siblings. In other words, you can have a marriage between the daughter of a brother and the son of a sister. Similarly, in some parts of Tamil Nadu state in South India, a girl can marry her mother's younger brother.

Do Animals Avoid Incest?

Do all animals believe in avoiding incest? There is one article that suggests that hyenas try to avoid inbreeding.[17] But there are other articles which suggest that inbreeding is helpful.[18] So the last word is not yet out on the topic. But we could safely presume that inbreeding (or 'incest') is certainly practiced more among some species than in others (probably because their genetic susceptibility to deformities is less). When we carefully observe most domesticated animals like dogs, cats, camels, pigs, cows and sheep with whom most humans share a good bonding, we would know that they do not have any severe instinctual taboos against incest. A dog would not think twice about mating with one of his 'daughters' and a rooster would not resist mating with one of his 'daughter' or 'sister' hens. Similarly, siblings among pigs or dogs that mate with each other do not seem to be producing too many defective members of their species.

It could be safe to assume that besides the possible in-born genetic aversion to incest, we also suffer from a deep societal, religious and cultural conditioning which makes even the slightest thought of incest an abhorrent one. However, if one really looks at the religious literature and wonders at the possible reasons for such strict religious prohibition, we would know that such prohibition exists primarily to prevent the dangerous genetic results of a pregnancy and offspring.

Towards a Changed Paradigm of Sexuality

We have to think of changing the paradigm of sexuality. This paradigm shift towards permitting incest would be even more severe than opening the chains of sexuality within marriage. In wedding parties where there is ballroom dancing, one can often see fathers dancing with their daughters or sons dancing with their mothers. No one seems to think of this as a guilt-inducing experience. This is ultimately the paradigm which we need to think of in the context of incest.

Does guilt have to go with incest? Is there a scope for guilt in love, joy happiness and pleasure? The answer is a resounding *no*. It is true that the offspring of close blood-relations are likely to have some genetic defects. This is probably nature's way of encouraging diversity within species. But has nature barred human beings or any other species from sharing pleasure with close family relatives? The answer is a big *no*. This bar is an artificial one created by social and religious conditioning that proscribes sexual relations of any type between relatives. It is another matter that as a result of this religious, social and cultural conditioning, many of us rarely get sexually attracted to our sisters. The girls who have grown up in our homes, the ones whom we have seen naked in their childhood are rarely the object of our sexual attraction.

Some readers might protest vociferously and argue, "How can sexual relations be equated with dancing?" Well, let us think of it for a moment. What if, for centuries together, dancing in couples was mentioned strictly as an activity between lovers/spouses? Imagine all religious books proscribing dancing between non-lovers or non-spouses. Imagine volumes being written on the terrible sin of dancing between non-lovers. Imagine that it was the secret fantasy of dancers to dance with different women. Would dancing a waltz, between a mother and son or the dancing of a father and his daughter not be done in secret to avoid social opprobrium? Would they not feel guilty that they are doing something terrible and sinful?

Community Traditions Which Do Not Make a Fuss About Incest

We can begin to understand the operation of an alternative sexually liberated society by looking at the traditions of the Mosuo people in China.[19,20] (The Mosuo people's outlook towards society as part of an alternative sexually liberated social model is also mentioned in the concluding chapter.) The Mosuo people are a Chinese ethnic group living on the border areas of Tibet. They have a matrilineal system of family, meaning that they trace their lineage from the female side of the family. The children in the family are often raised by their maternal uncle. Once the girls reach puberty, they have their own bedrooms. During social interactions and dancing, which happens quite regularly, the female who is interested in a particular male will skilfully invite him over to spend the night with her. Later in the night she will keep the door of her bedroom open and the male would come over and spend the night with her. In the early hours of the morning, he will walk back to his house. The children resulting out of these unions grow up within the community. Let us see the tremendous beauty of this system. The man has to earn the affection of his woman every time he is allowed to get into her bedroom. Similarly since a woman could change her partner once in a while (*although in practice, many women prefer to stick to the same partner for some time – in other words, the couple do 'fall in love'*), there is little record of who the real father of a child might be. The child grows up in their mother's family and there is every possibility that if it is a male child, when he grows up he might be sleeping with some of his stepsisters, since his father might have fathered some daughters through another woman. Does this kind of incest create guilt and terrible fear of sin? No. This is a fine example of guiltless, loving relationships between family members. Similarly in such a system, there are possibilities that a daughter might take a fancy to a man, little knowing that in reality he could be her biological father. The same could happen to the mother.

The Story of a Single Father and Disabled Daughter

For those who still exhibit a marked aversion to this very thought of incest, there could be another interesting story. Let us imagine a rare but plausible scenario of a man who has raised his daughter without the benefit of a mother – a single father. They live on a big farm in a house made of wood in the countryside. Being a large farm, they don't have many neighbours close-by. Sadly the daughter is deaf and blind by birth. But the father has raised this daughter painstakingly, imparting to her through the sense of touch the joy of perceiving the world around her. The daughter was always in the farm and had little formal education or outside interaction. At times when the father had to go to the town, he would get a babysitter – an old woman, who stayed in a small house near their farm. The daughter grows up, but not being extraordinarily attractive, does not have many suitors and lives with her father alone. The father loves his daughter as any father would.

The father and the daughter go for long walks holding hands together and enjoying the breeze. The daughter has a strong sense of touch. She likes to hug and sometimes rests her head on her father's shoulder. As he is grows older the father worries about his daughter more. One stormy day, when the daughter is resting her head on her father's shoulders in the house, she starts exploring her father's body and starts discovering the pleasures of touch. The father probably lets it happen knowing that she might not experience this joy in her lifetime.

When this father touches her and brings her joy and pleasure through this touch, he is acting more out of compassion than out of lust. But let us look at what the father feels and the daughter feels. The daughter who has had little education and not much idea of religion or anything else, keeps wondering why her father kept this treasure of tactile pleasure away from her all this while. On the other hand, the father feels terribly guilty and sad that he has done something taboo with his daughter. The daughter wants her father to give her the joy of that sexual touch and bring her to orgasm every now and then and cannot fathom the reluctance that her father shows in bringing her that joy. The same father who would do anything to make her happy is now acting like a terrible miser in giving her the pleasure he knows she is looking forward to every now and then. The father's side of the story is equally poignant. He does not know how he can tell her the kind of guilt that he feels and tries to avoid touching his daughter. Since the daughter was somewhat protected and isolated from the weight of culture, religion and society and has designed her paradigm of right and wrong based on the twin concepts of pain and pleasure, it is impossible for her to understand how what is pleasurable to her, and does not give pain to anyone else can be wrong. This imaginary tale is only meant to illustrate how the guilt of incest comes from cultural, religious, social and educational upbringing and a sense of taboo.

Perhaps the taboo against incest did not merely come from the fear of genetic deformities. Perhaps the taboo has also something to do with the social composition of family. Obviously, in a unit, where the mother and daughter both compete for the affection of the male, it can lead to a situation of hostility between the mother and daughter especially when the mother is expected to care for and love the daughter. Similarly, if the father and son both crave sexual joy from the female member of the household, it can indeed lead to a possible situation of jealousy between the father and the son, with possibly disastrous consequences for the stability of the family. As it is, even without this complicated angle to the relationship between a father and son, many father-son relationships are fraught with aggression and power conflicts.

More than the karmic results of incest, any ethically conscious person might merely avoid incest in our contemporary society owing to its complications of guilt and social taboo. Even if some enlightened person decides to embark on such a relationship, the social taboo might make it necessary for the person to hide even the most loving incestuous relationship from others, thus creating a false life, a life of lie. This in turn would lead to a high thickening of his Cosmic Sensitivity Barrier and prevent him from achieving his/her spiritual potential. The consequences of powerful guilt can lead to sicknesses at the physical level also. All this would be in addition to the fear of having deformed or disabled offspring out of such a union. Until our medical sciences evolve to a degree that these abnormalities cease to exist and the socio-religious taboo against incest is swept away, even the thought of living with a close blood relative like sister/brother or mother/father will continue to be one of the most forbidden 'sins' in our society.

11

Kings Love Kings, Let the Queens Do Likewise

Homosexuality

Another of the major taboos in human history has been the fear of homosexuality. Even in liberated, developed countries of the world, homophobia and the resultant violence is a constant problem. A popular gay website quotes FBI statistics to say that as late as 2009, there is an average of fourteen hate crimes *every day* against gays and lesbians in the country (USA).[1] In the UK, in the same year, within the first nine months alone, there were around 1200 homophobic hate crimes in London.[2] In several countries of the Middle East including Saudi Arabia and Iran, homosexuality is a crime punishable by death. In large parts of Africa, homosexuality is illegal and punishable by long imprisonment and even the death penalty. Amongst the giants of Asia, India and China, where the legal word of law has far lesser significance than the unwritten norms of social conduct, homosexuality is a great taboo. Men who enjoy homosexuality in such countries would either do it secretly or have a wife for the purpose of maintaining a facade of 'normal heterosexuality'. Even India's gay royalty, Prince Manvendra Singh, chose this route initially.[3]

Homosexuality has been prevalent in various forms, in the world. The resistance to homosexuality as a way of life is the main problem. The representatives of the Catholic Church have said that while having homosexual tendencies is not a sin by itself, having actual homosexual intercourse is sinful.[4] In other words, it accepts the fact that some people might have a tendency of sexual attraction towards the same gender. While it is true that people have started coming out of the closet in greater numbers in the last few decades in Western democratic societies, to say that homosexuality is only a recent phenomenon would be erroneous.

The biblical reference to homosexuality comes from the Old Testament story of Lot and the fate of the cities of Sodom and Gomorrah. Some of Christianity's most severe condemnations of homosexuality as anathema to God are based upon the biblical description of annihilation of these cities. The primary reason mentioned is the preference of these citizens for same-gender sexuality over 'normal' sexual behaviour. Similarly, in Greek mythology, the relationship of Achilles and Patroclus is often considered gay. Although some people insist that their love was purely a friendship between two war heroes, some of the ancient quotations and references lend more weight to the feeling that there was more than mere friendship between the two.[5,6]

Some psychologists have acknowledged that although two men (or women) are alike in terms of gender, it is possible for them to have a masculine-feminine interaction. Rosenfels calls it a victory of character specialization over biological identity.[7] Both psychologists and Catholics seem to inadvertently agree that people could have an inclination of attraction towards the same gender despite the norms of their physical, biological identity. Of course, whether a person acts upon this instinct to find homosexual partners or whether he remains 'celibate' is a different choice altogether.

The 'Active' and 'Passive': Another Possible Sexual Classification of the Future

Perhaps in the future, the sexual inclination should be considered irrelevant. Instead of classifying people as homosexuals, bisexuals and heterosexuals, people could consider themselves **active** or **passive** partners, meaning those who actively penetrate versus those who passively enjoy being penetrated. Unlike the biological and physical identifiers of gender these roles can easily be reversed. A person who is an *active* penetrator at one point might decide to become the submissive (*passive*) penetrated one on another occasion or with another partner. Like in a game of chess, where a person sometimes opts for the black pieces and sometimes for white, these roles could be changed easily. Perhaps this will remove the importance of physical gender as an important deciding factor while enjoying sexuality. Of course, in the case of two biological women, they might need some sexual aids to feel and enjoy the sensation of penetrator/penetrated. This is not to suggest that sexual enjoyment always needs to end with penetration, but the fact that large numbers of people enjoy orgasms as a result of penetration in one form or the other has the potential to make this the important factor in the choice of partner, rather than gender. In this situation even a male who might like to be 'passive' could enjoy the sensation with a female who loves to put on an attachable dildo and play the 'active' role.

Perhaps, this could also percolate slowly into our dating lingo instead of gender or gender choice. For instance, a woman who enjoys being penetrated could advertise 'seeking a penetrator of any gender'. On the other hand a male who enjoys taking the back seat could also place a similar advertisement 'seeking a penetrator of any gender'. Perhaps, instead of the word 'penetrator' or 'penetrated', a more benign terminology of 'giver' or 'receiver' could be used. Dating columns could be classified into 'Giver males', 'Giver females', 'Receiver males' etc. Those who are open to be 'receiver' or 'giver' as the occasion or partner demands can be classified as 'adjustables' or 'tractable'. Such an advertisement for example, could state that 'a tractable male seeks a tractable female for a long-term relationship'.

Reasons for Homosexuality

Although the Catholic Church and possibly other Christian denominations often find that the psychological genesis of homosexuality is 'unexplained'[8], when one understands karma holistically, it is not so difficult to comprehend. The karmic reasons for homosexuality can be summarised as follows:

1. **Result of a pre-dominant female (or male) identity that crosses the birth/death barrier:** The story of Amba as mentioned in Chapter 1, is a classic example of the gender identity crossing the birth/death barrier. Princess Amba who was in love with King Salva was kidnapped by Bhishma and later on due to various circumstances no one ends up marrying Amba. In her quest for revenge to kill the powerful Bhishma, she endures severe penances to please the gods, who appear before her and give her the boon that she will be instrumental in Bhishma's death in her next life. Not wanting to wait out the normal cycle of old age, she immediately commits suicide and enters her next birth. In this birth, although she is born a male named Shikhandi, her entire mindset and identity is a female one. (Leaving aside the few sources of Indian mythology which

state that she was born a female and later changed her sex.) Unlike normal people who forget their past life-history at the time of birth, in this case that does not happen, since Amba was focussed on seeking revenge from Bhishma. In the end, during the epic Mahabharata war, Amba, in the form of the male Shikhandi, gets a chance to shoot her arrows at Bhishma. However, Bhishma could immediately sense that his opponent is a female in terms of identity and immediately lowers his weapons. The rules of war in ancient India prohibited the use of weapons against women. Hence Bhishma refuses to fight against Shikhandi. Taking advantage of Bhishma's moral scruples, Prince Arjuna from the opposite camp shoots him down while standing behind Shikhandi. Hence Shikhandi (Princess Amba) achieves her aim of being instrumental in killing Bhishma.

2. **A noble spiritual entity takes birth to understand a gender better or for a special mission:** Souls like Helen Keller are often born to achieve some special mission in terms of being a guiding light for people who are born in this category. Similarly, sometimes a special advanced spiritual entity takes birth with inbuilt same sex attraction. This is often done to understand and experience the societal environment, reactions and milieu. Sometimes, the spiritual entity embarks on a life of homosexual attraction to balance some of the previous life karma in which he/she must have hurt homosexuals. Sometimes this brief sojourn as a homosexual is undertaken to achieve some mission.

3. **Environmentally created homosexuality:** Some evangelists and religious orders who claim to 'cure' homosexuality often address, with some success, this group of homosexuals. Children brought up in a very

homosexual environment often may want to emulate this tradition as they might misread it to be one of the cardinal 'norms' of acceptable social behaviour, even when they may not be 'born' with this inclination. For instance, a female adopted child of lesbian parents, who watches the great love between her foster parents from her early childhood and watches her lesbian parents interact with other lesbian couples, might assume that this is the right 'mainstream' home environment. Similarly, an impressionable boy born in a family of six children including five sisters who are close to the boy in age and interaction might start having similar mannerisms as the five sisters. At some point this boy might also get pulled in to the world view of his five sisters, and as he grows up, might start sharing their sexual attraction and fantasies for men.

4. **Hormonal imbalances, genetics and physical issues:** Hormonal imbalances, genes and physical deformities in reproductive organs might often incline people towards a certain gender identity or sexual preference and accordingly determine their sexual attraction. But very often, this is also part of a predestined karmic mandate.

Even when reasons 3 or 4 are the cause, it must be remembered that these are mere manifestations of decisions already taken by the overself. Sometimes the karmic blueprint might require the person to spend a few years experiencing homosexual attraction. In such cases, his homosexuality might be environmentally created and thus when his period ends (as per the karmic plan), then he might be 'cured' of his homosexuality by some psychological counselling etc.

There are other interesting reasons at a karmic level why a homosexual person might 'convert' to become heterosexual, giving enough reason for the 'psychological counselling' school of anti-homosexuals to feel triumphant. Sometimes the karmic plan decided by the overself for implementation can be altered. In this book, this is referred to as **mid-course corrections,** and explained below.

Mid-course corrections

As mentioned in Chapter 2, karma can be classified into 'hard' and 'soft' karma. Events which have an extremely powerful impact upon the trajectory of life are always the result of hard karma. For example a person born blind is often the result of previous hard karma, because blindness has a pivotal impact on the directions taken in his life. Similarly a person losing limbs in a factory accident or being paralysed as a result of a road accident are all results of hard karma. However, there are some mid-course corrections possible for all karma. Needless to say, minor problems in life (soft karma effects) are more easily corrected/straightened out. This can be done through interventions that are used to send specific messages to the overself to alter the karmic course and clean up the karmic results accruing in a person's life as 'obstacles'.

Common interventions which are used to **ameliorate** hard karma or **wipe** the effects of bad soft karma are as follows:

- **Prayers:** to spiritually evolved higher divine entities, gods, saints and so on. Some of the energy from these entities, as well as the psychological cleansing effect of prayers, clean up some karma or otherwise soften the hard karma. On the negative side, prayers can also be offered to darker spiritual entities that have some powers of intervention through energy transfer, but it must be remembered that darker spiritual entities always have a vested interest in multiplying negativities. Often their interventions are short-lived and they always endeavour to bring conditions into life that can create longer cycles of bad karma in the individual's life. Hence it is best avoided and one must stick to prayers to divine entities only.

Christians, Muslims and Jews, untrained in the Eastern tradition of meditation often use prayer as the best method for interventions. The thousands of prayer-request websites (mostly Christian) available on the internet attest to the popularity of this intervention.

- **Meditation:** A normal person's brain in its waking state is subject to the relentless assault of information. Most of the time the brain is occupied in analysing, understanding and processing this information. This information overload has only increased in recent years with the onslaught of 24x7 television, internet and mobile phones. As a result a person rarely gets a silent moment to relax his mind and concentrate on his priorities. Meditation works by silencing the brain and clearing the anomalies in breath. It also helps in connecting the person to his overself by silencing the ceaseless noise in his brain. It also clears some of the impurities of the overself and makes the 'hard karma' effects milder. How does that happen? Perhaps the metaphor of flowing water is appropriate here. Just like flowing water smoothens the rough edges of stones over a period of time, similarly meditation smoothens the rough edges of the hard karma and prevents its worst consequences. The Hindu ritual of *yajna* where offerings are made to fire accompanied by Sanskrit *mantras* can also be considered a form of prayer and meditation.

- **Rituals and Objects (*medallions, amulets, stones, taveej, yantra*):** Some mantra (chanting) rituals, medallions, amulets and holy objects often work in a similar fashion. There are two distinct effects that are seen. In some cases it is purely psychological. A person wearing an amulet gets an enhanced self-confidence. Perhaps it might be considered similar to a person carrying a gun while travelling alone at night. It reduces the fear. Imagine for a moment that the gun is a simple fake with no real bullets. If this fact is not told to the bearer of the gun, his confidence remains unchanged. He feels the same confidence that he would have while carrying a real gun. The medallions, amulets and so on often give this kind of enhanced confidence and psychological feeling of protection even when they do nothing. However, there is another angle to this. Some objects do carry the good vibrations of certain deities/personalities and therefore dispel some amount of negative vibrations. Good and bad vibrations cannot exist together, just like darkness and light cannot exist together. Hence, if the good vibrations are strong enough they dispel the bad vibrations/energy. There are other variations on this. Some objects create special energy due to their special sound combinations (for instance certain metal bells or special Sanskrit mantras). Other objects create energy due to their molecular arrangements (for instance certain types of metals or combinations of metals). Still other objects create special energy due to their shape (for example certain pyramidal-shaped crystals). Still other objects reflect or absorb a certain kind of energy emitted by different planets or deities and create certain vibrations (that is the reason several Hindus often wear stones on their fingers based on their astrological inclinations).

- **Donating positive karma:** Another intervention often successful in reducing the effects of previous karma is to create positive karma and expressly assign it for reducing previous karmic effects. For instance feeding hungry people free of charge and offering this generated positive karma expressly for reducing previous negative karma is often effectual. This must be stated verbally or in the mind of the donor, very clearly, at least three to four times, so that this positive karma is correctly noted and assigned to that previous negativity account.

Coming back to homosexuality, what is important is to note that despite the various reasons for homosexuality it should not be assumed that this book considers homosexuality as a 'disorder' in any way. We have only karmically analysed the reasons for homosexuality, because in most countries of the world, homosexuals are still less than ten per cent of their population and heterosexuality continues to be the mainstream sexual preference. (Of course, part of this low percentage can be explained as the result of difficulty in getting exact data during census owing to the sensitive nature of this question.) However, most organised religions take very little notice of the spiritual subtleties of homosexuality. They either treat it like a psychological aberration or a 'deliberate sin' (similar to murder or rape that should be punished).

The Catholic Church and Homosexuality

The main 'solution' offered by the Catholic Church for homosexuals is prayer and sacramental grace. It is like sending a man into the thick of a battlefield with rubber bullets. As mentioned earlier, doubtlessly, prayer has power and this power can never be underestimated. But to believe that a person can simply resist his natural homosexuality by prayer and grace shows a terrible lack of understanding and almost amounts to pouring out condescending sympathy on them. Why not try to curb the entire sexual instinct of 'normal' heterosexual human beings by the same 'grace and prayer'?

Even within the Catholic Church, despite a voluntary choice of priesthood and the religious life, a significant number of priests have been unable to keep strict celibacy. Some sources state that only fifty per cent of Catholic priests actually live a life of celibacy.[9,10] (The actual percentage of celibate priests might be *even* lower considering that in any research, only a few might actually reveal their moral failings.) While the Catholic Church is not able to maintain the celibacy of half of their priests, with all their 'prayers and grace', they still prefer to pontificate about the efficacy of prayer and grace to help their lay Catholics to beat their homosexual orientation.

In fact, all his life, Jesus Christ was critical of this same mindset of the Pharisees who used to look down upon all others as sinners and one grade lower than themselves. It is the same Pharisee-like quality that the church brings when it advises homosexuals to look for prayer and grace and showers pity on their 'helpless condition'. It is as if they are suffering from congenital blindness or some such cureless disorder. Although Jesus Christ himself never directly condemns homosexuals or lesbians, the ultra-religious among Christians always find refuge in some of the other biblical verses which condemn homosexuality.

One of the most oft-quoted references comes from the book of Leviticus[11], where '(a male) lying with another male' is referred to as 'an abomination' in the eyes of God. Although the word suggests a strong loathing, interestingly, a similar 'detest' is mentioned in the book of Leviticus for those eating fish without fins and scales (shellfish or crabs for instance).[12] Yet today, most Christians, unless they suffer from some shellfish allergy, merrily eat shellfish. The same book of Leviticus also has other outlandish prohibitions. It prohibits cross-mating of animals, use of diverse type of seeds while farming and wearing of mixed-fabric garments.[13] Other interesting prohibitions in the same chapter of Leviticus include cutting hair at the sides of the head or clipping the edges of the beard. All these prohibitions are merrily ignored by Christians and underplayed by the Bible preachers today to avoid ridicule from others. There are few priests or reverends that condemn shellfish from their pulpit with the same vigour they devote to anti-homosexuality.

There are other oft-quoted biblical verses against homosexuality. There is the 'argument' that homosexuality is 'unnatural' and therefore punishable by God.[14] This 'unnatural' argument has also been used by various countries to prosecute homosexuals. The unnatural argument is also closely tied to the belief that the primary purpose of sex is procreation. This argument is also generally used to condemn all sex outside marriages. These 'unnatural' and 'procreative-purpose' arguments have already been dealt with in various previous chapters. As mentioned before, most of our present-day behaviours and styles of living, socialising, eating and so on are absolutely 'unnatural' when compared to our closest animal relatives. Yet this 'unnatural' argument continues to be used with respect to homosexuality. Interestingly, other churches have taken their cue from the Catholic Church and condemn homosexuality in a similar vein.

This procreation argument and the strong animosity against homosexuals could be perhaps understood in the context of early emphasis of various religions on fertility. In the early stages of human evolution, human population was not yet at the gigantically overblown stage that it is today. It is not surprising then that Hindus, Christians and followers of Islam all rejoiced at the increase in their numbers. Anything which increased the fertility of men and women was considered desirable. Rituals, mantras, prayers and religious methods to improve fertility were common. In this sort of background it is very easy to understand, why a preference for same sex pleasure would have been sharply discouraged. After all, any normal homosexual activity would really not bring in an increase in the population. There was the danger that if large groups of people started going down the homosexual route, it could put a serious brake on population growth, which would not have been desirable at that point in history.

Islam and Homosexuality

In the case of strict Islam the idea of homosexuality is even more abhorrent. Some Islamic scholars have called it a moral disorder. In countries like Iran and Afghanistan several hundreds of people accused of homosexuality have been executed mercilessly. A prominent Islamic scholar from the Islamic Society of North America comments that 'homosexuality is a moral disorder. It is a moral disease, a sin and corruption... No person is born homosexual, just like no one is born a thief, a liar or murderer. People acquire these evil habits due to a lack of proper guidance and education'.[15] This pairing of homosexuality with immoral and criminal activities over the years has often blinded people in these countries to the obvious difference between coercive, violent activities like robbery, murder or rape and consensual homosexual activities. As is explained in Chapter 4, Islam's parameters of life and living, as dealt with in the Quran, should be seen through the life and context of the period in which the Prophet Muhammad lived.

Arguments Against the Homosexual Family

The other argument often advanced against homosexuals is that a homosexual family is not a 'normal family'. Some among the Christian clergy and religious groups argue that tolerance of a homosexual lifestyle ultimately leads to demand for homosexual marriages which is often followed by a demand for permission to adopt children. Since many developed countries have already allowed (or are about to) homosexuals to get married legally, the permission for them to adopt or otherwise bring up children is only a matter of time. By allowing homosexual couples to adopt children, the religious argue that we are effectively permitting the children to be deprived of a 'normal' heterosexual family. These children, the argument goes, may often grow up believing that having two 'mothers' or two 'fathers' in the house is quite normal. They further argue that by allowing children to be adopted by such families, we are depriving them of the right to enjoy a normal father-mother figure in the household.

Although this seems to be a strong argument, it does not stand detailed scrutiny. To begin with, we must understand that, presently, there are millions of children all over the world who are being brought up by single parents. In other words, a child brought up by a widowed mother maybe deprived of the full filial love and companionship of someone called a 'father'. Similarly, the child brought up by the single father is deprived of maternal love and companionship. Yet many of these children go on to lead full, happy lives and create full, wholesome families. It would be difficult to argue that children who grow up in single-parent families always think of that as the 'norm'. Obviously, as these children grow and see the world around them, they gradually do realise that *all* families are not single-parent families and understand and assimilate this cognitively. In a similar way, one could surmise that children who will be raised by homosexual gay or lesbian couples would also realise that all families do not necessarily consist of two parents of the same gender.

Regarding the question of deprivation of a masculine or feminine parent in homosexual-couple families, every child grows up in an environment where he/she is deprived of one important perspective in life. A child who grows in an abysmally poor family is often deprived of the perspective of a financial worry-free existence. Similarly, a child born in a prosperous family might never get the perspective of near-starvation or struggle for the most basic needs. A child born in an atheist family might never gain the religious perspective of a child born in a church-going, devout Catholic family. Hence whatever the circumstances that a child is brought up in, there is the danger that the child will automatically be deprived of some perspectives and gain a closer experience of other perspectives in life. However, what is hoped for is that as a part of growth and learning, the individual comprehends situations, cultures and paradigms of life that are different from his/her own environment and develops a healthy respect for this amazing diversity.

Another argument can also be advanced to counter the viewpoint that a child in a homosexual-couple family is deprived of a male or female parent presence. Very often, even among homosexual couples, one partner may be more dominating and male-like. The other partner may be more feminine in keeping with the commonly accepted psychological stereotypes of women or men. In other words, a child growing in a lesbian couple family might find that there is indeed a psychological father and mother. The only difference would be that while the child's mother looks similar to the other mothers of his classmates, the 'father' looks physically different from the other fathers. While other fathers do not have breasts and might have facial hair, this child's father looks similar to other mothers. In other words, the child has a *physically* different type of father. But perhaps psychologically, the child gets some benefit of the fatherly presence.

Homosexuality and Karma

Karmically, consensual homosexual activities have few negative implications. Whether a person enjoys a homosexual or heterosexual pleasure exchange, it does not create positive or negative karma. Guilt is the only culprit. Many of the problems from homosexuality result from a sense of guilt or shame. Having said this, we also know that excessive desire for anything will result in a forthcoming birth, that leads to the fulfilment of that desire. Such a person, in a future birth, may be born as a king or a landlord with an opportunity to take several wives/other males and concubines. In the present life too, a person whose thoughts are filled with desire for sexual orgasm often misses other spiritual opportunities because the blood circulation and flow needed in the brain for good meditation is often absent since most of the blood continues to remain in the lower regions of the body.

While the gender is important, it is not really something inviolable in the story of the cycle of births and deaths. It is true that some individuals prefer to remain in the same gender from birth to birth. To use a metaphor, it is like some air travellers preferring to travel by the same airline every time they travel from New York to Los Angeles, despite there being many other alternatives. Despite this desire, once in a while, some 'male' overself may take birth in a female form. Similarly a predominantly female-preference overself may once in a while, take the male birth form. The Hindu god Krishna (an incarnation of Vishnu) is known to have taken birth as the beautiful Mohini, in order to trick the demons. Shiva, the male Hindu god of destruction gets attracted to Mohini and this relationship leads to offspring. Of course, being an omniscient god, Lord Shiva is said to be aware of the true self of Mohini and yet this does not stop him from making love to Mohini.[16] Hence this can be considered a proof of the ancient Indian sexual paradigm that homosexuality is not such a big deal. This whole mythology emphasises the fluid and non-serious view of gender in traditional Hinduism. This is quite different from the Christian or Muslim perspectives where gender is considered serious and inviolable. This view of gender as something written in stone is partly responsible for the hatred against homosexuality, transsexuals and for the various repressive rules and strictures against women.

It is normally understood that the circumstances of a child's upbringing till the child develops full cognitive faculties are often determined by the overself (refer to Chapter 1 and 2) even before the child's birth. Hence the peculiar circumstances of the first few years of a child's environment are pre-determined by the overself of that individual. Whether the child is born into a rich family surrounded by servants who pamper all the whims of the child or whether the child is born in a poor family and is forced to work alongside his parents for family bread, is determined before the birth itself. Only as the child grows and its cognitive faculties develop well, will the overself slowly start handing over the controls to the conscious brain and willpower of the individual.

12

Idiosyncrasies Galore

Frotteurism, Urophilia and Autoerotic Asphyxia

We in the West believe that the individual is the king. An individual decides what is best for him or her. If he wants to dabble in alcohol to the point of stupefaction, so be it. If she wants to sleep with a different guy every weekend, that is her wish. If they want to consume recreational drugs that are not illegal, that is their choice as long as they do not harm other individuals in any way. In other words, it is considered that the individual and what he/she feels at a particular point is the right thing, no matter how obnoxious the individual's choices may be. The individual is the unit for decision-making in Western 'free' society.

On the contrary, in the East, the society or the family is the minimum unit for decision-making. The family head and other elders often decide what is good for the entire family. The individual is merely a subunit within the family and the views of the familial majority often decide what the best course of action is, even when the decisions taken at the familial level often impact one individual's wishes adversely. Take for instance, the common practice of arranged marriage. The parents of the bride and the groom concerned sit together and finalise the marriage.

Does the Individual Need to Always Have the Last Word in Terms of His/Her Choices?

Those of us who believe in the supremacy of individual willpower would feel alarmed at the situation above where family or communities sometimes curb individual choices. Every individual has wishes, desires and aspirations. How can the collective of society, family or tribe trample upon those aspirations and desires of the individual? However, when we are asked about the obnoxious choices often made by individuals, we shrug and say, "Well, to each his own." Is it really? But this is exactly where the supporters of individualism diverge from the karmic reality of ethics.

The Karmic Reality of the Individual Choice of Cells and Organs

Those who have learnt deeper meditation know that each breath ultimately penetrates into each cell of the body. Each cell of the body has an intelligence of its own. When the cells come together there is an organ, and the organ then has an intelligence of its own.

So let us say that the man who is drinking twelve beers in one night is enjoying himself and says, 'It is no one's business but my own that I have so many beers.'

But if there was an instrument that could listen to this person's liver, it would be screaming loudly, "C'mon, , I am drowning in the alcohol you are ingesting, please stop it; you are torturing me."

Our Western societies have accepted that the father in the family does not have automatic right to beat up his children, *"Just because they are my children and I can do what I want with them."* Then how does our society not understand that it is unethical for a person's conscious brain to inflict abuse on his liver, when the liver has an intelligence of its own? Similarly, the lungs have an intelligence of their own, so when a person is chain-smoking, the lungs are screaming for help. Similarly, the digestive system may protest strongly against the individual who pumps in huge amounts of rich, sugary and fatty food to his digestive organs and tortures them additionally with huge quantities of alcohol. Sadly, our scientific instruments have not yet advanced to the level where we can pick up the vibrations and communications of different organs and cells that tell us different things.

Hence we refuse to believe that each organ of our body has individual intelligence, wishes and preferences. We need to realise that our body is not a small unitary system of government but much similar to a federal structure that consists of small units of organs and systems which are managed with their own cellular and functional level of intelligence and opinions. Simply put, each organ of our body is like an individual in a community. The head of this community of cells and organs might be the brain, but just like the king or leader of a community has the responsibility to govern his subjects ethically, the individuals' brains have the responsibility to avoid inflicting abuse and torture on their organs. This is the karmic reality. It is only a matter of time before we develop the precise instruments that will pick up these vibrations and interpret the communications of cells and organs. And then, just like how we punish violent, abusive dads who beat up their offspring, we will have systems to punish individuals who abuse their organs.

So this view of the individual being the minimum sovereign unit of our developed, liberal society and this focus on the rights of the individual may in the future be replaced by respect for the rights of every organ and cell which has its own intelligence and wishes. In the coming centuries, when a person visits his doctor and the General Practitioner (GP) attaches his listening devices to the person's body, the lungs may scream, "This man is smoking so much and causing me immense strain," while his skin may complain separately about it becoming dry in parts due to smoking, negligence and use of chemical perfumes. The doctor's job becomes easier because he simply has to listen to the organs, which will both tell the problem with the individual's body and also give insight to the doctor about the causes of the problems (ingrained in the individual's genes or his lifestyle).

Karmic Suitability of Sexual Idiosyncrasies

Hence all sorts of sexual idiosyncrasies must be seen through this karmic prism of an individual's consent + the consent of individual organs. It is in this context that we must look at the various sexual fads and idiosyncrasies that are enjoyed. Some of these fads amount to torture if we could take note of the views of the organs. For instance, if we had a way to ascertain the wishes of our nipples or tongues, they might tell us that they certainly do not wish to be pierced so many times, just so that the individual can look *cool*.

Having said this, the body can always be coaxed and persuaded into doing feats that it never thought possible. The legs and the body never thought they could achieve tightrope walking. The sexual activity of *fisting*, where part of the lower wrist is inserted into the vagina, could perhaps be achieved although the body part needs to be gently coaxed and the individual mentally prepared to do it.

But if the concerned body part firmly refuses to be part of this and continues to be stiff, then we need to respect the wishes of this body part. To ascertain the wish of a body part at the basic level is not so difficult. Does the body part which participates in this activity, bend, relax and generally go the way we want it to go? That is a good karmic indication of the consent of the body part. If the body part remains stiff, bleeds and expresses its anguish about the activity then we need to respect its wishes. Listening to the body needs to be more than just an abstract phrase and needs to be applied as if the body is an individual. This is the general principle to be followed for all sexual practices. Ask the body part, and try to persuade it to participate. Give the body part a preview of the pleasures by massaging the body part, making it feel that it is going to be a pleasure rather than a pain.

A List of Some Practices and Their Karmic Implications

A reputed psychologist Jesse Bering, in his book, *Perv: The Sexual Deviant in All of Us*, discusses close to forty-six different kinds of sexual fetishes.[1] Some of the more esoteric ones include arousal through the sun's rays, arousal with feaces, arousal with insects and so on. So where do these sexual idiosyncrasies stand with respect to karmic laws? It may be noted that the use of the term 'idiosyncrasy' does not imply any negativity in the practice, but merely to show that the practice might be a variant from the accepted sexual practices of large groups of people. Some of the more common sexual practices are listed below in terms of karmic laws.

Sodomy (Or Anal Sex): As long as it is enjoyed by two freely consenting people it does not violate any karmic laws. However, the following questions are relevant. Does it involve too much pain for the organ? Has the organ been given time to relax itself and to prepare for the pain, especially if it is the first time. Is it able to participate in the pleasure? That is why good foreplay is very important, because without good foreplay, very often the enjoyment is restricted to the orgasmic feeling of the brain. When there is good foreplay the local organs also participate in the feast of good vibrant sensations.

Sado-masochistic practices: As long as spanking or pinching contributes to the overall sense of pleasure and novelty, the organ concerned may not mind it. But if it involves bleeding, wounds and so on, is the organ willing to suffer much after the whole sexual activity is over? If there was an instrument which could ascertain the wishes of the buttocks which get wounded by the whipping, would it rather not be a part of this?

As long as there is human diversity, there are idiosyncrasies and efforts to make sexual orgasmic experience, even better. Even the Romans were famous for their orgies. Karmically, of course, the whole sexual experience is first to be seen from the angle of whether it is consensual at the level of the two individuals participating, and secondly, at a more subtle level, whether the organs involved actually do accept their participation in this game. After all, many organs have other non-sexual primary functions and yet may be used for sexual arousal and/or enjoyment. For instance, the eyes are used to see things and not just for seeing sexual imagery. Similarly the anus performs the most important function as part of the digestive system and not really a part of the reproductive/sexual system. Hence it is important that these organs are also persuaded to enjoy the symphony of sexuality before new things are tried out.

Rape, molestation or frotteurism (rubbing oneself against others in crowded places), exhibitionism (without consent), in decreasing order of severity, are sexual games which involve the violation of another individual's will and so have severe to mild karmic negativity respectively.

On the other hand unusual practices such as autoerotic asphyxia, where there is an intentional restriction of oxygen supply to the brain to heighten orgasmic experience can often go totally wrong and may result in fatality. If this happens it will be a terrible and avoidable waste of life and karmically the person is liable. Would this person be liable for the full karmic penalties of suicide? The answer is no. We have to remember that in karmic rules, the intention is important. In this case, it will be considered a mere accident, but if there is gross negligence, then there is more karmic negativity.

There are still more harmless sexual variances such as urophilia (the golden shower using urine), consenting exhibitionism and voyeurism, which often are used to increase sexual excitement. These are far less risky and painless means of excitement and diversity in sexual enjoyment. The present trend of sexual texting (sexting) and sharing of sexual pictures using the phone is a variation of this enjoyment. As long as both the parties are consenting, mentally sound adults and love this exchange, no karmic rules are broken. Use of vibrators and toys are all wonderful orgasm elevators that do not distress any human being or even specific organs of the body. The karmically prudent approach therefore is to stick to these methods.

PART III

CONCLUSION

13

Bringing Free Sex into Mainstream Marriage

A reader who has managed to reach these concluding chapters might ponder what the whole point of this book is? Do we need another book to propagate the idea of sexual liberation? Are the Western societies not liberated enough? Do men and women not go to singles bars and sometimes have one-night stands? Are short-term relationships not common in Europe and other developed democratic countries?

Yes, it is true that the idea of sexuality is better accepted in many parts of the developed world. Yet, as we saw in Chapter 1 of this book, sex continues to remain a taboo subject in social conversations. No one is yet able to say, "I went to a prostitute yesterday who gave me some nice oral sex," as comfortably as he could say to anyone, "I went to so and so restaurant and had a lobster burger for lunch," or, "I went for a haircut.". Can a woman say to her female colleague at the workplace in the USA or the UK, "I am going home a little early, because I am getting a nice male escort this evening," as comfortably as she can say to her boss, "I need to go home a little early because my parents and my sister are visiting us today. They are coming from Canada and I need to go and pick them up." Can a guy on the phone say to his friends who call him, "Can I call you back as I am busy having sex," as comfortably as he says, "Can I call you back after some time as I am in a meeting."

Politicians and Celebrities Continue to be Punished for Sex

In the press and media around the world, celebrities and their sexual relationships still make news. The trial of Anwar Ibrahim in Malaysia for homosexuality is well known. Also in the UK, USA and other so-called sexually liberated countries, politicians trying to enjoy sexual variety continue to make front page news. If a political leader in the UK or USA tried to have Chinese food one day or tried Japanese cuisine the other, would it make news? Why is seeking consensual sexual variety immediately linked to immorality? Why is it assumed that a person seeking sexual variety is 'sinful' and/or 'depraved'?

The plight of Tiger Woods, the golf superhero, is worth talking about as an example of this paradigm of sexual repression that we live in. Tiger Woods may have had affairs with five or six women other than his wife. Being a wealthy and healthy sportsman, he could afford to have mistresses and keep them happy. Since he wanted to stay married, he preferred to carry the guilt and concealed it from his partner. But as mentioned in Chapter 1 (under the section 'Contours of Jealousy'), most partners in marriages are slaves of our socio-cultural practice of jealousy. It is as well entrenched as our practice of expressing grief. When one of our close relatives passes away, we are trained to feel sad and sometimes even genuinely cry, even if that relative was not very close to us at the time of his/her death. Similarly in many cases, jealousy is a trained response. Society expects us to feel outraged and cheated. Most people dutifully oblige society on these two fronts. Some file for divorces immediately, even if they know that their partner still loves them at an emotional level. When Hilary Clinton did not divorce Bill after his world-famous (or 'notorious', depending on which side of the 'moral' spectrum one chooses to be on) sexual escapade with Monica Lewinsky, many people speculated on why she did not opt for this prescription of our society? Some media sources insinuated that Hilary had compromised on her 'self-respect' in return for Bill's support for her political ambitions.[1] Our society clearly prescribes that a married man found having sex with another woman must be 'thrown out' from the institution of marriage. Thankfully, in most of the developed Western world and Europe, this is the limit of the punishment.

As the society moves from freedom loving to repressive, the meaning of this 'thrown out' becomes heavier. In many societies in the East, where the focus is the welfare of society as opposed to freedom of the individual, the married man who is having sex will be 'thrown out' of his village as well. In some societies the level of sexual repression demands that the person be 'thrown out' from his job. In 2009, in India, the governor of Andhra Pradesh state was forced to quit because although he is around eighty years of age, he seems to have engaged in sexual variety.

In more repressive societies, this married man who sleeps around is not only thrown out of his village and job, but his freedom is also 'thrown out'. He ends up in prison. As we go into societies like Saudi Arabia or Iran, a person's right to life may also end with his sexual choices. The word 'his' in all these situations is used more for convenience and it applies to both males and females. Having said this, we must also remember that while the treatment of males and females under the laws might be the same, a woman has to bear far worse consequences than a man if she dares to explore sexual variety. If she becomes pregnant as a result of sexual enjoyments outside marriage, then her situation becomes pitiable.

One consequence of a woman seeking sexual variety is that she is immediately labelled a slut even when she is single. To some extent, a single younger woman having a variety of sexual companions is becoming more acceptable in liberal Western and European societies. While they may not exactly be appreciated or encouraged, the degree of societal condemnation has reduced. However, a single man in these societies in the same situation is often hero-worshipped by his friends. He is made to feel like an achiever. Such glorious 'achievement' treatment is rarely given to women who experiment with sexual variety. If we look at the situation of married women seeking sexual variety, it is far worse. Even in comparatively liberal societies like Italy, France or Spain where there is only some level of a benign disapproval of a philandering married man, the same level of tolerance is not extended to the married woman who indulges in promiscuous adventures.

Must Sexual Pleasure Always Come with the Package of Commitment?

Many societies continue to doggedly believe that long-term sexual pleasure must come in a complete package of emotional love and attachment, societal legitimacy (in the form of marriage) or other signs of commitment and physical enjoyment. This is the most acceptable package of sex for the society. As known in marketing parlance, this is a *product bundle* that society is loath to unbundle. For a politician to survive in the USA or UK, he must be having sex only as part of this package. And America and UK are symbols of the world's most free societies!

In partly liberal countries (still bound by oppressive social traditions) from India to Latin America and Japan to Lebanon, while the younger people in urban areas freely experiment with sexuality, keeping aside moral and social injunctions for later retrieval, older people still refuse to believe that this package can be 'unbundled'. Those whose ethical parameters are drawn from the religious traditions of Islam or Christianity, call sex without mushy romantic, sentimental love 'shallow', 'impure' or 'sinful'. They have deep difficulty in understanding this as a matter of personal choice.

Is Sex an Addiction?

It was mentioned that Tiger Woods had joined a sexual rehab centre after his sexual ignominy. If a married man wants to enjoy sexual variety with different women he is treated on par with a guy addicted to drugs. Never mind that unlike a hard-core drug addict, Tiger Woods is hardly likely to kill, murder, rape or loot if his mistress is not available on a day, or that, unlike drug addicts, his body will neither shudder nor his mind functions get clouded. All these are irrelevant details in our repressive sexual paradigm. When a person loves to read books, he might be called a 'book lover' or 'bibliophile', the word being generally meant as a compliment. Similarly when someone loves good food and becomes an expert in that, he will be called a 'gourmet' or a 'connoisseur of food'. If a wealthy lady likes to buy new clothes every week, there is nothing wrong with that. But if someone loves sex and wants variety, then he must attend a sex rehab centre. This issue has also been addressed in detail, in Chapter 8, under the section 'The Safety Argument: Psycho-emotional complications and solutions'.

The Terminology Used for Sex-lovers

If someone loves to talk of sex and wants to enjoy it, he will be called a 'sex maniac'. If he uses his imagination to observe and appreciate sexuality he must be a 'pervert'. Let us explore the example of our revered 'bibliophile'. Most people, even poor readers read fifty to sixty good books in their lifetimes. Even those who avoid reading books, go through magazines or newspapers. In fact many people even lie about reading books in order to look wiser.[2] Most people have a far lesser number of sexual partners than the books they read. Yet if a person admits to having sex with even one third of the number of partners compared to the number of books he has read, he will be labelled a 'sex fiend' or 'sex addict'. If the man in question is an older person who enjoys sexuality, he is immediately labelled a 'dirty old man'. And if the person happens to be a politician or a celebrity, then this 'deviant' sexual interest becomes a treasure trove for the media.

The Limited Options for a Sex-lover

To begin with, if a person wants to enjoy different sexual partners without facing legal problems or societal rage, he/she must live in a Western liberal democratic nation. This is in addition to the fact that one should not be married, because obviously being married immediately means that you are limiting all your other options. Some amount of social disapproval is bound to follow if a couple declare themselves as swingers. Some young men, at least in Western societies, perhaps for good reason, behave like wild bulls before their marriage trying to bed the maximum number of women (or men, as the case may be). The image of a raging, energetic bull, enjoying, mating with any female in sight and caring a damn about the world is probably the fantasy of many people coming true. Perhaps this might be the partial reason why a drink like Red Bull with its imagery of a powerful bull probably works on the imagination of people and makes it such a powerful brand, dominating the energy drinks market.

In much of the Eastern world, not to speak of Islamic countries, sex outside marriage is not just met with social disapproval, but is strictly illegal. In Saudi Arabia and many other countries in the Gulf, the person could be executed. This execution might even take an inhuman mode like being stoned to death. Countries like India, Nepal or Sri Lanka may not mete out such terrible penalties for enjoying sexual variety. But the social ostracism that one might face if one dares to reveal their love for sexual variety is so severe that most people who do enjoy variety, find some deviant, guilt-ridden way to achieve what they want.

Additional Problems for Women Who Love Sex

If it is a woman in some of the Asian countries, her life is even more difficult if she happens to enjoy sexual diversity. Even within an arranged marriage, if one's interest in sexuality is much higher than the partner's, then one has to merely suffer in silence. In Western societies, this situation could have been prevented because most women and men are expected to have at least checked their sexual compatibility before tying the knot. However, if one is born/brought up a practicing Roman Catholic and follows strict injunctions on pre-marital sex, one is again doomed to suffer.

However, even if these women had taken the precaution to marry someone of their own level of interest in sex, it is possible that people do change as they age. People who loved books in their youth might lose their extraordinary interests in books. Food lovers may also slowly change their eating habits for health or other reasons. There is a possibility that some people's interests in sex might diminish drastically. What if a married woman finds that her husband is not as interested in sex as he once was? What are the options in front of her? In a Western liberal country like USA, UK or Australia, it might not be extraordinarily difficult for a married woman to get a male escort to help her. But unless her spouse is unusually broad-minded she cannot dream of revealing this to him. If she doesn't, her guilt about lying and cheating and the anxiety about being found out would become overwhelming as the years go by.

Sex in the Land of *Kamasutra*

The present situation in the land of origin of *Kamasutra* is sad indeed, but despite government hypocrisy the situation is improving. As mentioned in Chapter 1, in India, till the late nineties, the Bollywood movies would not even depict a lip-locking kiss on the screen. When a husband and wife were shown in a romantic scene in their bedroom, what one could expect is the hero in the movie to tentatively touch the clothing of the woman and then promptly put off the light. Songs in the rain with clinging wet clothes were another common sight. The remaining was left to the imagination of the audience. Generally since movies in a society often reflects the social situations of that culture, we know that in real lives also, in much of South Asia, sex was something done in total darkness and with limited conversation. Driven by spontaneity, the questions of contraception, female orgasm etc. would be left to the understanding of the partners. Women who wanted orgasms, would have to somehow make the husband slow down and last longer. In countries like India, Pakistan and many other parts of the Middle East, where marriages are arranged by the parents and family, there would be little chance of knowing what the person will be like in bed before one is stuck with him/her for a lifetime.

And if you are a woman in India with a husband uninterested in sex, you might as well join a monastery. The concept of male prostitutes does exist in some cities like Mumbai and other mega-cities in India, but even here, the social and legal acceptance of this situation is extremely poor. And if a woman takes the unimaginable risk of taking a man as a temporary lover, the risk of blackmail, crime or social implications of it becoming public knowledge are so fearsome that such a woman might as well resort to mere masturbation with the help of fantasies. However, things are changing for the better in urban India very fast, thanks in part to the liberalizing influence of internet. It is becoming increasingly possible for even married women to have affairs and relationships using social media such as Facebook to befriend men. The world of the internet where sexual conversations with real people can be done from the privacy of their homes and easy access to pornography has revolutionised the lives of such women. But at the official levels, there is no reduction in the hypocrisy. Recently India's Supreme Court reinstated the law that makes gay sex a crime.[3] The Hindu nationalistic party BJP, presently governing India, has strongly opposed any lowering in the age of consent for sex from eighteen to sixteen stating that it will 'encourage pre-marital sex which is against Indian culture'.[4]

In India, where the great treatise on sexuality has been written, the departure from sexual liberalisation is probably one of the impacts of liberal Hindu India's long Mughal rule and British colonial history. Interestingly, the Mughals also, in course of time, understood the true beauty and art of poetry, etiquette and romantic eroticism that was steeped in the Indian tradition. One result was the *tawaif*, an institution similar to the *geisha* in Japan, where beautiful ladies who excelled in poetry, dance, music and erotic love-making became epicentres of cultural discourse in Northern India in the eighteenth and nineteenth century.[5] Another result was the development of Urdu, a language suitable in many ways for romantic poetry, having the beauty of some Indian words and the best of Persian linguistic traditions.

In a way, this book is also for countries like India, to exhort the people of this great country to reclaim the sexual liberties that were part of its glorious ancient heritage.

Simplifying the Availability of Sex and Liberalizing the Concept of Marriage

Even in most 'liberated' cities in the world the quest for sexual entertainment by a married or committed person is a very complex quest, riddled with guilt and devoid of straightforward systems. This lack of simplicity for a situation when two people want to enjoy sexuality has created a market for shadowy prostitution, brothels and unnecessary complexity in relationships. In several developing countries with cultural and/or religious baggage any quest for sex is breathtakingly complex. These situations must be simplified in developed countries. This unwritten prison of marriage must be broken to free our sexual selves. A life without freedom of sexuality between two consenting adults within marriage can be suffocating for the person with a healthy sexual drive. As the episodes of Bill Clinton, Tiger Woods and Schwarzenegger have shown, our present system of marriage is not able to keep a lid on this powerful drive. When people say marriage is an 'institution', did they mean an 'institution' like the prison? Things are only going to get worse in an environment where we are bombarded with sexual images all the time, reminding and igniting our sexual needs. Despite all the books on monogamy, experimentations with positions and other creative manoeuvres, there is a limit to how much change one sexual partner can provide in the sexual activity. While it is true that a pizza can have an almost endless variety of toppings (maybe one for each of the 365 days in a year) at the end of the day it is still a pizza. Similarly, a single partner can perhaps provide some differences in style and positions in sex, but at the end of the day it is the same partner. The time has come for marriages to be more liberal and allow multi-partner sexual experimentations. Hence the Western society, even in its present sexually liberalised state, needs further openness. The most important part of the premise of this book is its advocacy for the removal of guilt from mutually consenting adult sexual relationships.

How can this Change in our Sexual Paradigm Change Our Society?

What are the other ways in which this paradigm of fundamental freedom of sexuality for all adults is likely to change our world? There are myriad implications. For instance, today when we walk into a reasonably good resort or hotel for a short or long stay, we find that it has facilities for food (restaurant), drinks (bar), sleep (bed) and recreation (TV, billiards table, swimming pool). Some hotels go further and have facilities for beauty treatments, massages, gymnasium, casino and so on. (We are not talking about dodgy hotels that use the word 'massage' euphemistically for sexual activities.) The change in our paradigm of sexuality could see these hotels openly advertise facilities for sexual activities for adults where men and women while on their short business trips could enjoy sexual activities without any hang-ups.

Some hoteliers might argue that if someone wants sex, they could always visit a brothel. The simple rebuttal to this argument would be that hotels also have restaurants and beauty parlours inside their premises despite the fact that people could eat outside or have beauty treatments in other establishments. Hence, why is there such discrimination against sexual enjoyment? After all, most people like to enjoy sex as much, if not more, than going to a gymnasium or gambling or even drinking, so why are these activities being allowed while pretending sexuality does not exist? Moreover, the brothel is a connotation of a non-liberated era where sexual enjoyment is considered the preserve of men where women merely concur and tolerate a man's sexual urges. Most brothels stand for something shabby or shady (or both).

On the other hand, in the liberated sexual paradigm, we could have facilities in a luxurious hotel where the services of both men and women are available for a sexual experience. Moreover, since people have different sexual preferences, they could opt accordingly. Some upscale and decent hotels could also have swinging parties for their hotel guests without fear of being forced to close down (in some parts of the world) or fearing complete loss of reputation. Just like how a swimming pool is today part of most luxury hotels, a sexual services centre or a swinging lounge could also be a normal part of luxury hotel services.

Changes in Workplace

What are the other areas of everyday living that the paradigm mentioned in this book will impact? Existing professional rules of conduct are another part of the debate. Reforms in our laws on workplace practices will result. Today, there are ironclad rules which bar sexual relationships between consenting adults in unequal positions of organisational hierarchy. Often even where there is full consent, it is referred to as 'sexual harassment'.

If the boss and his subordinate have a coffee together every day or a beer after work sometimes, why should the employee *not be allowed* to sue her employer afterwards for 'caffeine harassment' or 'alcohol harassment'? Today a manager and his subordinate can enjoy coffee, alcohol, cigarettes, meals and even an ice cream with each other, but a healthy sexual romp, which is certainly less harmful than all the above-mentioned, is certainly not permissible. Similarly, sexual relationships between an adult postgraduate student and his/her teacher is still considered 'inappropriate', even when the student is willingly part of such a relationship without there being any quid pro quo in terms of marks or results. Why is it not expressly prohibited for a student and teacher to have coffee and cupcake together? The main reason there are such elaborate and repressive rules against sex in the workplace is simply because 'it is a big deal' unlike coffee sharing or having a beer together.

Are we as a civilization, not yet ready to treat workplace sex in a mundane fashion like workplace coffee? Perhaps managers must also learn to accept *no* from their subordinates to sex just like some employees might refuse the offer of coffee when it is offered. Sex has to stop being the big ego thing, where men and women think of refusal as if it is a slap on the face. This can only happen when women are also able to freely ask men for sex, just like they ask male colleagues in an office, "Would you like me to get you a coffee?" Of course presently, women liked to be wooed and cajoled, because as mentioned in Chapter 5, under 'Sanctity of Marriage', women think of sex as 'giving'. That is mainly because society has conditioned them to think that sex, unlike coffee, is a big deal and must be given out only sparingly. Once this thinking and sexual generalisations are crushed, women will probably easily give and receive sex even with people they are clear that they are not interested in a long-term relationship with. After all, why must mutually pleasurable consensual sex between employees in workplace be out of place? There could be swinging parties in offices just like Christmas parties. Just like employees are free to opt out of office parties, these swinging parties must also be free to opt in or out.

The Economy of Sexual Freedom

Let us look at the kind of food experiences that are available to a human being today. There are hundreds and thousands of combinations of food available today. We are not at the same culinary experience level that a human being two hundred years back was. In our big supermarkets, we have pizzas, burgers, Indian food, Chinese food, ice creams, pasta, hundreds of variations of cakes, kebabs and so on. Within pizzas themselves, we have hundreds of different toppings and variations. Within cakes and pastries, hundreds of varieties jostle for our attention. Similarly, tens if not hundreds of flavours exist in the ice cream arena. Let us have a look at drinks. Hundreds of drinks in mind-boggling variety exist in supermarkets. We have hot beverages and cold beverages, alcoholic and non-alcoholic beverages, aerated drinks and non-aerated drinks. Then there are health drinks and energy drinks. Within each of these categories, there are hundreds of brands/varieties that meet our eyes. For instance, within the beer segment there are various varieties that boggle our mind from cider to lager, from wheat beer to astounding other varieties, sizes and flavours. As if the variety in alcoholic drinks were not enough, there are hundreds of other pre-packed cocktails that are available.

However, due to our culture of taboo, the sexual experience market has not yet developed. There are some sex shops in developed Western countries. We can only imagine what can happen if the sexual market opens up. From toys to books and various services and sexual events, one can only imagine the supermarket economy of sexual services section. This market and the variety of products and services in this market are going to explode like never before.

The Advent of Sexual Charities

There are some other implications of this book. Today there are charities that give shelter to the homeless and food to the hungry. In the future there could be charities which provide sex to the deprived. Men or women unable to find sexual companionship on their own due to their own tragic circumstances could be offered sexual gratification by charities dedicated to this goal. Handicapped men or women unable to have access to the same mental or physical attributes necessary to attract other men or women for sexual companionship could be offered sexual services by compassionate staff, hired by charities. Similarly men or women rendered extremely physically repulsive or grotesque by accidents, fires or other such tragedies and yet not finding the money to buy sex can find this charity helpful in satisfying their sexual needs. Handsome men and women can also donate sexual time to such charities (just like they donate their time presently for fund-raising activities or community services) giving beautiful sex to the disadvantaged. What a beautiful world indeed!

Will Divorce Rates Shoot Through the Roof?

Some outraged readers might still ask in injured tones, "What will be left of marriages where the concept of sexual exclusivity (or fidelity) is removed? Does it not mean that divorce rates will shoot through the roof?" On the contrary, when the concept of cheating and jealousy are removed from the marriage, divorces might reduce considerably. If a husband or wife loses sexual interest in her otherwise loving spouse, one (or both) of them could have interesting sexual experience with someone else transparently, without the baggage of guilt, lying or cheating. In today's society, otherwise decent and ethical people are forced to lie to their partners to hide their love for sexual variety. There is something wrong with this sociological premise in this day and age. When two like-minded friends (whether of opposite gender or same gender, depending on preferences) can have a sexual experience as freely as having an ice cream together without feeling the disastrous pangs of guilt, people will get married when they *really* feel like being together with a person for a longer time. The homing instinct is most probably, a stronger instinct than the sexual philandering instinct.

Besides the homing instinct, there are other pragmatic and logistical considerations. Let us revert to our analogy of a restaurant. Normal married men with families who are free to have food at any of the restaurants do not actually do so every day. Most of them prefer to eat at home, due to tastes and economics. In some cases, when the man (or woman) chooses to eat one meal regularly outside his home due to the exigencies of work or travel, there is little complaint from the spouse. The man (or woman) who enjoyed his lascivious meal outside also knows that his wife's meal is the regular one that he will return to despite the fact that good restaurants often offer tastier fare than the average housewife. Why can't we accept that a man (or woman) enjoying an occasional sexual tryst outside will do likewise? Similarly the working wife, who eats a meal outside her home every day, does not incur the jealousy or rage of her husband for not eating home food. What, other than prior pernicious conditioning prevents us from showing the same decent understanding behaviour when it comes to sexuality?

In fact several marriages simply break down because partners often (led by stringent social mores) expect unnatural sexual fidelity from each other. A wife expects that her sexually delightful and passionate husband who spends long hours in the office with his beautiful secretary, will unnaturally curb his sexual taste buds while at work. It is like seeing a beautiful piece of preferred food being laid on one's desk every day while being forbidden by thin moral laws to touch it. Is this a sustainable situation, especially if the beautiful secretary is also physically or emotionally attracted to the man in question? What is more likely to happen is that the man eventually decides to taste the cake and then gets into the loop of lying and deceit. Is this a desirable state for our society to be in? Isn't it easier to re-write the rules within marriages once and forever?

An Imaginary Situation

Let us imagine what the situation could be in such a sexually liberated and understanding marriage. Imagine a husband coming home late from work after an office party. When his wife initiates love-making he tells her that he is not so keen to have intercourse, because he just had some lovely sex with one of his office colleagues. This would be similar to a situation where the husband comes home and says that since he had to eat out with one of his colleagues unexpectedly, he does not want food. The wife understands the situation lovingly, although she might complain a little about why he did not inform her on the phone so she could have avoided some cooking. She might only expect him to give her some company at the dining table while she eats her own dinner. The loving husband gives her company at the dining table and there is no rancour or jealousy here. Similarly, since the husband does not seem in the mood for full intercourse but since she is in the mood for it, perhaps he can lovingly masturbate her. Or he could use some lovely toys to bring her to a wonderful orgasm, akin to the situation where he gives her company at the dining table. Then both of them retire joyfully and lovingly to bed.

Of course in this situation too, there could be some mild banter and envy, similar to the wife saying, "Wow, you had such wonderful food today," and asking him when he will take her to that restaurant. For instance, the wife could say, "Wow… you had such wonderful sex today with that colleague or with that escort, when will you pay for me to have such a nice treat?" In response to this, the loving husband could engage a well-built younger man for his wife's enjoyment one weekend. This would be similar to the husband buying some good food from a delicious takeaway restaurant for his wife. Or, like a visit together to a restaurant, the husband and wife could both go to some other good sexual establishment and enjoy some sexual services by males and females. Are the readers finally able to visualise the emerging institution of marriage – an institution free of hypocrisy, lies and jealousy?

Some of the more operational problems of our paradigm, for instance the problem of two people outside marriage falling in love is discussed in Chapter 5 under section 'What Happens if Married People Start Falling in Love with Others?'. Of course there is a possibility that eventually the two new people in love will move on and stay together. There are no easy solutions for this, but the next chapter on robust alternatives to the existing model of marriage might be useful. As for jealousy between existing partners, there are ways to break these calcified walls of jealousy in marriages and other forms of committed sensual relationships. If people can be trained to say please and thank you, eat with fork and spoon and flush the toilet (none of which are naturally occurring), they can be certainly trained not to be jealous when their spouse or partner has a sexual encounter with someone other than them. Jealousy, like selfishness, aggression and fear may be instinctive and traceable to our animalistic origins, but just equally possible to control and regulate. Jealous behaviour is often a result of the expectations of society, religious groups and communities, in a particular situation. For those who find particular difficulty in dealing with problems of jealousy or possessiveness, there could be courses/training sessions in jealousy management along the lines of anger management.

Will Monogamy Die?

Once we are free from the religious and socio-cultural bondage of sexuality, who would not like to taste the sexual company of other attractive men or women? Of course there will be some men and women who will continue to have single partners, just like there are men and women who never prefer to have food outside their home kitchen. But the point is of a choice here. The choice to enjoy the freedom of sexual maturity with mutual adult consent, without the baggage of guilt, shame and social blackmail, would be revolutionary. No society, however free, democratic or secular can achieve true freedom till there is sexual liberty within secure marriages. Until sober, God-fearing people are allowed to experience sexual proximity with others without having to break up a family, no society can really be called 'free'.

14

Alternative Models for Sexually Liberated 'Marriages'

The most important part of this book's message is the removal of fidelity as a precondition for marriage. Sexual liberation within marriage is an idea whose time has come. Perhaps incest would continue to be a terrible taboo for some generations, but sexual liberation within marriage is a contemporary idea, which is already being acted upon by thousands of couples through open marriages, spouse-swapping parties and other ways. If this idea is accepted into mainstream thought and society, we will finally break the chains of hypocrisy that now bind the institution of marriage in our world. In the course of one or two generations, jealousy, sexual cheating and conflict arising from these will disappear from our societies.

Some Ideas for Robust Alternatives to Marriage: Local Communities System

While the above idea seems to be fine, are there any robust substitutes for the existing system of marriage? The system of small local communes is a good example. Just like the Roman Catholic system of parishes by which almost the entire globe is divided into manageable parishes, we could think of small communities where men and women live together by mutual consent and the resulting children are brought up in a big community centre, paid for by the members of the community.

Let us see how this 'free community system' would work. A person who wants to enjoy the benefit of such a free community system would join up with his partner. When he joins this community, he will undertake that he will give up the children resulting out of his relations to the free community child centre where professionals will provide love, care and education to the children. He will also agree to contribute a chunk of his income to the centre where there will be children of many other free community couples. He will also agree to not make any parental claims on the child. He will be free to visit the community and meet the children as much as he wants. People would be free not to join this community marriage system if they do not like the idea.

There would be some free-community entertainment events every week and non-attendance in these events for more than two to three months could result in some punitive action. During the free community events the couples are free to mingle with other couples and spend time with them. After the events, couples or individuals who get along well with each other can continue to meet on dates. Suppose a person fancies another lady and the lady like-wise. They can simply decide to move in together. All that they would need to do is to inform the community officials who will collect the luggage and other belongings from the earlier partner's house and take it to the new partner's house. No fight, no jealousy, no questions asked. The children of resulting unions are given to the community centre without any questions. To begin with, such community centres could be purely voluntary and those who want to follow the system of life-long marriages can continue to do so. This community system has the potential to enter the mainstream as a robust, jealousy-free, fight-free and sexually liberated system of society. People will work, earn, have a house, but they will be able to change partners once in a while if one of them wants. Within the communitites, erstwhile pertners will continue to see each other and mix with each other. After some time they can again decide to move in back together. Those who end up single because their partners have left them can stay in a makeshift hostel, which would be, like council housing, a low-pay system of single studio apartments.

Of course like all systems, this system will have to be fine-tuned because there will be so many issues. What if the incomes are extremely unequal between two couples and then one partner in the high-income couple decides to move in with another partner from the low-income couple. Where do they stay? Will the houses be owned by the free community system? Will the free community itself allot houses for couples who are new? Can a person who joins such a community system and later on withdraw from it, be allowed to reclaim his/her child? These are implementation issues, which are difficult but not impossible to put in place. So far many of these commune experiments in different parts of the world have failed and not entered the mainstream because there were never any efforts to start a system that is well-integrated within the mainstream society. For instance, a person who worked in a regular job and led an otherwise normal life could not easily be a part of such a system.

A person with the desire and motivation for sexual variety would clandestinely join many secret groups, clubs and so on. Taking advantage of the desire for secrecy on the part of the joiners, many of these clubs/groups have had exorbitant fees and other types of scams.

There have been attempts to implement the commune system of living by semi-religious figures. But most of these religious communes were often destined to fail because they were driven by the dictatorship of a particular guru. Like a limited-life candle flame, the whole effort would get extinguished with the passing away of the guru. Moreover, since many such communities started by gurus take people away from mainstream life, there has rarely been any integration with the society. Mainstream society often regards the members of these communes with suspicion. Osho, a religious guru from India tried to do that in Oregon, USA, but there was no robust plan for continuing it and making it a systematic way of life for future generations.

Therefore it is possible that the friendly commune system not created by a sole person but incorporated institutionally with an intention to continue, can indeed survive. However, as of now, only tribal or ethnic societies in remote parts of the world have this style of sexually liberated, tension and jealousy-free lifestyle. In an era of environmental consciousness, when people in Europe and many parts of the developed world are becoming educated to the benefits of the bicycle over car, why is it difficult for us to learn from these simple societies and eradicate jealousy, stress and fights from sexual relationships?

Some Ideas for Robust Alternatives to Marriage: Registration System

Another proposed alternative is a system of registration, which takes into consideration the fact that jealousy in marriages is often the result of insecurity. This insecurity about not having the spouse around, when dissected properly, is often hinged on two major fears, namely, fear of lack of money and fear of lack of companionship (love and/or sex). One way of reducing this insecurity could be to ensure through a social and well-implemented legal, but optional system, by which a person who is married once, can never really sever all ties with his/her partner. The concept of 'registered' relationships would try to address these fears by ensuring that once a person had a 'registered' relationship with someone, it will be forever. The system should be such that every registered partner will have the legal obligation towards each other once in a year even if that partner is married presently to someone else. For instance, a person who had five registered relationships before his current wife/partner will be obliged to visit the five different partners at least once within a year. Similarly his existing wife might have another four or five registered visits.

How would this be different from a marriage? In case of a marriage, after divorce, the husband or wife is free to break all ties with their previous partner. In the case of registration, irrespective of whether they re-marry, remain single or have further divorces in future, both the partners will have life-long rights to each other's company – including sexual company, at least once in a year. Various technical aspects of this proposed system such as the time gap can be debated upon and tinkered. (Why not once in three months? Or two years? Or two months?)

To understand this proposed system better, let us assume a meeting period of once in a year and take an imaginary example of a man who had three divorces after joining this registration system. He would be under obligation to meet his three ex-partners at least once in a year and provide them with loving consensual sex, even if he does not 'feel' like meeting. In other words, even after divorce, if one previous partner makes a demand for companionship, it will be obligatory for the other partner who has moved on to provide sexual and loving companionship at least once in a year. Would this be implied rape? Not necessarily. There must be also some provisions for those who are not happy with the system to exit the system at different stages, with the caveat that those who exit the system once will not be allowed to re-join. However, what if one partner is not in the 'mood' on a particular evening? In that case, this partner can simply provide some loving action for the other ending in a nice orgasm. If one goes to a massage parlour after booking an appointment, does the masseur or masseuse refuse to touch because he/she was not in the 'mood' to give a massage on a particular day? Similarly in a family setting, does the housewife or househusband who provides meals for her/ his family refuse to do so, because one day she/he was not in the 'mood'. Even if they could not stand each other, if they have signed up for this 'registered' relationship, they would still have to meet each of their previous partners once in a year and be nice for the short time that they are together.

It is possible that this concept of permanency may finally kill jealousy forever by making every long-term registered sexual relationship *permanent*. This registered partner system could be the new real life scrapbook of sexual relationships, with every person whom you had a sexual encounter being listed as a 'registered partner' with obligations to meet (once in a year) and maintain the relationship forever. Simply put, no one with whom you had a loving, meaningful sexual encounter goes away from your life forever. To some people of course, this idea that a former partner can never truly go away from your life, will be intolerable. In that case they do not have to get into the registered relationship, in the first place. But to many who believe that even former partners can remain loving friends, this concept will make a lot of sense.

If large numbers of people adopt this system and visit all their former partners once a year, we eventually bring back the concept of a global village of loving relationships. Each partner can choose to live with anyone or have simultaneous sexual relationships, without feeling guilty, jealous or possessiveness that he or she is betraying the person with whom they are currently living. This provides a jealousy-free environment for sexual variety, even if it is with previous partners. Knowing that your partner will be there for you forever (even if it is just once in a year), also removes some element of insecurity from within marriages.

This has the potential to be a revolutionary system. Simply put, the more the number of registered partnerships, the more the chances of sexual variety after marriage. There are some pertinent questions. What if the obligatory visit to a former partner rekindles the relationship? Of course the existing registered husband might divorce his present wife and start living with his ex-partner or even marry her again. But the wife, knowing well that her ex-husband will remain her registered partner, should not grudge it so much. Of course the jilted wife still has her earlier registered partners with whom she will meet once in a year. This will partly remove her feeling of loneliness. It removes the system of 'winner takes all' in case of a divorce, when it comes to loneliness.

What if all my registered partners are now based in another continent, since I have decided to migrate to New Zealand? What if one of the registered partners is too ill to undertake visits? Who should do the commuting or accommodating in case of a visit? What if one of the previous partners decide to exit the system? Needless to say, to make this system robust, so many finer technical aspects need to be discussed. But the broad contour of the idea is as given above. In fact, if people start following this system it could also be a sustainable and ethically consistent system that says if you enter into a sexually long-term relationship anytime with anyone, that person will be in your life forever. This is broadly consistent with realities in the spiritual world too.

Towards a World Moving from Sexual Orgasm to Spiritual Orgasm

Many people would automatically assume this book is merely about sex. It cannot be denied that cosmic laws about sex are the main focus of this book. Another agenda of this book is to sever the connection of spirituality with sexual abstinence that has been tenuously maintained and propagated by religious organisations for centuries. The time has come to permanently sever this link.

There are other take-home lessons for those who like concise, pill-shaped learning parcels.

1. That sexual diversity even within marriage is permissible and must be adopted by societies. How, and in what form society will accept it in the decades to come is a matter of conjecture. Whether marriage as a social institution will survive this sexual openness within the established framework of marriage is yet to be seen. However, the perspective of this book is that it can survive provided some corrective mechanisms are incorporated.

2. The taboo against incest is a taboo based on the possibility of having offspring with deformities. In this age of genetic interventions and effortless contraception this can be clearly avoided. Therefore this terrible taboo against incest must go, just like the taboo against homosexuality is going away gradually in all freedom-loving countries. Other than terrible guilt that is a result of our cultural conditioning, incest does not have any severe cosmic spiritual repercussions.

3. Sexuality in human evolution has a limited shelf life now. For those who merely want to procreate, there are already other alternatives existing without sex. Unless humanity takes a regressive approach, our scientific progress and fast-moving research in health, medicine and mental faculties mean that our race will eventually discover the bliss centres of the brain and link spiritual practices like meditation to the bliss of orgasm, without taking drugs or having a sexual orgasm. In a hundred years, the human beings who are capable of being evolved will turn our planet into meditative and spiritual societies. When the joys of meditation and the almost orgasmic enjoyment of meditation become possible, from that stage of human development sexuality will start taking a backseat. However, as all the great meditators are aware, when meditation turns into an effortless activity, even sexual unions will become an activity done in a semi-meditative state. That will be the second stage in our spiritual evolution. The third stage is further away when physical unions will no more be required for pro-creation and other methods will be available for us. This is just a matter of time for human evolution.

With the possible exception of incest, these are all ideas whose time has come. No society can claim to have reached the pinnacle of freedom without untying these chains of sexual repression. Of course, the cause for concern is the growth in freedom-suppressing ideologies and the fear that they might take over the freedom-loving societies. In the sixties and seventies communism was the greatest such repressive ideology. Today organisations like ISIS and Boko Haram still operate on principles of violence, repression and brutality more appropriate to the dark ages. There are also organisations following communist ideology and fundamentalist versions of various religions which advocate violence to meet their ends. As mentioned in earlier chapters, the Prophet Muhammad was one of the greatest liberal figures, but the version of unchanged Quran clung on to by his supporters is most repressive. Unless vast cataclysmic changes on earth eradicate those with limited intellectual capacities to deal with these astounding freedoms, there is a real danger that even freedom-loving liberal societies could, at least temporarily, get submerged by surging numbers of those brought up in violent, repressive cultures or countries.

Having said all this, the enlightened world will eventually move from sexual orgasms towards spiritual orgasms. Some who are born with higher levels of spiritual powers might forego sexuality completely and move on to spiritual orgasms. For others still, this de-linking of sex-denial from spiritual paths will free their sexually repressed selves and allow them to progress on the path of spiritual growth, while enjoying sex without the huge rock of guilt. Whatever the end results for different people, this is an idea whose time has come.

ACKNOWLEDGEMENTS

A tree is often held strong by its roots. This work would not have been possible without the help of many visible and invisible hands. To begin with, I would like to thank my parents Chacko and Pushpa, whose significant sacrifices have made it possible for me to be educated in good schools, pursue university degrees and achieve whatever little I could in my life. I must also thank my intelligent wife and companion, Wenonah, who has helped this book at various stages with her constant flow of ideas. My young daughters, Tanisha and little Nikisha, who sacrificed a lot of their 'father' time, so I could focus on my work deserve my unstinted gratitude. Long discussions with my brother Stanly on various issues shaping the world today have helped sharpen several arguments in this book, while my sister-in-law Shaily has always encouraged me. My discussions with my erudite in-laws Trifonio and Aline have also greatly motivated me. My late sister's husband Manoj and his respectful, soft-spoken views have also helped.

I owe much gratitude to my various teachers, especially late Prof. A. Sreekumar and Prof. Tavakari with whom I often used to have a meaningful exchange of views on various topics. I owe my earlier manager at work, Dr. Subhash Sharma from Indus Business Academy, Bangalore tremendous gratitude for his contribution in shaping my world view on Eastern spirituality and ethics through his calm, but incisive intellectual observations. Despite being my boss, it was possible to have a robust argument with him on practically any topic under the sun without the weight of organisational hierarchy bearing down upon me. A similar role of gentle mentor was played by Dr. Ramesh Tagat, with whom I have exchanged views on many aspects. One of my managers and good friend in London, Dr. Michael Pinfold has read this book very thoroughly and engaged me in a powerful discussion of the various ideas propounded in this book. He has also painstakingly suggested various corrections in the language and grammar in the manuscript. I owe him a very special thank you.

I also thank Jeffrey Simmons, literary agent for his tremendous words of encouragement. He has also spent time, energy and probably money, in getting my book read by others and giving me suggestions on various aspects of the work including length, structure and possible market for the book. Prof. Geoffrey Alderman has also gone through this book and shared his opinion, which has helped this work. I am also forever indebted to all my friends in India and UK (too many to name), with whom I have exchanged thoughts and ideas. I also thank Fiona Lewis, my former teaching colleague, for her invaluable inputs towards improving this manuscript.

Thanks are also due to the publication team at Matador notably Jeremy Thompson, Lauren Lewis and others in the editorial, production, marketing, printing, website and finance departments who worked together with a very high degree of coordination. Without their utmost professionalism, this book would not have been possible. I must thank my freelance illustrator and friend George Grekas for this book cover and modification of illustrations inside this book. Chelsea Taylor from Matador has my special thanks for refining it to my rather exacting demands.

Lastly, with intense emotion, I would also like to record my unwavering gratitude to the various spiritually exalted individuals, whose unselfish sharing of ancient Indian wisdom has helped me shape the various arguments in this book. My *vipassana* meditation teachers and late Guruji Krishananda from the Manasa Foundation are but a few of these infinitely compassionate gurus. Without their spiritual guidance and positive energies, this book would not have been possible.

Needless to say, I own full and complete responsibility for any inaccurate facts or insufferable opinions.

A NOTE TO THE READERS

This book is not meant to be the proverbial 'last word'. If anything, this is a humble attempt to provoke thoughts and ignite debates on spiritual and sociological issues related to the welfare of humanity. Some ideas, suggestions and spiritual truths towards betterment of humanity have been presented in this book. If they make even an infinitesimal influence on our existing perspective of the world, I would consider it a worthy reward for all my efforts.

However, it is but natural that before you accept, or even consider my ideas worthy of your thought, you may want to discuss/argue with me. You may also have questions, opinions and/or clarifications on some of my ideas. You might also share with me some scenarios where you think my suggestions or ideas may not work. It is also possible that you may have better alternatives or more robust solutions to some of the problems that I have highlighted.

Whatever the reason, it will be a great privilege to engage with you, my reader and enrich my own learning further. If you write to me through my publishers, they will forward your correspondence to me. You can also email me on *karmasutra.karmaofsex@gmail.com* or get in touch with me through my Facebook page *Staju Jacob* or follow my Twitter handle *@KaRmasutraTKOS*.

I look forward to your company on this mutually enriching journey of Jnana Yoga, the path of knowledge and wisdom.

CHAPTER NOTES

Since the Bible, Quran and Bhagavad Gita are well–known and easily available religious texts, only the chapters and verse numbers have been mentioned and no hyperlinks or other details have been provided.

Chapter 1 – Introduction to Karma

1. *Police Corruption in India* by Ravikanth B. Lamani and G. S. Venumadhava, International Journal of Criminology and Sociological Theory, Vol. 6, No. 4, December 2013, pp. 228-234
2. The Bible, Matthew 9:2
3. The Bible, John 9:1-3
4. The Bible, Matthew 27: 24-25
5. The Bible, Luke 23:28
6. The Quran, Chapter 2:28
7. The Bhagavad Gita, Chapter 4: 19-23
8. The Bible, Mark 11: 14, 20

Chapter 2 – Karma and Marriage

1. Manusmriti, The laws given by Manu. Chapter V:147-166 also, Chapter IX: 2-3 http://www.hinduwebsite. com/sacredscripts/hinduism/dharma/manusmriti_2.asp; accessed on January 10, 2010.
2. Types of Karma

-*Four types of Karma & Soul Energy Correction* by Janardhana Guptha, 2006   http://ezinearticles.com/?Four-Types-of-Karma-and-Soul-Energy-Correction&id=174142; accessed on January 12, 2010.

-*ASHTAKARMA – Eight types of Karma*, part of the book ESSENCE OF JAINISM by Manubhai Doshi, 1992, available online on http://www.jainworld.com/jainbooks/images/22/ashtakarma_-_eight_types_of.htm; accessed on January 12, 2010.

-*Karmic Archery: Four Types Of Karma* by Alexys Fairfield, 2008, http://soulmeetsworld.com/2008/10/four-types-of-karma.html; accessed on January 12, 2010

3. The Bible, Matthew 22:23-31

Chapter 3 – 'Want Pleasing Harlot on an Empty Pocket' (Prostitution)

1. The Bhagavad Gita, Chapter 2:56
2. The Bible, Matthew 17:20 and Luke 17:6
3. The Bible, Matthew 5:5 and 8
4. The Bible, Matthew 21:19 and Mark 11:12-14, 20
5. *Magical Use of Thought Forms: A Proven System of Mental & Spiritual Empowerment* by Dolores Ashcroft-Nowicki and J. H. Brennan, 2002, Llewellyn Publications, USA.

Chapter 4 – Movie Stars Without Clothes Act the Best (Pornography)

1. *Porn Statistics* by Mike Genung, 2010, http://www. blazinggrace.org/cms/bg/pornstats; accessed on May 10, 2010.

2. Jerry Ropelato, http://internet-filter-review.toptenreviews. com/internet-pornography-statistics.html; accessed on May 9, 2010.

3. *How Big Is Porn?* by Dan Ackman, 2001, Forbes article, http://www.forbes.com/2001/05/25/0524porn.html; accessed on May 9, 2010.

4. *Statistics of Porn*, Lighted Candle http://www.lightedcandle. org/pornstats/porn_at_Work.asp; accessed on May 9, 2010.

5. *Banker caught on camera looking at porn in the office,* London Evening Standard, 2010, http://www.thisislondon. co.uk/*standard/article-23801388-banker-caught-on-camera-look*ing-at-porn-in-the-office.do; accessed on May 9, 2010.

6. 2010 SILF: Liveblogging with Ramachandra Guha, City Weekend, 2010 http://www.cityweekend.com.cn/shanghai/ articles/blogs-shanghai/silf/2010-silf-liveblogging-with-ramachandra-guha/; accessed on May 9, 2010.

7. *Colonialism, tradition, and reform: an analysis of Gandhi's political discourse, By Bhikhu C. Parekh, 2nd Edition, 1999, Publisher : Sage publications, New Delhi, Pp 210 -212*

8. *Catechism of the Catholic Church ARTICLE 6, THE SIXTH COMMANDMENT*, Vatican, http://www.vatican.va/ archive/ccc_css/archive/catechism/p3s2c2a6.htm; accessed on May 10, 2010.

9. The Quran, Chapter 16:90

10. Translations by various authors, The Quran, Chapter 16:90, http://quranexplorer.com/index/Sura_016_An_ Nahl_THE_BEE.aspx; accessed on April 20, 2011.

11. Islam online, http://www.islamonline.net/servlet/ Satellite?pagename=IslamOnline-English-Ask_Scholar/ FatwaE/FatwaE&cid=1119503543794; accessed on April 20, 2011.

12. *Islam on Pornography: A Definite No No* by Abdul Malik

Mujahid, 2011 http://www.soundvision.com/Info/life/porn/isporn.asp; accessed on December 10, 2011.

13. *Modernist and fundamentalist debates in Islam: a reader* by Mansoor Moaddel and Kamran Talattof, 2003, Palgrave Macmillan, USA; pp. 146-147

14. *The Life and Times of Prophet Muhammad*, Prophet Muhammad's Timeline, Manelelhag http://manalelhag.tripod.com/id3.html; accessed on May 16, 2010.

15. *Qur'an Contradiction, The Age of Marriage,* by Sam Shamoun, http://www.answering-islam.org/Quran/Contra/marriage_age.html; accessed on May 15, 2010.

16. *Rejecting the Myth of Sanctioned Child Marriage in Islam* by Dr. David Liepert, 2011, http://www.huffingtonpost.com/dr-david-liepert/islamic-pedophelia_b_814332.html; accessed on April 21, 2013.

17. *Why Hadith is Important* by Professor Shahul Hameed, 2014, http://www.onislam.net/english/shariah/hadith/hadith-studies/441273-prophet-hadith-sunnah-quran-importance-traditions.html; accessed on May 31, 2014.

18. The Quran, Chapter 4:3

19. The Quran, Chapter 4:4

20. The Quran, Chapter 24:31 and 30

21. Translations by Pickthal and Yusuf Ali, The Quran, Chapter 24:31, http://quranexplorer.com/index/Sura_024_Al_Noor_THE_LIGHT.aspx; accessed on April 20, 2011. Other scholars have used the term 'private parts'.

22. The Quran, Chapter 33:59

23. *Pornography: group pressures and individual rights*, by Hugh Potter, Federation Press, 1996, p. 30.

24. *Porn Statistics by Mike Genung, 2010, http://www*.blazinggrace.org/cms/bg/pornstats; accessed on May 10, 2010.

25. Adultwork.com, 2013, http://www.adultwork.com/Search.asp; accessed on May 01, 2014.

26. For *an* idea of salaries of teachers and counter sales staff of Harrods (one of the most Premium supermarkets in London), refer the following links.
- Further education lecturer: Salary and conditions, Prospects UK, 2013. http://www.prospects.ac.uk/further_education_lecturer_salary.htm; accessed on January 12, 2014.
- Harrods Salaries, Glassdoor, UK, 2014, http://www.glassdoor.co.uk/Salary/Harrods-Salaries-E6059.htm; accessed on June 03, 2014.

Chapter 5 – With Maidens I Roam, When Wife is Not Home (Marital Infidelity)

1. *What Is Marital Fidelity?* by Renee Miller, eHow, http://www.ehow.com/facts_5004622_what-marital-fidelity.html; accessed on 19 September , 2011.
2. *Sai Baba: God-man or con man?* By Tanya Datta, BBC, 2004, http://news.bbc.co.uk/1/hi/programmes/this_world/3813469.stm; accessed September 12, 2011.
3. *Nine arrested in India holy man sex scandal protest,* BBC News, 2010, http://news.bbc.co.uk/1/hi/world/south_asia/8549167.stm; accessed September 12, 2011.

Chapter 6 – Seduced to My Bed, You will Never Be Wed (Breach of Trust)

1. *Cosmopolitan Magazine United States edition cover page,* August 2005, http://www.whosdatedwho.com/topic/7920/kate-hudson-cosmopolitan-magazine-august-2005.htm; accessed on November 11, 2012.

2. *Cosmopolitan Magazine United States edition cover page,* January 2005, http://www.whosdatedwho.com/topic/7954/sarah-michelle-gellar-cosmopolitan-magazine-january-2005. htm; accessed on November 11, 2012.

3. *Cosmopolitan Magazine United States edition cover page,* December 2006, http://www.whosdatedwho.com/topic/7912/katherine-heigl-cosmopolitan-magazine-december-2006.htm; accessed on November 11, 2012.

4. *The politically Incorrect Guide to Women, Sex and Feminism* by Carrie L. Lukas, 2006, Regnery Publishing, Inc., Washington, USA, pp. 19-20.

5. *The Reality of the Male Sex Drive* by Roy F. Baumeister, Psychology Today, 2010, http://www.psychologytoday.com/blog/cultural-animal/201012/the-reality-the-male-sex-drive; accessed on March 12, 2012.

Chapter 7 – Peek and Be Peaked (Voyeurism and Exhibitionism)

1. *The Nude* by Kenneth Clark, 1980, Princeton University Press, USA, p. 8.

2. *Barenaked Laddies* by Amy Alkon, The Advice Goddess Columns, 2011, http://www.advicegoddess.com/ag-column-archives/2011/04/barenaked-laddi.html; accessed on September 30, 2013.

3. *Cybersex: The Dark Side of the Force* by Al Cooper (Ed.), 2000, A Special Issue of the Journal "Sexual Addiction and Compulsivity", 2000, Routledge, USA.

4. *The Joy of Cybersex* by Deborah Levine, 2011, Kindle edition, Ballantine Books, USA.

5. *Pornography and Difference* by Berkeley Kaite, 1995, Indiana University Press, USA, p. 83.

6. *Lady Godiva: A Literary History of the Legend* by Daniel Donoghue, 2002, Wiley-Blackwell publishing, UK.
7. *A Vision of Nature: Traces of the Original World* by Michael Charles Tobias, 1995, Kent State University Press, Ohio, USA, p. 30.
8. *Stealing the Garments of the Unmarried Gopi Girls,* Hare Krishna Temple Portal, http://www.harekrsna.de/stealing-cloth.htm; accessed on May 12, 2014.
9. *Handbook of Hindu Mythology* by George M. Williams, 2003, ABC-CLIO Inc., California, USA, p. 103 and p.160.
10. *Jamadagni* by Laura Gibbs, Encyclopedia for Epics of Ancient India, 2007 http://mythfolklore.net/india/encyclopedia/jamadagni.htm: accessed on March 19, 2012.

Chapter 8 – Not Seeing the Face, Other Things Are the Same (Delights with Strangers)

1. *The Holy Intimacy of Strangers* by Sarah York, 2002, Jossey-Bass (A Wiley Imprint), USA, p.19.
2. *Sex with strangers* by Lindsay Gordon, 2007, Virgin Books (Black Lace series), USA.
3. *Sex, Lies, and the Bible: How Human Sexual Behaviour is Controlled Through the Corruption of the Bible* by Francis D. "Frank" Ritter, 2006, Candid Press, USA, p. 184.
4. *ARANYA KANDA, The Ramayana* by C.N. Govindan and Alamelu Ramakrishnan, Vidya Vrikshah, http://www.vidyavrikshah.org/literature/ramayana/Aranya/ak18a.html; accessed on May 09, 2013.
5. *Maharishi Bhrigu curses Lord Brahma and Lord Siva*, Blog by Bangalore-Bangalore, 2012, http://thehindugod.blogspot.co.uk/2012/05/maharishi-bhrigu-curses-lord-brahma-and.html; accessed on June 23, 2013.

6. *Why is Hindu God Shiva Worshipped in the Form of Linga or Lingam?* By Abhilash Rajendran, Hindu Blog, 2008, http://www.hindu-blog.com/2008/02/why-is-hindu-god-shiva-worshipped-in.html; accessed on June 23, 2013.

7. *The presence of Siva* by Stella Kramrisch, 1994, Princeton University Press, USA, pp. 154-155.

8. The Quran, Chapter 4:57

9. *Man scandalises Saudi Arabia with TV sex confession* by Asma Alsharif, Reuters India, 2009, http://in.reuters.com/article/2009/07/30/idINIndia-41428720090730; accessed on December 11, 2012.

10. *Talk openly about sex and risk jail* by Ahmed Al-Omran, France 24, 2009, http://observers.france24.com/content/20090730-talk-openly-about-sex-risk-jail-saudi-arabia-mazen-abdul-jawad; accessed on December 11, 2012.

11. The Bible, Genesis 38:1-26

12. The Bible, Judges 16:1

13. *Bar Girl, Louise, 25 Has Slept With 200 Men She Met On Internet* by Matthew Acton, News of the World, 2009, http://www.newsoftheworld.co.uk/notw/news/150070/Bar-girl-bedded-200-men-after-surfing-web-for-sex-with-strangers.html; accessed on September 01, 2010.

14. *Female Condom*, AVERT, 2014, http://www.avert.org/female-condom.htm; accessed on May 23, 2014.

15. *Why do men prefer women with less sexual experience?* by Sheryl, Yahoo! Answers, 2010, http://answers.yahoo.com/question/index?qid=20100903071055AAHaZb5; accessed on March 22, 2012.

16. *Sex, Love and Friendship: Studies of the Society for the Philosophy of Sex and Love, 1977-1992* by Alan Soble (Ed.), 1997, Rodopi B.V.Editions, Amsterdam, pp. 308-309.

17. *Why should we not hoard material possessions?* by Jake, Instant Good Karma, 2008, http://www.instantgoodkarma.org/Aparigraha.html; accessed on July 18, 2012.

18. *Jain Dharma way of life,* Jainis, http://jainis.com/Jain%20 Society/JainDharamaWayofLife.aspx; accessed on July 18, 2012.

Chapter 9 – Do Not Covet Your Neighbour's Wife, Only Swap (Exchange of Spouse)

1. The Bible, 2 Samuel 11
2. The Bible, Genesis 29:10-19
3. The Bible, Genesis 29:26
4. The Bible, Genesis 29:23
5. The Bible, Genesis 29:31-35
6. The Bible, Genesis 30:2-5
7. The Quran, Chapter 4:20
8. *Another Choice, The Teaching of Ahmed Deedat* by Samuel Green, 2004, http://www.answering-islam.org/Green/deedat.htm; accessed on September 6, 2012.
9. *Towards Understanding the Quran,* Islamicstudies.info, http://www.islamicstudies.info/tafheem.php?sura=33& verse=35&to=40; accessed on September 7, 2012.
10. *Muta', Temporary Marriage in Islamic Law* by Sachiko Murata, originally published in 1974, http://www.al-islam.org/al-serat/muta/; accessed on September 19, 2012.
11. *Controversy, Conflict, and the Islamic Concept of Marriage* by Dr. Maqsood Jafri, 2009, http://familyofheart.com/10/09/May31/COMMENTS/COMMENTS-DMJ09.htm; accessed on September 21, 2012.
12. The Quran, Chapter 4:23-27

13. *Muta Marriage in Islamic Law*, Law is Greek, 2010, http://www.lawisgreek.com/muta-marriage-in-islamic-law/; accessed on November 11, 2012.

14. *Radha Krishna: A Divine Love* by Madhuri Guin, Dolls of India, 2003, http://www.dollsofindia.com/radhakrishna.htm; accessed on November 18, 2012.

15. *Marriage* (part of the book *India: A Country Study*) by James Heitzman and Robert L. Worden (Eds.), 1995, http://countrystudies.us/india/86.htm; accessed on December 19, 2012.

16. *Overview: Part I, SEX AND MARRIAGE: An Introduction to The Cultural Rules Regulating Sexual Access and Marriage* by Dr. Dennis O'Neil, 2009, http://anthro.palomar.edu/marriage/marriage_1.htm; accessed on December 19, 2012.

17. *Plenty of Smoke Over Fire* by Tim McGirk, TIME, 1998, http://www.time.com/time/world/article/0,8599,2054280,00.html; accessed on December 03, 2012.

18. *6 held over Valentine's attacks near Taj Mahal,* Associated Press, 2009, http://www.msnbc.msn.com/id/29194001/ns/world_news-south_and_central_asia/t/held-over-valentines-attacks-near-taj-mahal/; accessed on December 03, 2012.

19. *'How dare these people use my religion to terrorise young girls!'*, Rediff News, 2009 http://specials.rediff.com/getahead/2009/jan/28slid1-mangalore-pub-attack-young-women-speak.htm; accessed on December 03, 2012.

20. *IMF Chief Strauss-Kahn Caught in "Honey Trap"* by Mike Whitney, The Market Oracle, 2011, http://www.marketoracle.co.uk/Article28159.html; accessed on December 28, 2012.

21. *A town in fear: The fatal legacy of Doncaster's lady-killing bouncer* by Ian Herbert, The Independent, 1999, http://

www.independent.co.uk/news/uk/home-news/a-town-in-fear-the-fatal-legacy-of-doncasters-ladykilling-bouncer-743031.html; accessed on December 28, 2012.

22. *The man who gave Doncaster AIDS* by Jane Whitham, BBC Local, 2009, http://news.bbc.co.uk/local/sheffield/hi/people_and_places/history/newsid_8170000/8170707.stm; accessed on December 28, 2012.

23. *Berlusconi denies paying for sex,* BBC News Europe, 2009, http://news.bbc.co.uk/1/hi/8116003.stm; accessed on January 5, 2013.

24. *Clarification of contraceptive wording in clinical trials conducted in the UK*, Medicines and Healthcare products Regulatory Agency, UK, version 2, 2010, http://www.mhra.gov.uk/home/groups/lunit1/documents/websiteresources/con2033037.pdf; accessed on January 14, 2013.

25. *The Kama Sutra of Vatsayayana Part II: On Sexual Union,* The Sex Ezine, http://www.lilith-ezine.com/articles/sex/The-Kama-Sutra-of-Vatsayayana-Part-02.html#Union; accessed on January 14, 2013.

26. *Sex toys and artificial penis in Kamasutra*, Kerala Ayurvedics, 2007, http://www.keralaayurvedics.com/kamasutra/sex-toys-and-artificial-penis-in-kamasutra.html; accessed on July 25, 2011.

27. *Chinese wife-swapping charge sparks debate*, NBC News, 2010, http://worldblog.nbcnews.com/_news/2010/04/09/4376753-chinese-wife-swapping-charge-sparks-debate?lite; accessed on January 28, 2013.

Chapter 10 – My Brother is My Greek God (Consenting Incest)

1.   The Bible, Leviticus 20:11-21
2.   The Bible, Leviticus 20:19-21

3. *Putana killed, chapter 6, Krsna The Supreme Personality of Godhead* by His Divine Grace A.C. Bhaktivedanta Swami Prabhupada, originally published in 1970, available online on http://www.krsnabook.com/ch6.html; accessed on February 11, 2013.
4. The Quran, Chapter 4:23-24
5. Translations by various authors, The Quran, Chapter 4: 22, http://quranexplorer.com/index/Sura_004_An_Nisa_ WOMEN.aspx; accessed on March 8, 2013.
6. The Bible, Genesis 20:12-15
7. The Bible, Genesis 38:8-10
8. The Bible, Genesis 38:24-30
9. The Bible, Genesis 19:30-38
10. The Bible, Genesis 35:22
11. *Urvashi's Curse, Mahabharata* by Apam Napat, 2005, http://www.apamnapat.com/articles/Mahabharata032.html; accessed on June 11, 2012.
12. *Shiva to Shankara – Decoding the Phallic Symbol* by Dr. Devdutt Pattanaik, 2006, Indus Source Books, Mumbai, Pp. 43 -47.
13. The Rigveda, Chapter 10:10, http://oaks.nvg.org/rv10.html; accessed on June 11, 2013.
14. The Rigveda, Chapter 6:55, http://oaks.nvg.org/rv6c.html; accessed on June 11, 2013.
15. The Rigveda, Chapter 10:3, http://oaks.nvg.org/rv10.html; accessed on June 11, 2013.
16. *Why incest makes us so squeamish* by Dave Mosher, NBC News, 2008, http://www.msnbc.msn.com/id/22685942/; accessed on July 30, 2013.
17. *Female Hyenas Avoid Incest By Causing Male Relatives To Leave Home*, University of Sheffield, ScienceDaily, 2007, http://www.sciencedaily.com/releases/2007/08/070815135114.htm; accessed on January 29, 2014.

18. *Inbreeding Helps African Fish, Scientists Say* by Charles Q. Choi, LiveScience, 2007, http://www.livescience.com/animals/070205_inbreed_fish.html; accessed on January 29, 2014.

19. *Walking Marriage of Mosuo People,* Cultural China, 2007, http://traditions.cultural-china.com/en/115Traditions342.html; accessed on February 26, 2013.

20. *Mosuo,* Wikipedia, 2014, http://en.wikipedia.org/wiki/Mosuo; accessed on June 1, 2014.

Chapter 11 – Kings Love Kings, Let The Queens Do Likewise (Homosexuality)

1. *FBI Statistics show nearly 14 hate crimes every day,* The Gay Manifesto, 2010, http://www.thegaymanifesto.com/2010/11/22/fbi-statistics-show-nearly-14-hate-crimes-every-day-against-gays-and-lesbians-in-2009/; accessed on August 19, 2011.

2. *Homophobic crime rise in London* by Andy Dangerfield, BBC News, 2009, http://news.bbc.co.uk/1/hi/england/london/8316646.stm; accessed on August 19, 2011.

3. *India's gay prince appears on Oprah show*, Rediff India Abroad, 2007, http://www.rediff.com/news/2007/oct/26look1.htm; accessed on October 26, 2011.

4. *Pope – Gay Marriage Threatens Humanity!!!* by Terry, WordPress Blog, 2012, http://www.sdakotabirds.com/feathers_and_folly/?p=766; accessed on February 16, 2013.

5. *Was Achilles Gay?* http://www.angelfire.com/weird2/randomstuff/achilles2.html#; accessed on December 3, 2011.

6. *Alexander's lovers* by Andrew Michael Chugg, 2006, Lulu.com, USA.

7. *Homosexuality: The Psychology of the Creative Process* by Paul Rosenfels, 1971, Ninth Street Center Inc., New York, p. xx.
8. *Catechism of the Catholic Church ARTICLE 6, THE SIXTH COMMANDMENT* verse *2357*, Vatican, http://www.vatican.va/archive/ccc_css/archive/catechism/p3s2c2a6.htm; accessed on June 18, 2012.
9. *Secret sex in the celibate system* by A.W. Richard Sipe, National Catholic Reporter, 2010, http://ncronline.org/blogs/examining-crisis/secret-sex-celibate-system; accessed on May 7, 2013.
10. *Only Half of Catholic Priests are Celibate*, Ethics & Religion by Michael J. McManus, Virtueonline, 2004, http://www.virtueonline.org/portal/modules/news/article.php?storyid=499#.UEhjk42uZG: accessed on May 7, 2013.
11. The Bible, Leviticus 18:22
12. The Bible, Leviticus 11:10
13. The Bible, Leviticus 19:19
14. The Bible, Romans 1:24-26
15. A quote attributed to Dr. Siddiqi of The Islamic Society of North America by Mission Islam, http://www.missionislam.com/knowledge/homosexuality.htm; accessed on December 29, 2013.
16. *Mohini* by Mickey Weems, Qualia, 2011, http://www.qualiafolk.com/2011/12/08/mohini/; accessed on January 12, 2014.

Chapter 12 – Idiosyncrasies Galore (Frotteurism, Urophilia and Autoerotic Asphyxia)

1. This book has been mentioned in an article *46 Sexual Fetishes You've Never Heard Of*, Huffington Post Books, 2013, http://www.huffingtonpost.com/2013/10/23/sexual-fetish_n_4144418.html; accessed on January 26, 2014.

Chapter 13 – Bringing 'free sex' into mainstream marriage

1. *Why Hillary Clinton let husband Bill seduce any woman in sight* by Sally Bedell Smith, Daily Mail online, 2008, http://www.dailymail.co.uk/femail/article-507762/Why-Hillary-Clinton-let-husband-Bill-seduce-woman-sight.html; accessed on May 12, 2013.

2. *Do you need to read books to be clever?* by Denise Winterman, BBC News Magazine, http://news.bbc.co.uk/1/hi/7178598.stm; accessed on June 4, 2013.

3. *Homosexuality is Criminal Again as India's Top Court Reinstates Ban* by Nilanjana Bhowmick, TIME, 2013, http://world.time.com/2013/12/11/homosexuality-is-criminal-again-as-indias-top-court-reinstates-ban/; accessed on March 12, 2014.

4. *Govt's move to lower age of consent to 16 from 18 years runs into opposition*, Times of India, 2013, http://timesofindia.indiatimes.com/india/Govts-move-to-lower-age-of-consent-to-16-from-18-years-runs-into-opposition/articleshow/18996684.cms; accessed on March 2, 2014.

5. *THE TAWAIF, THE ANTI – NAUTCH MOVEMENT, AND THE DEVELOPMENT OF NORTH INDIAN CLASSICAL MUSIC: Part 2* – The Tawaifs by David Courtney, 2012, http://chandrakantha.com/articles/tawaif/2_tawaifs.html; accessed on March 4, 2014.

INDEX

"B-BETA," I CORRECTED HIM. "CAN'T KNOT ME."
It'll kill me.

"Ah, but I can," he murmured, pressing his impressive erection to my stomach. When had he lost his clothes? Why couldn't I focus for longer than a few minutes at a time?

And *how* did he plan to knot me?

"Y-you'll kill me," I breathed, arching into him. It was like my body refused to listen to my mind. "D-drugs," I added, hoping he would understand. *I've been drugged.*

Oh, no, little wolf. No more suppressants for you."

Ugh. He didn't understand! "Not… supp… ressants." I swallowed a moan as he rocked against my body, the water warm as it flowed overhead. It was confusing my senses, both pulling me back into a state of awareness while simultaneously drowning me in lust. "Vanessa w-wants to kill me. Tried, maybe. Drugs."

That gave him pause. "Say that again."

I shook my head, unable to focus long enough for so many words. "Help," I begged instead. "Need… help."

He frowned at me. "You're going into estrus, Snow. I'm planning to help you."

I shook my head, a whine catching in my throat. He didn't understand. "No knot." I couldn't accept it. This had to be part of Vanessa's plan, to make an Alpha think he could fuck me fully.

She'd planned to entice Enrique with this spell, to force him to knot me.

That was what she'd meant by having methods to induce the sensations. She'd cast some wicked enchantment that convinced Alphas I could handle them in a rut.

Tears collected in my eyes.

I'd escaped her clutches, only to fall into the hands of someone so much worse—an Alpha driven by need.

She'd won.

After all that… she'd still won.

I crumpled against him, sobbing beneath the crushing emotions of betrayal and defeat. And worse, arousal.

Because I wanted him.

X-CLAN SERIES

ANDORRA SECTOR

X-CLAN: THE EXPERIMENT

WINTER'S ARROW